CHRISTIAN VISION

of the

OLD TESTAMENT

(Synopsis & Exhortation)

James H. Kurt

© 2013, 2019 James H. Kurt
All Rights Reserved.

Children of Light Publications 11/30/2019
ISBN: 978-1-7332154-4-2

First published by AuthorHouse 05/23/2013
(ISBN: 978-1-4817-5500-9)

No part of this book may be reproduced, stored in a retrieval system, or transmitted by any means without the written permission of the author.

Nihil Obstat:
Rev. Donald Blumenfeld
Censor Librorum

Imprimatur:
+ Most Reverend John J. Myers, J.C.D., D.D.
Archbishop of Newark, New Jersey
April 16, 2013

The **Nihil Obstat** and **Imprimatur** are official declarations that a book or pamphlet is free of doctrinal error. No implication is contained therein that those who have granted the **Nihil Obstat** and **Imprimatur** agree with the contents, opinions, or statements expressed.

Conceived July 16, 2010 at feast day Mass,
Our Lady of Mount Carmel Church, Jersey City, NJ.

Revised Standard Catholic Version of the Holy Bible used throughout (except for two quotes on p. xiv)

Cover art: "Moses and the Burning Bush" by Marc Chagall; lithograph courtesy of Troy Wiles, Art's 400, Sarasota, FL (photo and design by James Kurt)

Final proofreading assistance: Louis Guerriero

"And Moses entered the cloud, and went up on the mountain.... And [the LORD] gave to Moses, when He had made an end of speaking with him upon Mount Sinai, the two tables of the testimony, tables of stone, written with the finger of God."

Ex. 24:18, 31:18

"And beginning with Moses and all the prophets, [Jesus] interpreted to them in all the Scriptures the things concerning Himself."

Lk. 24:27

Preface

This book is to be written seated on Mount Carmel with Our Lady at my side silently guiding all that is said. As I have long-consecrated my life into her hands, so especially shall this book be entrusted to her care.

The principal purpose of this writing is to contemplate and, in fact, defend the Word of God from the false prophets that abound in our day, much as Elijah did on Carmel against the prophets of Baal (cf. 1Kgs.18:17-40). I do not advocate the slitting of their throats, save perhaps in a figurative sense, but the words of Jesus should be remembered: "It would be better for him if a millstone were hung round his neck and he were cast into the sea, than that he should cause one of these little ones to sin" (Lk.17:2). And so, let all who are rightfully outraged at the servants of God who have abused young children know that the poisoning of the soul of Christ's little flock with the devil's doubt is an even greater offense against the LORD.

It is the fire of God I hope to bring to bear in these pages, a fire ignited by the blood of Christ, a fire that is of the Holy Spirit… one which reveals the absolute love of the Father for all His children. It is at Our Lady's side we shall find this fire of truth and love.

O let it be a fire that illumines and purges, that destroys only what is of the evil one, never harming even a hair of those dedicated to God. Let these words be only of truth, or let them be cast to the earth. To Holy Mother Church I submit all this writing, praying only to find ears open to the Word of God.

Table of Contents

FIRST WORDS	VII
CHRISTIAN VISION	XIII
GENESIS	1
EXODUS	16
LEVITICUS	24
NUMBERS	28
DEUTERONOMY	38
JOSHUA	46
JUDGES	52
RUTH	57
1 SAMUEL	58
2 SAMUEL	65
1 KINGS	71
2 KINGS	80
1 CHRONICLES	88
2 CHRONICLES	92
EZRA	97
NEHEMIAH	99
TOBIT	102
JUDITH	105
ESTHER	107
JOB	110
THE PSALMS	119
PROVERBS	144
ECCLESIASTES	150
THE SONG OF SOLOMON	154
THE WISDOM OF SOLOMON	157

SIRACH	161
ISAIAH	170
JEREMIAH	183
THE LAMENTATIONS	197
BARUCH	199
EZEKIEL	201
DANIEL	213
HOSEA	220
JOEL	222
AMOS	223
OBADIAH	225
JONAH	226
MICAH	227
NAHUM	228
HABAKKUK	229
ZEPHANIAH	230
HAGGAI	231
ZECHARIAH	232
MALACHI	234
1 MACCABEES	235
2 MACCABEES	244

ADDENDUM:
THE FINDING OF JESUS IN THE TEMPLE 253

FIRST WORDS

A.

YHWH:
On the Word, the NAME,
that is the Heart of Scripture

Where else to start but the heart of Scripture? And what else could be the heart of Scripture, the very Word of God itself, but His NAME – YHWH. And though this NAME be forgotten by the Jew and almost universally ignored by the Christian, should it not be resurrected from anonymity? Did the LORD tell Moses not to speak His NAME to anyone? Did God ever command this to His prophets? Did He not rather say: "This is my NAME for ever, and thus I AM to be remembered throughout all generations" (Ex.3:15)? And can we be of His generation if we do not know His NAME?

All generations will call the Virgin Blessed (cf. Lk.1:48), for she has conceived and given birth to the Son of God, He who has come in the flesh to lead us to the Father. But can we really say Jesus is leading us to the Father, that we know Him as we must (as is our first duty as Christians), if we are unaware of His NAME, or worse yet, if we willfully set it aside?

The Father is transcendent, but we must know Him. His NAME is ineffable, it is silent… yet for those who hear, it speaks volumes. If we have seen Jesus, we have seen the Father. But have we really seen Jesus, have we really seen the Father, if His NAME is something foreign to us?

I must encourage all souls to come to the LORD, to speak His NAME ("YHWH"), for His silence He has made pronounceable by the human tongue. And this great gift we should not shun.

Old Testament

Is this not the core reason the scholars of our day prophesy falsely – that they do not know His NAME, His silent wonder; that they have no faith, and so, no light to see? Faith is the core, the essence of our being (as God is the Truth of all that is and His NAME the heart of Scripture). Without faith how blind we are! Without God we should not go on. For why should souls be led into darkness by the doubt we bring? Why should we endanger others' salvation, not to mention our own? Would it not be better for those without faith, without the Spirit upon them burning truth in their heart's core, to resign their posts as scholars of the Word? Let them run from the pages upon which they write, and quickly, for indeed a fate worse than the millstone awaits them.

May all souls come to the NAME of the LORD and find their faith set firmly on the Rock that is God.

B.

The Witness of the Saints

Pope Benedict XVI, in the first volume of *Jesus of Nazareth*, speaks beautifully of prayer as "silent inward communion with God" (130), and he states well the significance of the LORD's calling Himself "I AM" ("He just *is*, without any qualification" (347)); but when addressing the divine NAME itself (YHWH), he calls it "enigmatic" (ibid). It should not be surprising that even such a brilliant Pontiff should not tie the silent communion found in perfect prayer with the Tetragrammaton, for in no writing of the Fathers of the Church or the mystic saints is this connection made.

Even the great Carmelites, St. John of the Cross and St. Teresa of Jesus, though they speak in an unsurpassed manner of spiritual union with our LORD and repeatedly of the silence that is so much its sign, and though they have likely experienced such silent union more intimately than any other soul (save, of course, Our Lady and the Beloved John)... yet even these extraordinary saints do not relate this transcendent wonder to God's holy NAME and the speaking thereof. Indeed, they seem unaware of the NAME's significance, never mentioning the Tetragrammaton at all.

First Words

This seeming ignorance notwithstanding, it can only be said, as has already been indicated, that these saints and so many others bear the greatest witness (as does Benedict XVI) to the silent wonder that is found most perfectly in the NAME of God.

One could point out countless passages in the writings of John and Teresa that poignantly describe the transcendent silence of God known in His NAME. The book *YHWH: Order of the Divine NAME* offers a quote from each. From John of the Cross: "The soul united to God and transformed in Him draws from within God a divine breath, much like the Most High God Himself..." (54); and from Teresa of Jesus: "In this temple of God, in this Mansion of His, He and the soul alone have fruition of each other in the deepest silence" (110). These are drawn, as I say, from numerous similar passages – one might even say that all their work (as well as their lives) addresses this silence of the LORD.

The same book on the Divine NAME also quotes St. Faustina: "Silence is so powerful a language that it reaches the throne of the living God. Silence is His language" (viii); and Blessed Elizabeth of the Trinity: "We must be silent; it is so simple" (187).... But if one were to search the writings of any of the saints, whether known to be particularly mystical or not, one would find such reference to the divine silence expressed in the NAME of God. For it is nurturing this silence within themselves that has made them saints and worthy of our emulation. Without it, they could not be united to the LORD.

Even within the month of the beginning of this writing (July 2010), Pope Benedict said of the hermit St. Celestine V, during a homily on the eighth centenary of his birth: "It is precisely in external silence, but above all in internal silence, that he succeeded in perceiving God's voice," later directly apposing "interior silence" and "the perception of the presence of the LORD" (*OSV*, 7/18/10).

And, of course, it is Our Lady, the Saint of saints, who best embodies this blessed silence of God. Benedict XVI told us on the Solemnity of Mary in 2006 *(Inside the Vatican*, May 2010) that Luke describes Mary as "the silent Virgin who listens constantly to the eternal Word, who lives in the Word of God." It is she who best hears "the voice of God who always speaks through the silence like the 'still small voice' of a gentle breeze (1Kgs.19:12)." (May she watch over and guide us always!)

Old Testament

To join our Blessed Mother in this holy silence that is the Word of God, we must speak the WORD of God, His Holy NAME, which is this pure silence itself. For speaking the LORD's NAME ("YHWH") serves to "suspend all the operations of the mind," which St. Bonaventure has instructed us is so necessary to "a sacred mystical experience."[1] "We must transform the peaks of our affections, directing them to God alone." And we do this best (the LORD knows) by silencing our tongue. And this is accomplished in speaking God's NAME:

> Physically, the "Y"
> poises the mouth for speech –
> but the "H" immediately
> opens the throat,
> preventing enunciation.
> Then, as the lips approach
> one another ("W"),
> perhaps to ask a question...
> they are left open
> by the final "H".
>
> (from *YHWH: Order of the Divine NAME*, p. 5)

And so we are left in a state of silent wonder. No words, no images, no power of our own – under the Cross of Christ we find the "silencing [of]... our passions and all the fantasies of our imagination" and "pass over with the crucified Christ *from this world to the Father.*" Thus we approach Our Lady and all the saints who live in the light of Paradise.

It is no coincidence that the three persons most intimate with Jesus, and so with God, are the three who stood beneath His Cross: Mary, His Mother, who was preserved from all sin and is ever one with her Son; John, the Beloved Apostle, who rested on His breast and was granted vision of His glory; and Mary Magdalene, the perfectly repentant sinner, who wept at His feet and at His tomb, and was the first to see Him risen. It is under the shadow of His wings,

---

[1] All quotes in the text of this page from Bonaventure's *Journey of the Mind to God*, as presented in the Office of Readings for the saint's feast day, July 15.

the arms of the Cross, we enter the Cloud of Unknowing[2], the utter forgetfulness of self by which we find ourselves in the Hand of God – by which we gain such intimacy with our LORD and God. We must remain with Him even unto death if we are to find new life.

O let us come to God's holy mountain and look upon His transfigured glory! Let us enter His Temple with Our Lady and all the saints. Let us listen to His Word speak to our hearts in Scripture and so find vision of His majesty.

C.
Into the Scriptures

We have already said that the Divine NAME (YHWH) is the heart of Scripture, is the WORD of God itself, for it is, indeed, His NAME. Before entering into our work proper, let us consider the place of the Tetragrammaton in holy Scripture.

The Divine NAME was given to Moses on Mount Horeb when the LORD called him at the burning bush to go and set His people free. Moses was to speak this NAME to the Israelites that they might know it was the LORD who sent him; and, YHWH tells us, this NAME of His is to be remembered by all generations.

It was also on Mount Horeb that God spoke His NAME as a "still small voice" (1Kgs.19:12) to the great prophet Elijah. It is this silence speaking the presence of the LORD that put fear of God into Elijah, a fear that could not be produced by a great wind or an earthquake or a terrible fire; a fear that comes only from being in the LORD's awesome presence. (We note that it was these two eminent men of God, Moses and Elijah, who appeared with Jesus at the Transfiguration, when His glory was manifested to His three principal apostles.)

Throughout the Old Testament the LORD is referred to by this blessed NAME, though, sadly, its use has been set aside in virtually all Bibles to this day. And so, that which is to be remembered by all, which conveys the very presence of the LORD, the Father of all, has

---

[2] Term taken from the book of this title, a seminal work on contemplation.

been all but forgotten. And so, the Spirit that moved upon the waters at the time of Creation, the Spirit Jesus breathed upon the apostles after His resurrection from the dead, is not well known. And so, to Jesus Himself do we remain to an extent blind.

Jesus reveals to us in Scripture that He is the Great I AM. He emphatically tells the Pharisees, "Truly, truly, I say to you, before Abraham was, I AM" (Jn.8:58). When the crowd comes with swords and clubs to the Garden of Gethsemane seeking to arrest "Jesus of Nazareth", what does He tell them but: "I AM He" (Jn.18:5). And what do they do but fall on their faces before Him, in awe of the presence of the LORD standing before them?

"I AM", He says to them; and yet more than these words does He say. For He stands before them in silence, perfect silence, speaking thus the NAME of God. Why is He silent? Why must He be silent? Moses had to stand in silence before the people because no man can pronounce the NAME of God, because the NAME of God silences our tongues. But Jesus stands in silence before the Pharisees and before His captors – and before us all – because He has nothing more to say than He Is. He must be silent that His *very presence* might speak the NAME of the LORD, might speak indeed the Presence of God.

God Is and He Is. He is God. The LORD of Heaven and earth stands before us in the Person of Christ. Here we look upon the face of God shining more radiantly than Moses' face when he came from conversation with YHWH. As Jesus answers Philip when he asks to see the Father: "Have I been with you so long, and yet you do not know me, Philip? He who has seen me has seen the Father" (Jn.14:9).

There is nothing more to say than these words of Jesus. There is nothing more to know than that His presence reveals the transcendent LORD of all, who is beyond words, beyond flesh. Through Him we come to the Father. He is the Way and the Truth and the Life.

Jesus is the Word that was in the beginning, the Word of God, His NAME, His Presence, made flesh. And it is He who speaks to us of the Father in all of Scripture, by the power of the Holy Spirit. And so, let us look with the vision of the LORD upon His Word, and so find Him present in every verse.

Christian Vision

Transfiguration

"Let us run with confidence and joy to enter into the cloud like Moses and Elijah, or like James and John. Let us be caught up like Peter to behold the divine vision and to be transfigured by that glorious transfiguration. Let us retire from the world, stand aloof from the earth, rise above the body, detach ourselves from creatures and turn to the Creator, to whom Peter in ecstasy exclaimed: 'Lord, it is good for us to be here.'"

Anastasius of Sinai

As I begin this work proper, it is the Feast of the Transfiguration. The above quote is taken from the day's Office of Readings. On Mount Tabor Jesus revealed Himself to His blessed apostles. In the radiant light of the Spirit He made Himself known. His glory shone forth to the eyes of Peter, James, and John. Moses and Elijah stood beside Him, and the Father overshadowed them and witnessed to His Son.

It is this same light of the Spirit that shines forth in Scripture; the glory of Jesus is evident on every page of both Testaments (Old as well as New). In this Word the Father reveals His Son, and so Himself – our eyes must be open to its light, and our hearts prepared to live there.

Old Testament

Prophecy

> "First you must understand this: there is no prophecy contained in Scripture which is a personal interpretation. Prophecy has never been put forward by man's willing it. It is rather that men impelled by the Holy Spirit have spoken under God's influence."
> 2Pt.1:20-21

Is there a Scripture passage as universally ignored in our day as this one, to the detriment of all? Is there anything to which people in general and Scripture scholars in particular are blinder than prophecy? The words of Peter could not be plainer; and yet it is as if they do not exist. For ever and always we hear the Word of God treated as if it were the words of men, as if it has come from their minds and thus is the product of their imaginations, rather than a reflection of the Mind of God.

A principal reason for such blindness is likely the secularization of society and the fact that science has become as the new religion, thought to hold all truth. Man worships his own mind and the products of his hands in a manner unsurpassed in history. He hardly even thinks of God. And so, how can one who never thinks of God understand the Word of God? He is unable to see beyond these passing things.

And this disease has infected even some in the Church, even those whose work it is to read and interpret God's Word to us. They, too, easily drift downstream with the dead things. They are, in fact, especially blind and deaf to the LORD's speaking to us in Scripture, for they are especially entrusted with its care.

And what is the source of such blindness? It is simply that they have no faith. Every drop of its heavenly dew has been drained from their souls by the incessant chatter of the material world. This noise is all they hear. And it is this which colors their vision.

Prophets speak for God alone. They do not "follow cleverly devised myths" (2Pt.1:16) to "tickle the ears" (2Tm.4:3) of their listeners. They speak what they hear, and what they hear is the voice of God, not their own, as impossible as that might be for a generation steeped in doubt and fear to comprehend.

There is but doubt and fear in this generation because this is all that can be produced when science is exalted as God. For science can tell us nothing of truth, of life itself, but only of passing things. And though there is certainly a place for knowledge of the world in which we live – one which would complement well the understanding of the ultimate reality upon which religion trains its sights – when it is made a god it can but disappoint, and strangle the life's breath from man.

God speaks, and we should listen. He comes to us with His Word, and thus would save us. Let us be attentive to what He says "as to a lamp shining in a dark place" (2Pt.1:19).

GENESIS

> "In the beginning God created the heavens and the earth. The earth was without form and void, and darkness was upon the face of the deep; and the Spirit of God was moving over the face of the waters."
> Gn.1:1-2

Here is the beginning of the prophecy of God, the Word that delivers unto us the origins of the universe. There was no man present when the world was created: only God saw what was, and only He knows what He did.

But He tells us. He tells us through prophecy what was and how things came to be. Try as they might, the ever-changing theories of science cannot tell us this – the mind of man can only be silenced before the great abyss. He looks but he cannot see. If he does not listen to the voice of the LORD, he shall never know who he is or whence he has come. Only God can tell him this.

And so, what foolishness it is to say that the Word of *Genesis* is not science, not history as we know it (as if what we mortals know might be greater than what God knows). Of course it is not! It does not fall under such limitations of understanding. It does not grope in the dark. It is not afflicted with blindness but shines with God's pure light.

This is what YHWH tells us of the beginnings of space and time, and of our own origin. If He could write it more clearly for us, He would. But this is the Word He gives to edify our souls, to reveal to our minds whence all things come. We must read it just so.

We must come to the Word of God with faith, with the belief that in these words God speaks to us all we need to know; that here He would share with us what He Himself sees and understands, that we might see and understand. But how shall we receive such glorious prophecy?

As a child. We cannot hear God's Word or understand what He would teach us if we don't come to Him as His children, with confidence in His love, that we might return His love as a child. If we are not humble (as He is), if we do not look to Him as our Father and open our mouths to receive His Breath… our souls will not be filled with the light of understanding. And we will remain blind.

In the Spirit of God we must come to the Word that is spoken by the Spirit. In this surpassing light we must dwell, if we are to have light at all. And if we come thus with faith in His Word, He shall indeed illumine our minds and our hearts, and speak to our very souls.

In the beginning was only the Spirit of God; and so, only He can tell us what was, and how things came to be.

Light

> "And God said, 'Let there be light';
> and there was light."
> Gn.1:3

It is by speaking that God creates all things; by His Breath He separates light from darkness. By the Word of His mouth the sky takes shape, and the earth and the sea…. At His command "the stars sh[i]ne in their watches, and [a]re glad" (Bar.3:34). And from the ground He makes man: "male and female He create[s] them" (1:27).

Yes, "even wind and sea obey Him" (Mk.4:41), even the very elements of the universe are pleased to serve Him. And so, why not us? If the angels happily do His bidding and nature falls in line with His will, who are we to rebel? At what cost do we fail to listen to Him?

At the cost of our lives – with the suffocation of our souls. From the dust of the earth the LORD raises man up; from his side He takes woman, his very heart before him. But how his heart can lead him astray if his ear becomes deaf to his Creator. And so, what can he do but hide from the eternal light; what can he do but die? What can he do but fall into darkness?

The Fall

And so, man becomes separated even from himself. Man and woman who were one, who are one, now run from one another, their shame too much to allow them to embrace.

How has this happened? How have those He has made to go forth and multiply, to bring His love, His presence, to the ends of the earth, become the bearers of division and death?

Pride. It is always pride that separates man from God and sets him against others. With what does the devil tempt Eve; what gift may she bring to Adam? That they might be like God! That they might be wise as their Creator. And what a temptation this is. What a great thing it would indeed be to be like our Almighty Father!

But what man cannot see, what Adam and Eve are blind to in the Garden, is that they *are* like God... but that they cannot be more than they are. Made in His image they reflect His glory, and He holds them in His own heart. But the devil convinces them they could be more – and so they become less.

Now they look upon their bodies and instead of seeing the light of YHWH shining through their flesh more brightly than seven suns, they see only how limited they are. They consume the lie that because they are physical beings, because they have bodies, they are but like the beasts of the earth. And so comes separation of body and soul, of man and woman... of man from himself and from God. (The LORD save us from such hell!)

O Jesus, come and show us we are indeed like God! Let us be one again with the Father through you.

Cain and Abel

And so, sin enters the world; and so, violence follows. And so jealousy is the offspring of such separation from God. Cast from the Garden of Eden, they no longer dwell in the LORD's light and are barred from the tree of life (lest they live for ever in their sin).

And so, how evil does grow in their midst, infecting all they touch with their soiled hands! Murder is wrought among them, the blood of a brother spilled to the ground... and so, further from the face of God man ever goes.

How the sins of man mount up before the eyes of God, ever tempting Him to enter in and destroy them. But a remnant the LORD does find amongst His rebellious sons, for His image remains in man despite the evil he has done. And so, though sin be ever "couching at the door...[we] must master it" (Gn.4:7).

By the hands of God man was formed, and by His Breath he is sustained; and even the arrogant pride that rises in his soul cannot utterly break the relationship of man to God. Hell is even this: that man stubbornly seeks to do what cannot be done – that he desires to kill the love of God within himself. But run as he might he cannot escape his Maker, and he cannot change His heart toward him. The LORD's love for man indeed remains.

Noah

In time the LORD will send His Son, the Righteous One, to redeem all those who seek return to union with Him; but now He finds a righteous man, Noah (a son of Seth, the third son of Adam), on whom to rebuild His Creation, from whom shall stem anew all the living. He alone enters the Ark with his family in tow. He takes a remnant also of all the creatures of the earth, that what was made by God might continue in a world washed clean of its stain of sin.

In the Flood is, of course, a sign of our Baptism as Christians. We who know Christ receive this cleansing in a complete manner, in the fullness that is Jesus; but in Noah's time a new earth comes, too... though this one will fall into corruption again.

After the rain, the bow in the sky brings hope for a fallen world. When our hearts turn to God and we sacrifice our lives to Him and for Him, there is a wonderful light that comes through the clouds to renew our spirits. YHWH is present to us. Our LORD and God never leaves us. In Him we are one with one another and find His blessing on our souls. Let us give all things to Him that, as with Noah, He might be pleased with the odor of our sacrifice and look with favor on our prayers.

O LORD, you buoy us up in the Bark of Peter, in your Holy Church. The rains and the waves of this world cannot overcome us, cannot even touch us as long as we are in your Ark. O let us touch down on the new land of Heaven! where peace reigns in men's souls, where we are for ever safe in your arms.

Babel

The sons of Noah are three, and from these the earth is now peopled. One in Noah as well as in God, they speak with one tongue. Their words are few, as this is all they need to be, since they are of the same family. But soon separation comes.

As they go forth, they come upon a plain and decide to build a city and a tower to the sky, even to God on high. So great has their pride so soon become that they think they can overtake the LORD in His kingdom. These heights of their pride reveal to the eyes of their God the remarkable depths of their foolishness. And so to prevent greater evils being conceived by the corrupted heart of man, He confuses their tongues and scatters them to the four corners of the earth. Such separation is here a blessing – much like the sword that guards the tree of life – necessary to keep man from devising his absolute destruction, to maintain the bow in the sky.

Now there will be time for man to learn the lesson that YHWH cannot be approached by human means, by his vain devices. He is not in the sky or across the sea (cf. Dt.30:12-14) or residing on another planet, but far transcends the reach of man... even while resting in his spirit. And only by grace will we find Him there. (In time Jesus will come to reveal the Father's transcendent presence.)

Abram

Generations pass and God calls Abram to go forth from his country to a land He will give him as a perpetual blessing. And from his home Abram goes, obedient to the LORD's Word. Leaving behind all he has known, he takes his wife and his nephew Lot to a place he does not know, going forth in faith as must we all in answering the call of the LORD. (How else shall we find the Promised Land?)

To the land of Canaan – he who was cursed by his father Noah – Abram comes. And after Lot follows the vision of his eyes to the region of Sodom and Gomorrah, the LORD blesses Abram with vision of His promise: He will give him all the land he looks upon, all on which his feet tread... and his descendants will be numerous, as the dust of the earth.

Should we not trust in God rather than the desires of the flesh and the attractions of this world? Is it not then we are truly blessed? Will the LORD not then turn even difficult and dangerous situations to our favor, protecting us and our loved ones from harm even as He increases our yield on this plane and prepares our place in Heaven?

O let us have the faith of Abram, dear LORD! In you we become very rich. What is not ours if we follow your Word? The stars in the sky, the grains of sand on the shore – these indeed can be numbered. But your blessings extend beyond the reaches of this universe. For it is you yourself you would give to us; your own life you desire to share with your children. And so, let us follow in faith the way you mark out for us.

Abraham

The Covenant made with Abram seems in jeopardy, for Sarai is barren and now well beyond childbearing years. And so Abram takes matters into his own hands: listening to the voice of his wife rather than the Word of God, he goes in to her maid. And though the boy conceived in this union shall be blessed, though at his father's request the LORD hears the child's cry... there is yet another son to come. Ishmael is not the one through whom God's promise is to be fulfilled.

The father of many nations Abram will become, and so his name is changed to Abraham. And the LORD reassures His patriarch that the promise to him shall yet be fulfilled – the aged Sarah shall indeed conceive and bear a son.

Who could believe a woman of ninety could give birth by a man of a hundred? And as Abraham and Sarah laugh at such a prospect, scholars of today scoff at the possibility. But he will be born just so, this Isaac; and still the Word of God remains.

Let us laugh only in wonder, never derision, at the hand of God at work in our lives; and perhaps in us, too, His Word will be fulfilled. For if we cannot believe the birth of a child from a centenarian, how will we believe in the One born of a Virgin?

O LORD, in the darkness of this night confirm your Covenant with us; through our poor offering send your blessed fire. It is but in you that we must trust – it is only you who could fulfill our every desire. O let us be fruitful in this land and come at last to Heaven! Let our hearts be circumcised.

Sodom

After Abraham is circumcised with Ishmael and all the men in his house, YHWH appears to this father of nations, this father of all those of faith in the one living and true God. In this mystical scene, the LORD comes to him as three wayfarers, who sit beneath a tree at Abraham's request and eat the food he prepares. After speaking of the imminent birth of Isaac, Abraham and the three men walk together toward Sodom. With Abraham God shares His plans, and gives him opportunity to participate in them.

Does the LORD not want us all to pray to Him, to ask Him for what we need, for whatever good intention is on our hearts? And if we come humbly before Him as does Abraham, if we recognize His righteousness and His power to do all things, He will hear our requests. The LORD would have us stand before Him in faith, and as He saves Lot from the terrible destruction of the city of Sodom at the poor begging of our father in faith, so He will do for us as we ask.

O LORD, we are not worthy to stand in your presence, in the otherworldly light of your kingdom, and speak to you who hold our lives in your hands. How can we poor creatures converse with our Creator? Yet in patience and in love you wait for us to come to you. You bend your head to listen to the beating of our hearts and share with us your very life and will, making us as your children. Save all our brothers from impending doom!

Lot's Wife

O let us not be as the wife of Lot! who looks back toward Sodom with the desire of its sin in her heart, and so is turned to a pillar of salt. Why should we become useless, good for nothing but to be "thrown out and trodden underfoot" (Mt.5:13), worthless in all our words and works?

If we hold evil in our hearts, if we look longingly on the iniquity of this world, saying to ourselves, "If only I could participate therein," what shall be our fate but to be cast from the LORD's presence, even as His angel strives so diligently to keep us on the path to His City, to safe haven in the arms of our God?

Lot himself is so weighed down from living among the sinners of Sodom that he finds it difficult to flee its destruction. (Does the city's influence not cling to him as remembrance of Egypt will later cling to the departing Israelites?) Only because the angel is so persistent and the LORD makes an exception does Lot not die along the way.

And do not the daughters of a mother so lost to wickedness prove to be as she was? Is not the offspring of sin ever the works of evil? For what do Lot's daughters do but go in to their own father? O how the iniquity of the place from which they have so recently come still clings to them! And do not the sons born of such unholy union become the enemies of Israel?

We must rid ourselves of all attachment to sin and prove ourselves indeed the children of God, made in the image of our Father in Heaven and so not giving our members to the wickedness of this corrupt generation. In no other way will we be saved. In no other way will we share in the Sonship of Jesus.

Dear Savior, may our exodus be successful as your own!

Isaac

The promise of YHWH is finally fulfilled as now Isaac is born, the one over whom all laugh with joy for the blessing of a child at such an advanced age. He is Abraham's legitimate son, the only son of Sarah, through whom his promised descendants shall come. This one has both the love of Abraham and of God... yet the LORD calls for him to be sacrificed at the hand of his father.

To the mind without light it would seem a strange request, against all logic and the love of God itself. But one must first remember that Isaac is *not* sacrificed, and never would have been: if Abraham had not obeyed, the LORD would not have killed Isaac anyway; and Abraham's obedience is answered with his son's protection, and Abraham's greater blessing. It was never the will of God for Isaac to be sacrificed, but rather that Abraham and all who follow him in faithful adherence to the Word of the LORD might know precisely that He does *not* require such sacrifice of us, indeed, that it is only *He* that can offer true sacrifice – only His Son will die, will be offered up, for only His death is fruitful. All who die apart from Jesus, die in vain.

Do the eyes of Abraham not see most clearly now that it is the LORD who provides, that He is always watching over us and leading us to His presence, to His light, to His care? Does he not see now that all things are in God's hands? And so, does his heart not brim over with joy? Does he not truly laugh in wonder at all the LORD can do? He is now thoroughly confirmed in faith; and his generation will be most fruitful.

O what a blessed God we have! who would reveal His love so clearly to us, and work so fully in us. Alleluia!

Rebekah

Sarah dies and is buried in the cave at Mamre in the field in Canaan bought by Abraham. To this resting place Abraham himself will soon come, and so he turns to his son, to seek a wife for him from among his kin. And so he sends his servant to the land from which he has come.

And O how the Father blesses the mission of Abraham's servant! How He answers his prayers! For at the man's request, even before he is finished speaking, the LORD sends a fair woman, the daughter of the son of Abraham's brother, to bring him water and to water his camels. (Does He not know what we need before we ask (cf. Mt.6:8)?)

In silence the servant looks upon the maiden as she performs her gracious tasks, and what does he see but the LORD's hand at work? What does he find but that YHWH has answered his prayer in a manner beyond his imagining?

And could there be a more poignant scene of love, of the coming together of bride and groom in the Spirit of God, than the meeting between Isaac and Rebekah? "Isaac went out to meditate in the field in the evening; and he lifted up his eyes and looked, and behold, there were camels coming. And Rebekah lifted up her eyes, and when she saw Isaac, she alighted from the camel…" (24:63-64). She discovers the man walking toward her is her husband, and "Isaac [i]s comforted after his mother's death" (24:67). (Even so should all men be wed to the will of God, and come into His bridal chamber.)

Jacob and Esau

Abraham is indeed the father of many nations; in addition to Ishmael, after the death of Sarah he has several sons of another wife and his concubines. But he gives all he has to Isaac, who greatly prospers, sending the others far away from him. Abraham dies at a hundred and seventy-five, and is buried by Isaac and Ishmael.

Rebekah soon gives birth to twin sons, who strive against one another even in her womb. It is the younger who proves stronger, for though Esau finds favor with his father, God's favor rests on Jacob. And so, supplant his brother he does.

A slave to his belly, Esau first trades his birthright to Jacob for a bowl of red lentils; then even the blessing of his father, Jacob eventually wins. Isaac has grown quite blind, and so, by his senses he is easily deceived as Rebekah dresses up Jacob like the hairy Esau. Mistaking Jacob for his brother, Isaac unwittingly pronounces the blessing of the firstborn over his younger son.

It is Isaac's wife who inquires of the LORD, who speaks with God about her sons; and so she becomes the instrument to bring His will to fruition. And the words Isaac speaks over Jacob cannot be taken back; and so, nothing is left to Esau but to serve his brother.

O LORD, let us not fight against your will. Help us to be obedient to your voice and follow in your way, whatever sacrifice it might entail, for only by walking humbly with you will we be saved. And what good is it if we gain the whole world but lose our souls (cf. Mt.16:26)? Let us rather be ready to give up all of this life and serve our brother, even as Jesus has done. May our spirits not be enslaved to our flesh but let your Spirit set us free, that we might dwell for ever in your tent.

Israel

On his way to his father's homeland (while fleeing his brother's wrath), Jacob has a dream, a rock under his head in the open air. In the dream the promise made to Abraham and Isaac is again confirmed – he will be the one through whom all nations are blessed.

In his dream is a ladder stretching from earth to Heaven, upon which the angels ascend and descend. What is this ladder but the Son of Man (cf. Jn.1:51)? What does Jacob have but vision of the Savior the Father will send to carry His children to the Promised Land? And it is through Jacob this Son shall come. Truly the blessing of all generations is upon him. His is the house of God.

Jacob wrestles with the LORD and then is able to make peace even with his brother ("truly to see your face is like seeing the face of God" (33:10)) as, limping and bowing before Esau, he returns to Canaan with his wives and children and all the many possessions he has gained serving Laban, his uncle, for twenty years.

This man who strives with God (and men), desiring to see His face and know His NAME, is blessed by the angel with a new name: Israel. He is the model for all the faithful, seeking always to embrace his LORD and Savior. Tenacious as Israel we all must be.

O LORD, let us come to you and remain with you, trusting in you for all things of Heaven and earth, and we will be blessed as Israel with vision of your face shining in the face of our Brother, with knowledge of your grace upon our souls. Preserve and prosper the work of our hands in this world and the one toward which we climb. May we come in stages to your kingdom…. Let us walk ever with you.

Joseph's Dream

YHWH blesses Israel with twelve sons, fulfilling his call to be fruitful and multiply, to attain the promise of his father. Of all his sons, Joseph is his favorite; son of his beloved Rachel (who dies giving birth to Benjamin), he is a son of his old age. Thus, a long coat with sleeves He gives to him that he might be as a prince in his house.

It is not only Israel who favors Joseph; God, too, blesses the boy, giving him dreams to reveal his position among his brothers: they shall bow down to him, along with his father and mother.

Such exalted position seems to his brothers great presumption, and they are filled with jealousy for Joseph's place above them, both with their father on earth and their Father in Heaven. And so his coat they strip from him, and even his life they conspire to take, though he is their own brother.

But Israel's favor upon the boy, as well as, of course, God's own, cannot be turned back – Joseph's dream will be fulfilled. There is not a soul who can gainsay the Word of God, and how foolish are those who try. His will shall be done.

Joseph's Slavery

Joseph is sold into slavery by his brothers; to Egypt he is taken captive by Ishmaelites, those who are themselves sons of a slave girl. But the LORD is with Joseph, as He is with all who devote themselves to Him, and He brings him first into the house of one of Pharaoh's officers, then into the house of Pharaoh himself, where he serves to prosper the nation to which he's come in chains. The LORD lifts his head even from the dungeon into which he is thrown for his fear of God and his loyalty to his master. He enables him to see with Heaven's eyes, to interpret the dreams brought before him... and so he finds favor in his slavery.

And the land is saved from impending famine because of the preparations made by Joseph, who is put in charge of everything in the nation. All peoples come to receive rations at his hands, for only in Egypt is there food. God is with Joseph in his rule – and so we see how the LORD blesses those who carry their cross in this world.

What need we fear at the hands of our jealous brothers within the Church or the threats of the powerful of this earth? The LORD is with those who are faithful to Him; even from death they shall be raised with His Son.

The Dream Fulfilled

All the world comes to Joseph to beg for food, and his brothers with them. They bow down before their younger brother whom they sent away in chains. And so is the dream of Joseph fulfilled by the LORD, who alone prospers the work of the just man.

Will we, too, bow down before our lowly Brother, He who has made Himself a slave for our sakes? Our eyes, as were those of Joseph's brothers, are prevented from recognizing our Brother; because of our sins His identity is hidden from us. But He holds our very lives in His hands – without His grace no soul can be sustained.

The favored Son stands before us now, ready to forgive our sins against Him that His Father's will might be accomplished. He weeps over us as for a brother who has gone astray and so become separated from His love. It is His love He longs to give us; His identity He thirsts to reveal to us.

O let our hearts be repentant for what we have done! that we might be reconciled to Him and so find the free gift of Himself and the kingdom He wishes to share with us. Though we crucify Him, His concern is for our souls – in the Brother we have wronged we shall find our salvation.

Israel in Egypt

Then Jacob comes to Egypt with all his offspring, seventy persons in all, for there he will be provided for by his son in this time of famine; and there he will prosper and become a great nation, even as God foretells.

With all their flocks and herds come Israel and his household; with all their possessions they leave the land promised to Abraham to dwell in this foreign place. But indeed here they will be blessed.

And if we question *why* we should live in this land of exile, apart from the saints in our heavenly homeland; if we find our time in this world burdensome and wonder when we shall return again, when the Son shall come to carry us to the Father's side... we will certainly be given the LORD's assurance that all is for our good, and that He blesses us in the trials of life – He is with us wherever we are.

And let us know and remember that soon we shall return, and for ever, not only to a favored piece of earth, but to the kingdom of our God, to Heaven, where there shall be no more fear or weeping but only rejoicing with the full number of saints in the LORD's holy presence.

Jesus is with us now to bring us there; and so, let us pray for the Pharaoh and accept whatever grace we find, even in this desert land.

Israel's Blessing

Jacob blesses his twelve sons – the heads of the twelve tribes of Israel – with the blessing each deserves. Before he dies he imparts his words so that the favor of the LORD might continue forth through his generation, as YHWH Himself has promised. It is in accord with the will of God he now gives his blessings.

Blessed be Israel for the truth upon his lips, for his accomplishing the Father's will! His own will he does not seek to invoke, for he has learned from the blessing he himself received that the will of God is not the will of man. He was not the firstborn and yet the blessing of the firstborn came to him, though his father Isaac would have done otherwise. Ephraim is not the firstborn of Joseph's sons yet he gains the firstborn's blessing from Jacob, despite the wishes of *his* father. And it is Judah to whom Israel's sons shall bow down, through whom the Messiah shall come. Though he, too, is not the firstborn, nor a son of Jacob's favored wife (like Joseph himself), yet "the scepter shall not depart from [him]" (49:10) – he shall rule over his brothers.

And the blessings he gives to some of his other sons do not sound like blessings at all, for he pronounces only what his sons deserve and not what a father might contrive.

O LORD, may we merit a holy blessing from your sacred mouth and accept your will in all things.

The Death of Joseph

Jacob dies and is buried by his sons in Canaan in the cave near Mamre where Abraham and Isaac and their wives (and Leah) were buried. And Joseph weeps again at his brothers' repentance, as they fear now retribution at his hand. But his promise of protection remains upon them and their children, even after the death of their father; for he knows that God did all for good, that the enslavement he suffered has caused many lives to be saved.

How Christlike Joseph is in accepting his sacrifice for the sake of others. How he cares even for brothers who have brought about his suffering. Such obedience to the will of the LORD and trust in its goodness may we all find, that our souls may be saved as we lay down our lives and so become one with the only Son of God.

Joseph soon follows Jacob to the grave, requesting that his bones be taken to the same place, that when the house of Israel returns to Canaan, as Joseph foretells, he might rest with his fathers. But before that time comes, there shall be the suffering of enslavement for all the people: the memory of Joseph shall soon pass from the mind of the Pharaoh, and so Israel be put to hard labor.

Old Testament

EXODUS

The people of Israel multiply greatly and fill the land in Egypt, becoming a strong nation. Thus the Egyptians fear the Israelites, and so their king sets them to hard labor, that their spirit might be crushed. "But the more they [a]re oppressed, the more they multipl[y] and the more they spread abroad" (1:12).

So it is with the people of God that the more we are made to suffer as Christ Himself has suffered, the stronger we become. The chastising hand of the LORD is upon us only for good, only that we might grow more like Him who died for our sins – only that with Him we might become one with the Father.

But the prince of this world will not cease his vain attempts to exterminate God's chosen ones; his jealousy knows no bounds. And so, after Pharaoh does not succeed in getting the midwives to kill them at birth, it is decreed that male Hebrew infants be drowned in the Nile.

To what ends will the powers of this world of darkness not reach to bring the children of light into their grasp? But whatever they might try – even the murder of the only Son, He who dwells in the House of the LORD all His days – shall indeed be in vain, shall indeed be turned back upon them. For even the passageways of death are controlled by God's Hand.

Moses

He is taken from the river, this Moses, saved by the hand of Pharaoh's daughter herself from the death to which all male Hebrew babies have been condemned… and then raised as her own. But it is his mother who nourishes him at her breast.

Just so are all God's chosen ones saved from the watery depths; even the powers of this world He employs to accomplish His will. For all His blessed children are precious in His sight and evoke the pity even of hardened hearts, for who can hide his eyes from the light of the LORD?

And just so are we nourished by our Mother, the Church. Though raised up here in this world amongst this corrupt generation, we are kept free of its temptations and snares by the grace of God. Though reared in Pharaoh's house, Moses does not become as one of those with whom he eats, but remembers whence he has come by the teaching of his mother. And so, when grown he defends his people against the oppressive arm of the Egyptians.

For his zealous concern – which even those he saves do not appreciate – Moses has to flee from the face of Pharaoh and take refuge on God's holy mountain; but soon enough at the call of the LORD he will return to lift the heads of the Israelites from their slavery.

The Burning Bush

The LORD hears the groaning of His people under their heavy burden, and so after forty years He appears to Moses in a bush that is burning but not consumed. On this holy ground on Mount Horeb, the LORD reveals His NAME to His servant; to the ears of this meekest of men He speaks His silent Presence: "YHWH". God Is. He is who He is and will be what He will be and no man can put his tongue upon Him or tell Him anything – He is beyond our words and our comprehension and is only made known to us by His grace and by our admitting that we cannot know Him.

God calls Moses. He promises to be with him, to give him all the strength he needs to carry out his mission. The LORD's NAME will be written upon his soul and so he need not fear speaking even to Pharaoh – no power of the world can stand before Almighty God.

But Moses fears; he doubts his ability to bring the Israelites out of slavery, to call upon Pharaoh to set them free. He thinks of himself and the weakness that afflicts us all, and not of the power of the LORD God of Israel... and so he falls short of his call, and so provokes the LORD to anger. Thus YHWH puts Aaron, his brother, in his place, allowing him to speak the words the Most High delivers to His servant. We see in this that even the great Moses is not fit to speak the Word of God.

Old Testament

Pharaoh's Hardened Heart

To no one before has YHWH made known His holy NAME, and no signs and wonders such as those worked at the hands of Moses and Aaron have ever been seen. But that which is obvious, Pharaoh refuses to acknowledge – that God is calling His people to Himself.

Pharaoh sees from the first that the LORD is with Moses, yet his heart is hardened. And though the severity of the plagues upon Egypt ever increases, nothing can sway the sense of this stubborn king. For try as he might he cannot let go of his subjects, those whom he has convinced himself are his own. Though he knows there is no hope of keeping the Israelites under his thumb, that the LORD's will must necessarily be done... nothing but death will change his word.

And so he thinks to increase their burden, to pile the bricks higher upon their backs, to make it impossible for them to complete their tasks. And though he breaks the spirit of the people and works doubt in the heart of God's chosen servant, the will of the Father is only strengthened, hardened beyond alteration.

He who fights against the LORD can only lose; he who would put himself in God's place shall be deposed. He will lose everything he thinks he owns.

Passover

Not even the darkness in which he sits for three days can Pharaoh see; not even this convinces him of the LORD's hand against him. (And will the three days Jesus spends in the belly of the earth be remembered by us? Will this darkness be enough to open our eyes to the depth of our sin?) And so the LORD's wonders are multiplied – and so the firstborn of Egypt must die (and so Christ is sacrificed).

On this night the LORD God will make a distinction between Egyptian and Israelite. On this night He calls for the sacrifice of a lamb by every household of Israel; on this night its blood will serve to save His people. For the angel of death will not enter the doors anointed with the blood of the lamb. These he shall pass over. But every house of the uncircumcised he shall enter: every Egyptian in the land shall lose his firstborn.

And now the wailing rises, as death comes close to their own skin. Now they beg the people of Israel to leave their land, that utter doom not come upon them. Now they even shower silver and gold upon their slaves as they depart. And this very night the LORD's Chosen go forth as one man, their unleavened bread and staff in hand. Finally they find escape from their slavery, and the grace to worship God freely.

The Crossing of the Red Sea

The LORD leads the Israelites en masse (six hundred thousand strong) out of Egypt to the shores of the Red Sea. In triumph they march out of slavery. But Pharaoh soon pursues them, his army cornering them before the water. It seems they are trapped and will soon be overrun by the gleaming chariots.

But the pillar of cloud which had led the people forth now goes behind them, preventing the Egyptians from coming any nearer. Then Moses stretches out his hand over the sea, and all night a driving wind from the LORD separates the waters before the throng of the Israelites... and they pass through on dry ground with the waters as a wall to their right and to their left. The Egyptian troops follow them even into the sea but, once Israel has made its way across, at a word from God and by the outstretched hand of Moses, the walls fall in... and every one of the Egyptians is drowned. Their bodies wash up on the shore.

The pursuit of sin is relentless, but the LORD is with us with His surpassing power. A mere breath from His mouth is all that is needed to preserve us from destruction, to do away with all our enemies, however dire the circumstances may seem. With the blessing of our God, there is no wall we cannot scale. Let us turn to Him in great faith and praise His goodness in bringing us from the snares of this world to the shores of His kingdom.

Old Testament

The People's Complaint

Upon first crossing the Red Sea, the people of God are greeted with springs of water and palm trees, and all sing the praises of YHWH. But they do not come immediately into the Promised Land. The cloud of the LORD and His fire soon lead them into the wilderness....

A brief sense of their ultimate home, God gives the Israelites; and then they moan when it is taken away. In the desert wilderness the people complain against Moses and the LORD, for they are hungry and thirsty. And so they desire even to return to Egypt, where at least they had food.

There is no place in this world we should seek to remain – even the Promised Land will soon disappoint the Israelites, as the Israelites so soon disappoint the LORD and turn from His call. While we are yet in this flesh we are away from home, away from the presence of the One to whom our dear Jesus would carry us. And so, let us rejoice in the glimpses we have of Paradise, of our dwelling in Heaven... and let us learn to rejoice, not complain, even when such blessing is taken from us, knowing by faith (which is thus ever strengthened) that God is worthy of trust and that to greater glory He does lead us – He hears our prayers and never removes His love. Even the hiding of His light is but to prepare us to receive the eternal grace and blessing of being with Him in Heaven, which we might otherwise spurn.

Manna

What is this? What is this Bread from Heaven the LORD gives us to eat, to nourish us on our journey here? How wonderfully He provides! Indeed, what we need He gives, no more and no less – let us gather in what we require for the day and never fear for tomorrow.

What a great lesson is the manna for the Israelites in the desert! What grace is shown to them! And what grace is shown to us in the true Bread from Heaven, our Lord Jesus Christ, and in His flesh, of which we partake in the Blessed Sacrament. Let us here find our daily bread.

The Father in Heaven watches over us. He sees all our needs and answers all our prayers; He feeds us poor humans with the bread we require. As in the wilderness He gave manna to the people of Israel, so this day He gives all believers His only-begotten Son. Let us come to this table and eat.

But let us keep to His Word; let us follow His instruction and that of His Church. Let us not eat unworthily or greedily seek more than our share. There is enough for all, and no more or less should we desire. Let us be neither gluttonous nor wasteful, leaving nothing over for the next day and never taking more than necessary, more than that which in His grace He offers every hungry soul.

The Commandments

On Mount Sinai YHWH reveals Himself in thick cloud, in smoke and in fire, in thunder and lightning speaking with Moses and warning all that He alone is to be worshiped and adored, that apart from Him and His commandments we surely die.

Moses it is who sits in judgment of the people, for the power of the LORD is with him; God's Word comes through His servant to instruct us in the way we should go. Only on his seat can any find wisdom and means to understand and apply the Law. (And by the rod of the LORD in the hand of Moses, Joshua defeats Amalek in battle.)

Where would the people be without the Law to guide them? How could they know their right hand from their left? Would we be ready to worship God alone and love our neighbors as ourselves if He did not tell us to do so? The heavens must shake for the Israelites to comprehend, for the blindness to be taken from them. And though with the coming of the New Moses we are now freeborn men and slaves of the Covenant of Sinai no more, still, not a letter of the Law will pass away until it is all fulfilled – until heaven and earth pass away and the Word that is Jesus is all we know, we remain in need of these words inscribed in stone.

The Golden Calf

Even while Moses is on the mountain of God, receiving the commandments inscribed by His hand; even though the LORD has promised to send His angel before them to lead them to the Promised Land; even though they have entered into covenant with their God, vowing to do all He commands... in fewer than forty days the Israelites turn from Him to worship the image of a grass-eating bullock.

How stiff-necked the people are! How deserving of death are we all. If we had not Jesus to stand in the breach for us as Moses stands in the breach for the Israelites, despite the gravity of their sin, all would soon perish. If the LORD did not forgive those who sin against Him, there would not be a soul remaining on this earth. Yet those who harden their hearts will not go unpunished – they shall be blotted out of the Book of Life.

How ready we are to revel in our sin. How easily indeed we forget Him who saves us – how little our word is worth. To the golden idols of this world our eyes eagerly turn, and our hearts are quick to follow. Let us listen to the voice of the LORD, let us be stripped of all attachment to sin, for if we are not faithful in our promise to love Him alone, what hope have we for tomorrow?

Moses' Face

Moses alone speaks with the LORD face to face, and so the skin of his face shines like the sun. To Moses YHWH reveals His NAME, and with it His very Presence. Moses is the faithful servant of the LORD to whom He gives His Law inscribed upon stone; and so all the people are commanded to follow the words he delivers to them.

But the light of his face they find too much to bear – too awesome for them is the glory of God upon him. And so when he speaks to the people, Moses is asked to wear a veil. And so even in the Law come from the mouth of the LORD, His presence remains hidden from their eyes.

There is a shadow over the Testament of old, the Covenant made on Mount Sinai with the Israelites and renewed by the Father even after His children so severely stray from worship of Him. He will again go with them; He will be with them as they enter and conquer the Promised Land… though He knows they shall soon turn away again.

All that Moses can do, he does for the people, in fasting and in prayer, in calling on the merciful LORD to be present and make known His NAME – but how can such weak hearts hold to such a gift? And so, until the coming of His Son, His glory remains covered over.

The Tabernacle

In the wilderness the tabernacle is built according to the word the LORD imparts to Moses. By skilled craftsmen and through the generosity of the people, the tent is made and the ark of gold placed within, guarded by the cherubim. And the glory of the LORD fills the tabernacle in a cloud by day and in fire at night. And by His glory the Israelites are led on their journey.

The altar is made for sacrifice and the lamp to give light in this holy place. And to this day the sacrifice is made, and in the Holy of Holies the LORD remains. Nothing has changed. Nothing has changed but all has been brought to perfection by the sacrifice of the Son and the offering He has left with us – His own Body and Blood, of which we partake every day in His Church. And in our tabernacles He stays, awaiting our worship of so great a gift.

Now the manna is the Bread of Life; now the Word is among us as Man. Now the staff of the Holy Father leads the children of the Righteous One on their journey to His kingdom. And YHWH will be with us till the end of the age – from us His presence shall not be taken until we are one with Him in Heaven, until the Day we leave this wilderness and enter His eternal Dwelling.

LEVITICUS

Without blemish must all offerings be made to the LORD – a male without blemish is the norm. Though a peace offering may be female and the sin or guilt offering of the common people female, the whole burnt offering must be male, even as our Jesus (who offered His whole life for our sakes)… or it shall not be a pleasing odor to the LORD.

And the blood is splashed against the altar, the blood which, with the fat, may be eaten by no man but is reserved for God alone. In the blood is the life of the creature, and only God Himself is Life to all. But when Jesus gives us His blood, poured out upon all holy altars throughout the earth, we may drink of this cup He offers. For He calls us to be infused with the divine life of the heavenly Father found in Himself.

And the cereal offering must be unleavened, and a portion of it burned as a memorial. And this most holy offering, which is the food only of the priests, becomes food for us all on the table of Christ's sacrifice. Indeed, we are all called to eat His Body and drink His Blood to become holy as only He is.

O may the fire of the altar of sacrifice never go out! May we add wood to that flame each day, burning ever with the Spirit of God.

Aaron

Aaron is consecrated as priest of the LORD; he is anointed along with the tabernacle and the altar, clothed in the garments of God… and so the sacrifices begin. In the tent he must stay with his sons seven days, and how obedient they must be to the commands given them through Moses! For when two of Aaron's sons offer fire not prescribed by the LORD, they are killed immediately.

The priesthood is no light occupation but one which demands the utmost attention, the utter sacrifice of one's life. One cannot play with the things of God, for He will not be mocked (lest all souls lose respect for their Maker and find themselves unable to stand on His Day). Yes, the LORD is a forgiving God, but he who sins against the Spirit shall not be forgiven – he who makes light of the things of God and so turns them into a lie, cannot but die.

And as Christians we are all called to the baptismal priesthood. We are all inscribed with the Name of Christ, anointed for His mission. Let us be attentive to our call that due sacrifice be ever made to God on high. If a priest cannot play games at the altar of the LORD, neither can we fool with the sacrifice our own lives must become. Let us do all things as the Spirit prescribes, never forgetting the gravity of the work at our hands.

Uncleanness

We must be kept free of all uncleanness that we may enter the House of God and give Him due worship, that we might ever be His children, holy as He is holy. And so YHWH gives Moses instructions on what the people of Israel may eat and not eat, and so He makes distinctions for them about what is clean and unclean among the animals, that they might understand there is a difference between what is of God and what is not, and so learn to desire the good in all things.

And though the laws governing what might be eaten or not are no longer in force, though Jesus has done away with such dietary restrictions, the underlying principle has not thus been weakened but strengthened; for though the flesh has been shown to be of no avail in the things of God, the necessity of a clean spirit is now accentuated.

Which form of leprosy may (or may not) have made a man unclean and caused him to be separated from his community in days of old is now not so important in the eyes of man or God; for all to do with the flesh is now revealed as but skin deep and passing – nothing of the flesh abides – and so only the impurities of the spirit, discharged by a corrupted heart, separate us from the LORD. Let us keep ourselves clean in His eyes.

Atonement

If we are to be holy as God is holy, then atonement must be made for our sins. Even the priests of this earth cannot freely enter the sanctuary, but must first make reparation for their own sins before making reparation for the sins of the people. We must be kept apart from the sins of the nations, the abominations the pagans commit in the eyes of God, else we shall not stand in the holy place to which all the sons of Israel are called.

In matters of sexuality in particular we must not sin against the LORD and His command of purity. Kept free of all lust and all illicit unions, we shall find our way to God; but giving reign to our desires shall lead us only to death. For none who do so shall stand before the face of YHWH, who is all pure, all holy, and cannot countenance our wayward hearts.

But there is an offering to be made for our sins, a goat who will bear them into the wilderness, away from our camp, that we might be free to enter God's presence. Upon His own head Jesus takes our iniquities; the iron weight of the Cross we build He carries on His shoulders… and upon the fulfillment of His sacrifice, we see our sins no more. Let us be faithful to this offering made for our salvation.

The Feasts

The feasts of the LORD must be kept with due diligence. On these days, or for seven days, no work may be done but all must observe the Sabbath rest. On the seventh day the LORD God rested from all the work He had done, and we must ever rest in Him, trusting in His providential care.

And so, on the feast of booths and the feast of weeks, on the day of atonement and at the time of Passover – on every Sabbath day appointed by the LORD, all His children must remember that it is He who is our Creator, and return to Him in peace. Every seven years let the land have rest, and in the fiftieth year let all come back to their inheritance, all be set free to walk with their God, until the day we dwell with Him eternally in Heaven.

Our jubilee shall come; it is upon us now, every day, in the merciful presence of the only Son. In His blood we find our freedom, we find our reason to rejoice as at a feast. For the rest we had lost by our sins against the Father is within our grasp again; the toil with which we were cursed even from the Garden has been removed, and we may walk in liberty as flesh of the only Son of Man.

O let us rejoice all our days! Though the Cross be upon us as it was upon the One who saved us, yet the Word of God cannot be chained, and He cannot be crucified again... and so we rest in Him.

The Blessing and the Curse

O what blessings are in store for those who follow the commandments of the LORD! For He shall walk with them and be with them in all they do. In war they shall conquer, though few in number. Their fields shall produce fruit abundantly, for His rains shall be upon them. There is nothing they need fear – no beast, no foreign nation... for the LORD God shall bless them; He shall watch over them in all things.

But for those who refuse to hearken to the Word of God, sudden terror will come upon them and their lives will waste away in vain. Whatever they attempt He will confute, and they shall flee at the drop of a leaf – their enemies shall easily pursue and overtake them. No children, no cattle, no land will be left to them, for they shall become a desolation.

But those who heed the chastisement of the LORD and return to Him and His ways, He will bless again – He will not utterly destroy the people of Israel or take His Covenant from them. Those who continue in their sin will be punished sevenfold, but those who recognize the evil they have done and seek God's mercy will be received by the land once again. For the LORD desires to draw all souls into His kingdom.

Value

What is the value of a man's life in the sight of God? Fifty shekels or thirty, twenty or ten? Let every man, woman, and child devote his life to the LORD and it shall be beyond value, beyond the standard valuation of men. Infinite in the sight of God is the value of a man's life, for, made in His divine image and restored to that image by the sacrifice of His Son, he becomes as the Person who created him – he becomes one with the LORD. And who could put a value on God Himself?

But let no man seek to take back from the LORD what is His; let him not fail in his devotion to the one God. Our lives are ever in His hands and if we look to remove them from there, what hope shall we have of finding any meaning, any value, to life at all? With Jesus let us offer ourselves as a holy sacrifice. With Him let us place our bodies on the Cross. In this laying down of our lives we shall find their value, we shall take them up again with the Son in the heavenly kingdom.

Blessed are those who dedicate themselves and all they own to the service of the LORD! Blessed are they indeed, for they become His own. And when the Day of Jubilee comes, what glory will be ours as we are gathered into His loving arms.

NUMBERS

The Israelites are numbered according to their tribes; tribe by tribe they are numbered by Moses and Aaron and the chosen leaders of the people. A half million men of age for war are numbered among them, and all the Israelites in their tribes find their place around the tent of meeting, the tabernacle of God.

Three tribes each are placed to the east, south, west, and north, but all face the tent at their center, where the presence of YHWH dwells. And the Levites are positioned in a square within them, closest to the tabernacle, with care over the tent and all its accouterments. These

Levites are holy to the LORD, taking the place of the firstborn sons of all the tribes of Israel, and only they may serve Aaron and his sons, who themselves alone are called to the priesthood.

This is what we see as we look upon the tribes in the wilderness: a people set neatly in place by the LORD, in their ordered rows, with all the congregation focused on their God. This is the vision Balaam will have of the blessed people of Israel. Is it not a model for the Church to follow? Are we not all to stand in our place around the LORD, ready ever to go to battle for Him, ready ever to serve Him as He calls? Let all our attention be given to God as we present ourselves as one Body before Him.

The Aaronic Blessing

"The LORD bless you and keep you:
The LORD make His face to shine upon you,
    and be gracious to you:
The LORD lift up His countenance upon you,
    and give you peace."
                               6:24-26

YHWH, let your peace, the peace your NAME bears, be upon us. Shine your face upon us this day – let us never be separated from you.

Let there be no jealousy or unfaithfulness among us, no infidelity of any kind spoken in our midst. For you shall find out our sins, and truly bitter is the drink we would then have to consume.

Rather, let us consecrate ourselves to you, freely and completely. Let our lives be a total offering to you, as are those who take the vow of the Nazirite. Let no bitter drink pass our lips, but let us be holy as you are holy, clean of all grave sin, and so, blessed to be called your children.

From the corruption of human society we must remove ourselves if we are to know the light of your face shining upon us, if we are to stand in your presence and serve you. O let our days be completed in faithfulness to you, our dear Husband! Make our spirits one with your own by your grace.

Old Testament

The Altar Dedicated

The altar is dedicated to the LORD, and all the tribes bring their offering to Him; day by day, tribe by tribe, in perfect order their offering is made to God. Each gives an ox, and between two a wagon, for the service of the tabernacle. Each brings a silver plate, a basin, a golden dish with incense... and all the animals to be offered on the altar in sacrifice.

And the lamps are set up to give light; and the Levites are consecrated to the work of God. These are given to the LORD in place of all the firstborn, to do service for the people at the tent of meeting and to make atonement for all Israel. They are cleansed and so made ready to enter the tent and serve Aaron and his sons.

And now the Passover may be kept at its appointed time. Now all the Israelites are commanded to remember the night on which they passed from slavery to new life. Now all must eat the Lamb of sacrifice as prescribed by their LORD and God, that they might remain His people till the end of time.

To the altar let us all come this day, to offer the Passover Lamb in freedom and in joy. Let us all share in this sacrifice of the only Son, joining Him as a holocaust to the LORD. And then the cloud of His holiness will cover us... and we will be led forth by the Spirit of God.

The Cloud and the Trumpets

YHWH is present to His people in a cloud that settles upon the tent of meeting, and which has the appearance of fire by night. This cloud serves as the people's guide all their time in the wilderness; by it the LORD leads them forth.

Indeed, Israel follows the movement of the cloud, breaking camp only when the cloud rises, and settling again where it rests. With remarkable faithfulness the people of Israel follow the cloud in the desert; with remarkable faithfulness the LORD leads them.

And when the time to break camp comes, two trumpets Aaron and his sons blow; and those on the east, south, west and north set out in order, the tabernacle of the LORD in the midst of them. To the trumpets all remain obedient, falling into their ranks at the sound.

Numbers

These trumpets also serve as a call to war and a call to celebrate the feasts of the LORD.... And when the angels blow the trumpets at the end of time, it shall be a call into the kingdom for all God's faithful people.

Do we hear the call of the LORD; do we follow in His way? Are we faithful as the Israelites in our journey through this desert? Do we have obedient hearts set on serving the will of our God? O let us set forth in faith and in strength as He calls, that we might dwell with Him for ever. Let His Spirit be always upon us!

The Complaining Continues

Though the LORD dwells with His people and scatters their enemies before them; though He gives them manna, the food from Heaven... the people complain against God and Moses and desire to return to their slavery in Egypt, that they might fill their bellies with flesh of the earth.

So the LORD burns with anger against His people and answers their crying with quail up to their necks all around them. But with this food, which they eat till it pours from their nostrils, the LORD sends a plague, that they might learn that sin has its consequences – no one can spurn the love of God and live.

Then to answer Moses' plea that He kill him if he must bear the weight of all this people, the LORD places His Spirit on seventy men chosen by His servant, to help with the burden upon him.... O that all might indeed be prophets of the LORD! that He might put His Spirit on all souls – let the prophecy of Joel be fulfilled in the Spirit of God's only Son.

But when Miriam and Aaron speak against their brother and presume to take equal place with him, the LORD strikes Miriam with leprosy to prove to all that none is blessed as Moses. And so, who is there like Jesus among the sons of men, He who is the very face of God? Let us never complain against this New Moses or against His Father, but simply rejoice in the Spirit, whatever cross we must bear with Him.

Refusal to Enter

Moses sends a leader from each tribe to spy out the Promised Land which the LORD calls the Israelites to conquer; and though it is a land flowing with milk and honey, though its fruit is rich and it lives up to all the promises God makes, these leaders instill only fear in the people as they doubt their ability to overcome the natives of the place.

And in doubting their strength, they doubt God, who has sworn to be always with them – they make Him as small as themselves. And so the people long again to return to Egypt; and so they would stone Moses to death along with Joshua and Caleb, the only faithful sons. And so the LORD desires to destroy them all.

Because of Moses' intercession, the LORD spares the lives of the people for a time but vows they will all die in the desert, where they are doomed to wander now for forty years. Only their children will come into the Promised Land, with the faithful two. Here is witting sin against the command of God; and so their blood will be on their own hands, as so soon the LORD brings their death about.

Why should we doubt the Word of God? How can we who have known His love fail to remain faithful to Him? Why do we question His power? His arm is not shortened and all that is just He shall accomplish in His holy will.

Korah's Rebellion

Then Korah and his men stand up against Moses and Aaron and challenge their authority. Though Levites called to serve in the tent of meeting, they want more: they desire to enter the sanctuary and approach the altar of the LORD God – they want the priesthood itself. They would arrogate to themselves what is only the Father's to give, and so they accuse Moses and Aaron of being presumptuous as they, saying the brothers speak their own words and not the command of the LORD.

For such grave offense against the Word of God and against His will, the punishment cannot but be severe. For who can approach the altar who is not called? Will they not be burned in unholy flames before Him? And so, as these men stand before YHWH with their censers in hand, indeed they are consumed by fire. And all their families are swallowed by the earth, going down to death with their sins upon their heads.

Yet on seeing all this, the people do not fear but accuse Moses of murder. They rebel as well. And so a plague goes forth from the LORD that would kill them all... but Aaron stands in the breach between the living and the dead.

It is Aaron and his sons who are called to the priesthood, to share in the LORD's choice portions. It is his rod alone which sprouts with almond blossoms. And today, who can come before the altar apart from the call of the Pope or a bishop? Let no man (or woman) take the priesthood upon himself, or he shall surely die.

The Waters of Meribah

Seemingly never cleansed in the water for impurity, the people contend again against Moses and Aaron, for they have not the food or drink they so greatly desire. To Egypt their eyes are again turned, as once more they look back with longing upon their slavery. But the LORD shows patience with His people and calls Moses to tell the rock to bring forth water for them.

But Moses has not the patience of the LORD with the complaints of the people. With anger he comes before them, striking the rock two times, as if in hateful vengeance. And for this failure to display the sanctity of God, for making Him seem less than holy in the eyes of Israel, Aaron is kept from entering the Promised Land... and Moses shall soon follow him in death on the mountaintop.

The LORD will provide water for those who love Him, who sing His praises day to day. For He loves His people and is concerned only for their welfare; it is not His intention that any die in the desert but that all enter happily into His presence.

But how hard our hearts can be! And so, the fiery serpents are sent into our midst. Yet, on a pole He will mount His Son, that all who look upon Him shall be saved, all their sins washed away.

Old Testament

The Vision of Balaam

The Israelites begin to show the power of God that is upon them, destroying Sihon king of the Amorites and Og the king of Bashan. And so Balak, king of Moab, calls on Balaam to curse God's people, for fear of them has fallen upon him.

But what the LORD reveals, the prophet must make known; what he hears from God, he must speak. And though he may be distracted by the silver and gold offered him, though he might like to please the king, Balaam realizes he himself will be destroyed if he follows not the path the LORD sets forth. And so, saved from the sword in the angel's hand by his donkey's vision and speech, the prophet comes to the king of Moab and repeatedly blesses the children of Israel.

Balaam sees not only the glory of the encampment of the people, that they are set apart from the nations and shall devour all in their path by the power of God; he sees also their future glory – that the Son of God shall arise from them.

O that we had eyes open to see and hearts brave enough to speak of the glory of God on all who love Him, on all who are His faithful children! O that we might be among them, in their blessed ranks in the light that has come forth from Jacob!

Phinehas' Jealousy

How fickle is the heart of the people. For after Balaam's refusal to curse the Israelites, they serve to curse themselves by going after the gods of Moab and bowing down to the Baal of Peor. And so, what the king of Moab could not accomplish, the people indeed bring upon themselves.

Through harlotry with the daughters of Moab, the people are seduced, drawn away from worship of the one true God to that of false idols: to the evil one they yoke themselves. But when even in the sight of Moses, even as the people are weeping for the plague they suffer for their unfaithfulness, one of the men of Israel brings in a Midianite daughter of a tribal head that he might marry into this foreign race... the righteous anger of Phinehas is aroused.

In his jealousy for the LORD he runs through with his sword both the man and the woman, thus atoning for the sins of Israel and staying the plague upon them.

No one can destroy the men of God but themselves. Nothing can kill us but our own sins and our refusal to turn from them to the blood of the Lamb. If our hearts go out from the love of God to the lust of this world, what can the Father do? We are free to bring about our condemnation. But know that He has sent a Savior.

The People Numbered

All the men twenty years of age and above are numbered again in their tribes, in their tens of thousands, in their half million as a whole. They are numbered that it might be known the size of each tribe and so the length of land to be assigned to each when the Israelites come into their promised inheritance. Indeed, the time is upon them to enter in, for all those have died who rebelled against the LORD and His command to take possession of the land, all those who refused to embrace such a gift for fear of the people living there. Now only Joshua and Caleb remain of all the men present at that time; the rest have perished in the wilderness.

And soon enough Joshua shall lead them in. Though Moses will die on the mountain, he lays his hand on his assistant... and so Joshua is given power from God to accomplish his mission.

Who among us is worthy to enter Heaven? Who shall lead us to our inheritance? We are destined to dwell for ever in the LORD's holy kingdom, but who has been prepared for such a call? All fall short of the glory of God; all should be held back from entering in. But by Jesus and His blood we are made ready to receive the gift the Father offers His humble children. And so let us pray we shall be among the number of those who find their place in the Promised Land.

Offerings to the LORD

The offering of animals and cereal and drink marks the days and the weeks, the months and the seasons of the year, consecrating all time to the LORD God. The people are commanded by God to remain faithful to these sacrifices, that their lives might be blessed, that they shall indeed themselves be consecrated to the LORD.

There are offerings prescribed for each day, for every Sabbath, for the beginning of each month and the turn of the seasons. Time is in the hands of God; all Creation is His own. And if we wish to remain in His hands, as His own, we must continually give all over to Him – we must ever recognize His supremacy over everything. Then we shall be living in the truth, and the truth, the presence of the LORD in our lives, will make us free men and women.

O LORD, you are our Husband and Father, with the final say over all that proceeds from our mouths. Let our vows be blessed by you, or let them not be at all. Let all our offerings be acceptable in your sight, or let them fall to the dust. May our very lives be as a fragrant offering rising to you each day, every hour of each day throughout all the days of all the weeks and months of all our years!

O LORD, make us holy as you are holy, as your Son is the holiest sacrifice.

Vengeance on Midian

YHWH calls Moses to avenge the people of Israel on the Midianites, those who have served to lead Israel astray with their worship of false gods. It is to be Moses' last act before he dies. It is a sign of the purity the people must have in the sight of the LORD – they must not be polluted by the idols of the nations to whom they come.

And the five kings of Midian are slain along with Balaam and every man among them. But the warriors bring back the women – even those who themselves have seduced Israel into false worship – as well as all the children. And so the anger of Moses is enflamed and he orders the death of all these women and all their male children, that Israel might not again be led into sin; only the young girls who have not lain with a man are spared.

Let it be known that there is nothing more important than pure worship of the only LORD. Without this, all are dead. And so, the lesson of Scripture must be learned: that life is found only in God and in His Word.

The sheep and cattle and all the booty are divided between the warriors and the people, and the priests and the Levites receive their share; but all gold is given to the LORD as atonement, for the lives of every one of the twelve thousand soldiers has been preserved by Him alone.

Transjordan

The Israelites come by stages to the end of their journey in the wilderness. From place to place they have passed these forty years, and now the time approaches to come into the land promised them.

As they prepare to enter and take possession within the boundaries the LORD has set – each tribe to receive land according to its size – the sons of Gad and Reuben and the half-tribe of Manasseh request of Moses to take their inheritance this side of the Jordan River. Though at first angry, believing them to be repeating the sins of their fathers (who refused to enter the Promised Land at the LORD's command), Moses relents to their proposal after they vow to go with their brothers to war until all have found their places.

And cities of refuge for those who kill without intent are commanded to be set up in land appointed for the Levites to dwell. In these places alone will he who slays by accident remain safe; but he who murders shall not escape punishment.

The inheritance of the daughters of Zelophehad is confirmed (as long as they marry within their clan), as is that of every tribe… and so all is set for the people indeed to come into their inheritance. But first a final word from Moses.

Are we ready for our eternal inheritance? We must ask ourselves.

Old Testament

DEUTERONOMY

Before he dies, before the Israelites enter into the land promised them by the LORD, Moses recounts for the people how they have come to this position, then reminds them of the Law.

It is the end of their fortieth year in the wilderness and all those have died who disobeyed the command of God to enter and take the Promised Land. Moses stresses to the people the foolishness of their fathers that they might not make the same mistake, that they might not be afraid despite all the graces with which the LORD has blessed them. He was with their fathers in power and might, yet they had no faith in Him. Let their sons not also turn from their God.

They have destroyed the kingdoms of Sihon and Og and taken all their land; with them the LORD has already shown His mighty hand. Did He not give these kings over to His chosen ones? Have not some already come into possession of their inheritance this side of the Jordan? And so, will the LORD not be with them in the same way as they cross into the Promised Land? There is no place for doubt of the providence of God.

And so, why should any doubt that the LORD is with us, that He is true to His Word and well able to do all He promises? Is it not His will that we enter Heaven? And so, with Him, how can we fall short?

The LORD Is God

"The LORD is God;
there is no other besides Him."
4:35

The LORD has taken the people of Israel from the midst of the furnace in Egypt, rescued them by His great power from the land of false worship, and now He calls them by the voice of Moses to enter into the inheritance He would give them. And the first word Moses must declare is that *The LORD is God*. All their future rests on remembrance of Him.

He has spoken to them out of the midst of fire in the theophany on Horeb. There they heard a voice but saw no form that spoke the words, for YHWH indeed transcends all the images of this earth: His NAME cannot be formed by any tongue. And yet He has come to them and revealed Himself to them, so much so that they asked to be spared such vision of His glory, begging that Moses alone might speak with Him.

And will they now turn to the graven images of the nations they are about to conquer? Will they worship the sun and gods of wood and stone in the form of the creeping things of this earth rather than the one true God who has saved them and entered into Covenant with them? Even if they do He shall forgive them when they seek His face again, for indeed, He alone is God and His mercy endures for ever.

The Ten Commandments

That they may live long in the land they enter to possess, the LORD gives His people His commandments; if they abide by them, they shall not lose their blessing.

He tells them first they must indeed worship Him alone who is the only God, keeping His NAME and His day holy, never attaching themselves to any corrupt thing of this earth. Then they must give honor to those who gave them birth and be certain never to kill or lie or steal, or fall into lust or the desire for anything that is not their own. They must keep themselves pure as He is pure, seeking always to do His will, remembering always that they are His own.

His Word must be written on their doorposts and gates, on their hands and foreheads, and kept ever in their hearts. With heart, mind, soul and strength they must love the LORD their God and speak of Him always, wherever they are, and especially to their children. All must know Him and love Him and draw closer to His eternal love in the light of Heaven.

How shall we come to His kingdom if we do not remember Him here? How shall we find His blessings if we do not desire them? And so, let us praise the LORD for the path He marks out for us in the Commandments written on stone by His own hand; and let us praise Him most of all for His Word made flesh in the Person of His only Son. Through Him we shall come to the kingdom.

Old Testament

Holy to the LORD

The people of Israel are called to be holy, they are called to utterly destroy all the wicked images and altars of the nations into which they come; for nothing abominable can stand before the LORD, and they are to stand with Him.

It is not because of their righteousness that Israel is called to be God's chosen people, to reflect His image in this world. And it is not by their own power they shall conquer the land of Canaan. It is the LORD's will and the LORD's power that are at work, as it is with any of us who follow in His way. All is sheer grace.

The Israelites will receive abundant blessings in the Promised Land, but they must beware, as must we all, of becoming bloated by the good things the LORD shares with us... lest we lose ourselves in them, lest we begin to think we have gained all good ourselves – lest we forget God.

We should never fear the obstacles that are set before us, the threats of the evil one that surround us. YHWH is with us with His power to save and build up His people, and there is no greater power than His. But let us remember always that it is indeed *His* power and not our own by which all good things are done, and we shall remain holy before Him, with no stain of sin, no pride, to corrupt our souls or lead us into temptation. Let us leave no false idol standing.

Rebelliousness Remembered

What a stubborn people Israel is! How they readily turn from God. Moses reminds the people how they have sinned against the LORD so that they will realize it is certainly not for their righteousness they are being blessed. Indeed, they deserve death.

How many times the LORD would have destroyed the Israelites in the desert; but for Moses' intercession, but for his fasting and prayer on the mountain of God, they all would have died for their worship of the golden calf, or for their failure to enter into the Promised Land... or for their constant complaining against the LORD. And He would have been justified in killing them.

How right the LORD would be to destroy any and all of us, for we have all been rebellious toward Him and none deserves to live. This we should fix in our hearts. Remembering our sinfulness in the eyes of God, how could we fall into a vain pride which would be the death of our souls? What should we do but treasure His commandments and serve Him and praise Him for His goodness in sparing our lives at His Son's Word, by His Son's blood?

It is only by grace we live at all; let us indeed keep this fact firmly in mind. Let us ever recall that we are nothing, and less than nothing, for our sins. But by God we are graced to become His children: in Him we find life everlasting.

The Place God Will Choose

The Temple is already foretold by Moses here in his final words to the people. To this place all must come with their tithes and offerings; in this House alone will worship be acceptable, and not under every green tree. Here shall be eaten the meat of sacrifice, here alone. Let no man persuade you to go elsewhere, lest death come to you as well as him.

Unclean things shall not pass the lips of the Israelites, for they are holy to the LORD. They cannot eat everything nor believe every word that comes to them. For they are being tested, as are we all, to see if they will follow the LORD's righteous path, or go aside according to the desires of their own heart.

Should we listen to every prophet that comes to us, speaking as if from God? And if he should lead us then to things that are not of God, will we listen to him still, will we be fooled by the glamour cast upon our eyes? Let every false and empty vision be put to death.

The LORD chooses for us a place to dwell, a City and a House in which to offer Him due praise. Only in His Church is truth known and our sacrifice made worthy. If we do not come into His Temple, we shall not find His blessing. Let us rejoice before Him alone, with those whom He ordains.

Year of Release

The people are to show the kindness of the LORD, His merciful love, to all, and especially to their brothers. And so, every seven years they are to release their fellow Israelites from any debt. Thus there will be no poor among all the people, for all the people will reflect the LORD's generosity toward one another.

Indeed, they are to give freely to those who are poor, not only releasing them from all debt at the appointed time, but also lending to them even if the seventh year is near. Thus hearts must not be grudging toward their neighbor but indeed reflect the great generosity of God, from whom all good things come.

And all their Hebrew slaves the people are to set free after six years of service; in the seventh year they are to let them go, furnishing them liberally with the goods they need. The Israelites were redeemed from slavery by the hand of the LORD, and this they should celebrate by releasing their brothers from bondage in like manner.

How generous is our God! With what mercy He looks upon our poor souls. He makes us rich by His grace, setting us free from sin and giving us all we need to thrive before Him. No weight of debt do Christians know, except to love one another. What joy is ours in reflecting the image of God!

Eye for Eye

YHWH calls His people to keep the appointed feasts; three times a year they are to appear before Him with hands full of offerings. For the feast of unleavened bread, the feast of weeks, and the feast of booths, they must come to the place He will choose.

But those who go and serve other gods and worship them, what shall become of them? They must die. Those who share in the abominable practices of the nations, those who burn their children in the fire and practice divination and sorcery – all of which the Israelites shall do – what can come to them but death? The LORD cannot look upon such evil.

The LORD gives cities of refuge for those who slay without intent, for He does not judge those who kill by accident; but the murderer shall not be spared – he shall be stoned to death at the gates of the city.

The LORD will appoint priests and judges whom the people must obey, and He will even give them a king.... But that king is commanded never to multiply houses or wives, or silver and gold (all of which King Solomon will do so prominently). He is not to rule in a vain pride but follow closely the Law of his God. For how shall a kingdom stand apart from the light and love of YHWH? How shall any live removed from Him? They shall not; they cannot, for He Himself is Life.

War

It is the LORD who fights for Israel; He goes with them to war. And so their trust must be in Him, and in His command.

If any is fearful, let him turn back to his house – only those of courage are needed in battle. And if a man has any business undone with his house or fields or bride, let him turn back and take care of these pressing matters.

The Almighty does not need many men to gain victory in battle, but He does need their faith. As they enter into war, their hearts must not be faint or in any way distracted; they must but know the LORD is with them and in Him they will triumph.

And though they must act humanely in their battles, though they must offer peace to each city they would conquer, not destroy the fruit of the fields barbarically, and give the women they take a period of mourning for their families... all the men are commanded to be put to death, that all the evil come from them might be blotted out.

The LORD has a purpose for war; He calls the Israelites to fight in His NAME. The killing is never to be arbitrary, but serve to accomplish His will and prove that He is determined that goodness reign among us. And so we should not be afraid at the specter of death or to effect God's chastisement. We must trust that He is always with us in battle and remains with us even in death, ever bringing about a greater good. The rebellious son shall be killed, but innocent blood must not be shed.

Keep His Statutes

All the statutes and commandments must be carefully kept if the Israelites are to be God's holy people, as they are called this day. Justice and purity are with Him and must be with those who enter His house.

And so, tithes must be given and a just weight maintained; a brother's goods must be protected and the widow and orphan never oppressed. The worker must receive his wage and opportunity be given to the poor to glean the food they need. But above all, the marriage bed must be free of defilement.

Sexual purity and justice are a particular call to the people of God. Women must guard their virginity and men must respect it. Once taken, responsibility must be accepted. Life and death are tied to the sexual act and the organs thereof, and the Word of God is not bashful about acknowledging the critical importance of this gift. Children must be borne, and borne according to His Law – let no one abuse this privilege.

Ultimately the Law of the LORD is one of reason, of truth, of perfect justice. It is written for the man of earth and his humble state. Those who would go beyond it vainly seek to make themselves gods; those who fall below it become beasts. Life is found only in keeping to the way the LORD marks out for us.

The Curses

How severe the curses on the people if they should turn from the LORD their God and fail to keep His commands. Blest are they when faithful to Him, but what woes shall come upon them when they do not obey!

All that they have shall be attacked, shall be stricken – their land and their cattle, their wives and their children, and their own bodies He shall smite. Fiery heat and drought, fever and consumption and violent nations shall fall upon them. Covered will they be from head to foot by boils; driven away will they be to another land.

Their enemies shall indeed utterly overtake them and all they possess, and they will be struck with "madness and blindness and confusion of mind" (28:28). So great shall be the affliction upon them that they will eat the flesh of their own children: there will be no love left even between mother and child.

They shall be all but blotted out from the face of the earth – those once numerous as the stars of heaven shall be very few. For what punishment is too great for a people chosen by God to be His own who turn to worship of wood and stone? How shall those be made to see who have given their eyes and hearts to profligacy? They will languish many days, becoming even less than slaves.

Return

Though all the curses Moses prophesies upon the people of Israel shall come to pass, though they shall suffer like the innocent Job for all their guilt in spurning the LORD their God and be sent into exile far from His face and the blessing given to Abraham... though their walls shall be broken down and they find themselves again as slaves in Egypt, yet their walls will be rebuilt when they return to YHWH with all their hearts and seek to worship Him alone.

The Law Moses inscribes for the people, the blessing and the curse He invokes upon them in the Father's NAME, shall remain with the Israelites all their days, never losing its effect. But there will come a Savior from among them to free them from the weight of the Law, to take on Himself the punishment for their rebelliousness and so release them from its bondage and lead them to salvation.

Let all hearts turn to Him and recognize His speaking in our every breath. He is near and calls to us to leave behind our blindness, our lack of love for Him, that we might come into His Promised Land and there dwell in His peace for ever.

Let the curses we suffer serve to open our eyes to the futility of our ways apart from Him, that we might choose life and not death and so find His eternal blessings in the kingdom of Heaven. Let Moses' song be remembered by all.

The Death of Moses

On the very day Moses finishes speaking God's Word to the people, He invokes blessing upon the twelve tribes of Israel and goes as called to the top of Mount Nebo to die. He is granted vision of the Promised Land in all its goodness, but he is kept from entering there because of his failure to reflect the holiness of the LORD at Meribah.

The LORD must hold a special place for His servant in the heavenly kingdom, a place of rest from all his labors here. As Elijah the great prophet will be taken up by the fiery chariot, so it seems that Moses, whose place of burial "no man knows…to this day" (34:6), is also taken from this plane to God's side in Heaven. There may be blessing in his being kept from entering the land of Canaan, a Promised Land which will not stay – the LORD likely brings to the true Holy Land His servant who knows Him face to face. (With Elijah, Moses appears at the Transfiguration; does this not show he is in heavenly light? For how can a man be seen beside the Son of God in His glory if he is not in a place set apart?)

The hands of Moses are laid upon Joshua now; the spirit of wisdom is with this savior of the Israelites. Let them follow him faithfully to the blessed land held in reserve by their mighty God.

JOSHUA

Now that Moses is dead, the LORD calls Joshua to lead the people into the land He has promised them. The time has come to cross the Jordan and conquer Canaan, and Joshua must stand in the place of Moses and be of great faith and courage in accomplishing the Father's will.

First he must indeed be faithful to the Law Moses set down; day and night must he meditate on the Word of God, for there alone he will find his strength – by the LORD alone he must be guided.

Thus Joshua calls the people to readiness, to go in and take possession of what the LORD gives to them – wherever their feet tread shall become their own, as long as they remain faithful. And the people vow allegiance to Joshua; they express their willingness to follow his command. May the LORD God be with him!

Salvation is upon the people now; their hopes will finally be realized. But even as they prepare for battle, even as they treasure the call of the LORD and fortify themselves in faith and in His Word… even as the Promised Land they enter to possess, we know this possession shall not last for ever, that only our Heavenly homeland can satisfy our hearts. And so, Jesus waits for us at the gates; and so, in Him we must put our faith. Upon His Word let us meditate, and we shall be saved. He is the new Moses.

Rahab

Joshua sends out two spies to view the land, and to Jericho they come. There they find refuge in the house of the harlot Rahab, who hides them on her rooftop. And so they are not discovered; and so the LORD keeps them safe and they accomplish their mission.

Perhaps as good a deed as saving the men Rahab does in informing them about those who stand in the path of the Israelites: great fear has fallen upon all who await these impending conquerors, for it is clear that YHWH, the LORD of Heaven and earth, is with them. And no one can stay His hand.

As Rahab preserves the lives of the two spies, and with them the hopes of Israel, so the promise is made that she shall be spared with her whole family at the time of Israel's invasion. And through this harlot the Son of Man shall descend, showing most clearly how all may find welcome in the House of God.

O may all our hearts be so converted to the LORD that we might serve Him in such a profitable way! Like the Magdalene is Rahab, upon whom the grace of God has come, and so there is hope for all of us sinners so far removed from the LORD's presence, that we shall in wisdom turn to Him and have our lives preserved with all our loved ones. The scarlet cord we wear shows we are but sinners, yet the LORD has mercy on those who recognize His power. All faithful souls shall be saved on the Day of His coming.

Crossing the Jordan

Now the LORD manifests Himself to the Israelites to make clear to them that He is with Joshua as He has been with His servant Moses, for as He parted the Red Sea that they might pass through on dry ground, so does He do with the Jordan River, that they might pass now into the Promised Land.

And it is the priests who lead them, carrying the ark of the Covenant; and so it is truly God who leads them, who goes before them to eliminate any obstacles to the fulfillment of His will. Even as the feet of the priests enter into the river, the waters cease to flow (disappearing in the other direction) and stand in a mound as a wall beside the blessed children of God. Safely goes this great multitude on dry ground, protected by the Hand of the LORD.

And once across they are commanded by Joshua to take twelve stones from the midst of the Jordan, from the ground on which their feet have trod, that when the river overflows its banks again they will remember whence they have come and what the almighty God has done for them, that they might have faith in Him; they set up these stones that indeed they might never forget how blessed they are. And in this place all the men are circumcised, made clean in the sight of the LORD – the reproach of Egypt is rolled away from them.

The Israelites then keep the Passover. And on the very next day the manna ceases and they eat of the fruit of the land.... A wide country opens up before their eyes.

Jericho

Michael comes and stands before Joshua, drawn sword in hand, to call him to his conquering mission in the LORD's NAME. This commander of God's Army will be with the leader of Israel's army, for it is the LORD and His angels who fight for them. On this holy ground Joshua is entrusted with the destruction of Jericho, the first city to fall before the arm of God.

Specific instructions are given to the people's chosen savior: the priests must circle the city once each day, seven trumpets blowing before the ark, the army of Israel before and behind them. Thus the

Joshua

inhabitants of Jericho, who have barricaded themselves within the city walls, will grow even more afraid of what is upon them. Then, on the seventh day, when the priests and the army circle the city seven times and raise a shout unto Heaven (after having remained silent the first six days), the walls surrounding Jericho shall collapse... and the wrath of the LORD destroy all its inhabitants.

And so it is. Every man, woman and child, along with all the animals, the Israelites put to the edge of the sword. But it is indeed the LORD who cuts them down, who destroys their city with fire for all their sins against Him... for their holding so dearly to iniquity, to false gods and errant ways.

Let no man who persists in sin think he shall escape the wrath of the Just One; only those repentant as Rahab shall be spared on the LORD's holy Day. Here is a sign of the coming destruction held in store for the city of man.

Ai

Even in the midst of great victory is wrought the downfall of the Israelites, for though the LORD blesses them mightily in their first conquest of the Promised Land, they do not obey His command. (How lacking in faith all men are!) And so defeat soon follows.

The tiny city of Ai sends Israel's troops fleeing, and a number of men are put to the sword. How can this be? Is the LORD not with His people? Has He not promised to deliver the land of Canaan into their hands? Yet now they seem forsaken.

YHWH has made a covenant with His people, and as long as it is kept, they shall be blessed. But there is a man among them who has taken that which was under the LORD's ban, and for his greed the fate of all Israel is put in question. For the LORD God can countenance no disobedience; we must love Him with all our hearts to enter His gates.

And so the man must be utterly purged from their midst, he and his whole family. Only then do they regain the grace to conquer their enemies. In the second battle at Ai the Israelites are indeed victorious, and this time the LORD allows them to take of the spoils.

Old Testament

And Joshua proves Himself a faithful leader of the people, for upon their destruction of the city of Ai, he builds an altar, makes sacrifice to God, and inscribes the Law of Moses upon the stones. This he reads out before the whole assembly that they might remember whence their victory comes, and their great need to be faithful to His Word.

The Sun Stands Still

The time comes for the Israelites to make conquest of the whole land before them. Certain that the LORD will give all the land into Israel's hands and destroy all its inhabitants, the Gibeonites pretend to come from a faraway place that they might make peace with the Chosen race and so save their skins by becoming their slaves. Failing to consult the LORD, the leaders blindly accept their proposal. (How vigilant we must ever be!)

In defense of Gibeon the army of Israel goes forth and utterly destroys the five kings of the Amorites, the LORD fighting for them in mighty fashion. Hailstones He throws down from the sky, killing more than those who die by the sword; and in answer to Joshua's prayer, the sun stands still in the sky at Gibeon till the destruction of the kings is complete. For a whole day the sun stays in its place – never has any such thing been seen!

Then the whole land is conquered by the power of God working through the Israelites. All the kings gather as one against them, but every man they smite with the edge of the sword – they do not leave any that breathe. Yes, the time has come for the LORD's will to be done, for the hardened hearts of those who war against Him to be exterminated... even the greatest of giants now fall like flies; thirty-one kings in all Joshua destroys. And will there not be greater destruction at the end of time, on the final Day?

Joshua

Apportioning the Land

After five years of war the time comes for the Israelites to settle into their places in the Promised Land, and so the LORD calls on Joshua to divide the territory among the twelve tribes. First he gives the two and a half tribes beyond the Jordan their inheritance, then two and a half tribes in Canaan, including Judah, and Caleb in particular. (There are half-tribes because Joseph was given a double portion; yet the number of tribes remains at twelve since Levi has no portion among them but only cities with their pasture lands in various places throughout the whole territory.)

Joshua then sends three men out from each tribe to divide the rest of the land into seven sections for the remaining tribes. This is done, the cities of refuge are set up... and the Israelites have rest from war as they enter into their inheritance. But in each of the territories there are yet natives whom Israel has not cast out; these will serve as a continual temptation to them, and be the cause of their downfall.

YHWH, strengthen us for the mission you set before us. Help us not to fall short of your glory. Who among us can fulfill your will without the assistance of your Son and the Spirit you send upon Him and all His children. To our place in your House let us all come.

We Will Serve the LORD

The time now comes for Joshua to die, but before he goes he finishes his work by emphasizing to the people their need to worship God alone. They find peace all around as they settle into their places, and do seem ready to fight against all idolatry. In fact, the other tribes are prepared to war against Gad and Reuben when they build an altar at the Jordan as they cross back over to their land. They mean the altar to be a witness that they are of the people of Israel (lest their brothers should forget), but it seems a call to worship apart from the LORD's tent... and war is averted only by clear reassurance no sacrifice is intended apart from the place the LORD sets up.

Abraham was called from a foreign land to Canaan by God that he might worship the LORD alone; Israel has been taken from Egypt and all their false gods by the LORD's mighty hand; and now foreign nations are cast out before them by His power. All this is to show that the LORD is God and worship must be reserved for Him alone – and so Joshua elicits from the people promise to be just so faithful.

All foreign gods must be put away; our hearts must be inclined only to YHWH. He is faithful to all His promises, fulfilling His will for our good. So let us not turn from Him, lest we be cursed, but till death keep our word to serve the LORD and love Him with all our souls.

JUDGES

Because the Israelites fail to expel all the native tribes from the land God gave them, they indeed become a deadly snare to the people, leading them astray to worship of their idols. The LORD leaves these as a test for those who have not known war or Moses, who have not witnessed His hand at work for His Chosen in all the wonders He has performed. Will they remain faithful to Him? Will they continue to follow His commands and so find life for themselves and their families?

Upon the death of Joshua and the elders who were with him in the conquest of Canaan, the answer quickly becomes clear. No sooner have these souls gone to their rest than the hearts of the Israelites turn to the false and empty gods of the foreign nations; and they give their sons and daughters to them in marriage.

So begins the sad history of the people of Israel, who will continually turn from love of God and their own salvation to vain worship and their destruction. When they cry out, the LORD sends a judge to serve as a savior of the people from the nation that oppresses them; but when he dies their sin only becomes worse, and so the oppression they experience.

This troubling refrain will repeat itself through the generations of kings and their exile... until the time the Son comes to set all men free for ever.

Deborah

There is Othniel and Shamgar, and Ehud, who thrusts his sword into the bloated belly of the king of Moab till it disappears and the dirt comes out of him, till he dies and Ephraim is able to subdue his country, that Israel might have rest from its enemies. And then there is the prophetess Deborah.

This woman judges Israel when they are oppressed by Canaan; it is she who sounds the alarm, she who calls Barak to go forth and conquer... and she who goes with him into battle. And though this man and the army that follows him from Naphtali and Zebulun destroy Canaan and their king, it is a woman by whom that king's general falls to the dust: at Jael's feet Sisera lies, a tent peg through his skull. This descendent of Moses' father-in-law gains the glory of victory this day.

The LORD fights for those who are obedient to His will, to His voice speaking through His prophets. He goes into battle with those who put their faith in Him. For He is almighty and gives strength even to the weakest among us; with Him at our side we all become mighty warriors. He needs not sword or scimitar, horse or chariot, to defeat His enemies – what we have at hand will suffice in every situation. Always the victory is His, and so let us sing His praise!

Gideon

Now Gideon is of the least of the clans in Manasseh (which is the least of the tribes), and the least in his family... but the LORD chooses him when Israel is overrun as by locusts by the hand of Midian for seven years. They have no food, since the Midianites readily destroy any sign of grain, but Gideon prepares a meal for the angel who comes to him – and the angel consumes the food in the fire of God.

Gideon then destroys the altar to Baal his own father built, and cuts down the Asherah beside it; and no man defends Baal when challenged by Joash, though a moment before they would have killed his son.

Old Testament

Gideon gathers a huge army from the tribes of Israel. Convinced by the fleece which is wet with dew, then dry (opposite the grass both times), he goes forth to battle against Midian. Though the multitude they face is as the sand on the shore of the sea, only three hundred men the LORD has him take. For the battle is the LORD's and His the victory, and with these few, the men of the East are conquered. Their trumpets and torches set their enemies into a fitful anxiety, causing them to kill one another and flee... and then they are pursued by all the men of Israel.

But when the people come to Gideon to make him ruler over Israel, he refuses, saying quite rightly that it is YHWH who rules over His Chosen. Let us put our faith in Him alone.

Abimelech

Gideon refuses to rule over Israel, but he does make a golden idol, which serves the downfall of his family and causes a straying of the people. For where he has demurred, one of his seventy sons stands arrogantly and, aided by his fellow men of Shechem, slaughters his brothers on a single stone that he alone might rule.

Such evil comes back on the head of Abimelech and on the city of Shechem. Yes, the curse of Jotham, the youngest brother and only one to escape slaughter, soon comes to pass: as ruin descends upon Shechem at the hand of the wicked Abimelech, Abimelech himself is crushed by a millstone thrown from a tower by the hand of a woman.

Evil has no place in the House of God; and though it may seem to triumph for a time, quickly the crimes of the wicked are repaid. And those who presume great might and strength, who appear as a tower among men, are cast to the dust from which they come. And nothing is remembered of them.

We cannot by our own hands devise positions of power in the sight of God. These are reserved for whom He chooses, and are given ever to the lowliest of souls. Let us all learn the lesson of Abimelech, that wickedness soon comes to a terrible end.

Jephthah

After Tola and Jair judge Israel, the men of Gilead call on their forsaken brother Jephthah to come and lead them in battle against the Ammonites, who oppress them and all the tribes either side of the Jordan. This renegade son of a harlot accepts their offer, with their promise that he will be their head if successful in war.

When the king of the Ammonites refuses to listen to reason, the Spirit of the LORD comes upon Jephthah to lead his people forth into battle; and he makes a vow to offer to God whomever comes out to meet him on his return from victory. Jephthah thoroughly smites his enemies, but when his daughter greets him first from his house, he is much grieved. Now, does his faithfulness to his word cause Jephthah to burn his daughter in unholy fire – something clearly against the will of the LORD and the Spirit which inspired him at the time of his vow – or is it her *virginity* that is the sacrifice, a sacrifice perhaps even greater than a woman's life? It is this she bewails for two months, and this the daughters of Israel perpetually mourn. (But how can we understand the gravity of this sacrifice in a day when conception is considered more a curse than the greatest of blessings?)

We know that either way Jephthah soon dies without an heir (though not before slaying 42,000 of his brother Ephraimites as they try to cross the banks of the Jordan), for he has no other child.

Samson

After Ibzan and Elon and Abdon judge Israel, YHWH gives His people into the hand of the Philistines for forty years. Then an angel appears to the wife of Manoah and foretells the birth of a son to this barren one. A Nazirite he will be from the womb, and so she is to take no wine or strong drink… and no razor is ever to come upon his head.

This son is the mighty Samson, the twelfth judge of Israel, who tears apart a lion with his bare hands and eats honey from its carcass, who slays a thousand Philistines with the jawbone of an ass. But he is undone by his love for women, and by their persistent cries. First his wife presses him for the answer to his riddle; then Delilah draws out the secret of his strength and betrays him to the Philistines for several thousand pieces of silver. (How weak the mighty can be!)

But once his shaved head gains its hair again, strength, too, returns to Samson; and in revenge for the gouging of his eyes and his enslavement to them, he kills more Philistines in death than in life: for the house whose pillars he pushes apart falls not only on his head but also all his taunting enemies.

What shall we say of this sacrifice? Though he is wrought with moral weakness and unbounded anger and resentment, Samson foreshadows the sacrifice Christ will make… but His shall be for the redemption of all, not for anyone's destruction.

Micah's Idols

In these days every man does what is right in his own eyes, and so the man Micah makes of his silver a graven image and a molten one and sets them up as a shrine, also appointing a priest at his own discretion – a wandering Levite happens upon his house and Micah hires him to preside over the shrine and its idols.

Does not the same occur today with great regularity among those who do not recognize the authority of the Church and Peter? Do they not simply make themselves priests and pastors as they see fit? Should these not ask themselves if this is truly the will of God; does He desire such lack of obedience to rightful authority?

Then warriors from the mighty tribe of Dan come and take by force of arms the idols and the priest from Micah's house, for how can he stop them? And the priest reasons that now he is blessed to be able to preside for a whole tribe of Israel. There is in his mind no concern for what is right or wrong (as there had been none in the Danites, nor Micah), but only for what is for his benefit.

Beware, all souls who seek your own gain while presuming to stand in God's stead – your lack of self-sacrifice or concern for what is right will bring you to an inglorious end.

War against Benjamin

From Ephraim to Bethlehem a Levite comes to recover his concubine, who has fled to the house of her father. As he returns he stops overnight in Gibeah, a town of Benjamin. But the men of Gibeah do not welcome their brother in his wayfaring. Though a certain man eventually shows the Levite hospitality, others come to the house desiring to rape him, instead abusing his concubine till she lies dead on the threshold. How like Sodom is this town of Benjamin!

And for such abomination and wantonness toward one of their own (by one of their own!) the tribes of Israel gather as one against Gibeah. But Benjamin will not give up the evil men, choosing rather to fight against their fellow Israelites.

Twice the Benjaminites are victorious in battle, but the third day they are destroyed, and left with no wives and no recourse to any… for the other tribes swear an oath not to marry with them.

And so, will one of the tribes cease to exist? The thought brings great woe to Israel, and so peace they make with the Benjaminites, providing them wives from a house that has not gone up to the battle, that their tribe might endure.

How ready we should be to care for the needs of our Brother! And O how our very lives are threatened when we turn against Him! Let us not do what seems right in our own eyes, but submit ourselves to the will of God the Father.

RUTH

"Where you go I will go, and where you lodge I will lodge; your people shall be my people, and your God my God."
1:16

Here is the story of Ruth, grandmother to King David, who though from a foreign land proves herself of greater faith than any in Israel, and so is blessed by God. Though bereft of her husband, she clings to her mother-in-law and becomes more to her than any daughter or son.

Old Testament

By her hard work and faithful service to Naomi, Ruth wins the favor of Boaz, and gains for herself and her mother-in-law not only abundant grain but a son to renew the hearts and lives of both, and to carry on their name.

How humbly this maidservant comes to Boaz in the night, lying at his feet! How obediently she follows Naomi's every word. And how just in doing his part as next of kin is the man to whom she comes. It is no surprise their blood flows in the veins of the LORD's humble servant David. Indeed, this Ruth is blessed as Rachel or Leah in building up a house for God. Through David greatly does she prosper, and her name is remembered; she who comes from among the enemies of Israel is a true child of the LORD.

1 SAMUEL

He is asked of the LORD, this Samuel. His mother is barren and mocked therefore, but she entreats the LORD, begging in anxious prayer that she might give birth to a son and promising to leave him in the service of God in the temple in which she prays. And the LORD hears her prayer and answers her with this blessed boy. And so indeed the barren one becomes most fruitful; Hannah is lifted from the dust and Samuel sits with the princes in a seat of honor.

Yes, YHWH calls Samuel from his youth to take the place of the wicked sons of Eli, the priest of the temple. Their house will be torn down and Samuel rise in their stead, a priest and prophet respected throughout Israel. None of his words fall to the ground for the LORD is always with him; a sure house God indeed builds for this anointed one.

O LORD, let our ears be open to your call upon our souls; may we hear our name spoken by your own mouth. Let us never despair of your blessing, dear God, but come to you ever in holy prayer, unafraid of what those around us might say… set only on the accomplishment of your will. "Speak, YHWH, for thy servant hears" (3:9). Take all that we have, and make it your own.

The Ark Is Captured

The glory of the LORD now leaves Israel. After being soundly defeated by the Philistines, the Israelites try to strengthen their ranks by bringing the ark of God into their camp. A shout rises up and the Philistines fear; yet Israel is defeated again and the ark itself is taken.

They think the LORD is with them, but indeed He has already departed their ranks because of their sins, seen so clearly in the two sons of Eli, Hophni and Phinehas, who are slain in battle with thousands of others. Eli himself falls off his chair and dies at the news of the ark's capture. How the glory of God departs from Israel!

But the ark does the Philistines no good, for the LORD is not with these pagans either. Their god cannot stand beside Him, for there is no God but Him. Cursed by death and tumors are all the cities to which the ark of God is sent, till they desire only to be rid of it. And so they let it leave on a cart pulled by two cows.

It comes back to Israel, but not to Shiloh: "Who is able to stand before the LORD, this holy God?" (6:20). The men of Kiriathjearim come and take the ark, but it will be twenty years before it is carried by King David to its rightful place in Jerusalem.

How shall we make a home for your presence in our hearts, LORD, we who are so corrupted by this age?

Saul Anointed

Samuel intercedes with the LORD and the Israelites are delivered from the Philistines by God's mighty hand. But the sons of Samuel are not like this great seer; rather, they take after the sons of Eli in their greed and wickedness. So the people demand a king to rule over them and lead them into battle, that they might be like other nations.

Israel has not only rejected Samuel but, more importantly, the rule of God, for they are a nation peculiarly His own – YHWH is their King. But the LORD relents to their plea, though not without prophecy of the oppression they will suffer at the hands of their king.

It is Saul the LORD chooses first to rule over Israel; He leads him to His prophet as this king-to-be searches in vain for the missing asses of his father. Saul gives every appearance of a king, for he is taller and more handsome than any man in Israel. But this child of Benjamin, the least of the tribes of Israel, is reluctant to accept the anointing upon himself, hiding amongst the baggage even as his name is made known to the nation. Although the Spirit of the LORD has fallen upon him and made him a new man, he still fears the call of the prophet's tongue.

Perhaps it is with good reason Saul seeks to avoid the kingship, for despite his majestic appearance he will not prove himself a man of God, and so soon lose his blessing.

Saul's Disobedience

The people have sinned greatly in rejecting God and desiring a king to rule over them, but Samuel promises the LORD's favor if the king and the people hearken to the voice of their God and all His commands – though cursed they will be if they rebel.

Obedience seems something the Israelites cannot fathom (can any man?); certainly it is something they cannot practice. Their obedience is indeed fickle… as is their king's.

Saul leads Israel to victory over the Ammonites and over the Philistines. He defeats Moab and Edom and the Amalekites. He seems a mighty man of war successful as the head of God's chosen people. But the Word of the LORD he does not follow.

First he presumes to make sacrifice himself when Samuel is late and the people are leaving his side before battle. His fear tells him he must do something, and so he breaks the command of God (instead of trusting in His providence). Then the blood on his hands is compounded when he spares oxen and sheep for sacrifice (as well as the king himself!), against the express command imparted by Samuel to utterly destroy Amalek and every creature among them.

Saul cannot be faithful to the Word of God but is prepared to kill his son Jonathan to remain faithful to his own hasty oath barring anyone from eating as they go into battle. He does not do so only because he listens to the will of the people.

How great is the ignorance of genuine obedience among Israel (and among us all)! And for his disobedience the kingdom shall be rent from Saul.

1 Samuel

David Anointed

Then the LORD calls Samuel to anoint a king in place of Saul, a king after His own heart… one who is humble and faithful to the Word He speaks.

To Jesse and his eight sons in Bethlehem Samuel comes, waiting for the LORD to reveal who among them He will have as king. And we see that the eyes of Samuel are in ways as blind as the rest of Israel, for he looks upon the height of the firstborn and presumes YHWH will choose another impressive figure like the forsaken Saul – but the transcendent God teaches Samuel and us all that His eyes are not like our own: "For the LORD sees not as man sees; man looks on the outward appearance, but the LORD looks on the heart" (16:7).

It is in the youngest son tending the sheep that the LORD God finds reflection of His own heart. Finally a man who will follow Him and not his own mind! Here the salvation found only in Christ begins to be wrought among the chosen people, for here, finally, is a man who will give himself to the will of the Father. It is indeed his Son who will save us; and with David the sacrifice commences.

The Spirit of God rushes upon David as he is anointed; with him it remains even as it leaves Saul. Saul is now troubled by an evil spirit and will soon seek to kill the very man who brings him relief with the music of his lyre, he who proves himself a faithful son most worthy of his love.

Goliath

Samuel's hidden anointing of David begins to become manifest as the boy comes from tending his father's sheep to Saul and his troops lined up for battle. He hears the defiant words of the Philistine giant and the promises Saul has made regarding anyone who kills him.

Where all the other men of war tremble in fear of facing Goliath, this youth steps forward with sling in hand and races toward the pagan worm unfazed by his sword or spear or javelin, or the curses he hurls at him. In defense of the living God and with His Spirit enflaming his soul, he slings a stone into the Philistine's forehead, and this mighty warrior falls on his face to the ground. David then beheads Goliath with the giant's own sword.

This poor Bethlehemite proves himself meet for any battle and so becomes not only musician to the king but leader of his army... and none can stand before him. He slays his ten thousands and captures the hearts of even Saul's son and daughter: indeed, Jonathan gives David his own robe and armor, and Michal is given to him as wife. Thus does David become twice a son to the king, despite Saul's festering jealousy and hatred of him, and thus the will of the LORD for David shall be accomplished soon.

Jonathan's Love

Saul is determined to kill David and indeed repeatedly tries to pin him to the wall with his spear, so great is his jealousy toward him. Jonathan intercedes and speaks well of David to his father, and Saul seems to listen to reason, bringing David back into his presence.

Michal also helps David escape her father's wrath, and Saul is even overcome by the spirit of prophecy as he pursues his enemy.... But nothing can stop his determination to eliminate David.

When Saul becomes bitterly angry that David is not in his place for a feast, Jonathan knows his father's determination is piqued, and again defends David before him. So livid does Saul become that he even attempts to kill his own son, whom he is so desperate to see take his place as king.

But Jonathan loves David more than any desire for the kingship, more than his own father and his own life, for the righteousness of God is in him and he recognizes the blessing that is upon David. And so he helps him to escape one final time, informing him of his father's wrath.

What can be said of a man who so loves his brother that he would give his own place to him? And what can be said of the tears these two shed as they depart from one another? Here is a love greater than man for woman.

Bread and a Sword

As David flees from Saul he stops at the house of Ahimelech the priest, seeking food and a weapon. It is the holy bread set before the LORD that Ahimelech gives him, for there is no other bread in his house and David and his men have kept themselves pure. He gives him also the sword of Goliath enshrined there, for who has a better right to it? And so, David is provided for.

He must feign madness to escape one king; then takes refuge in a cave, where he is joined by his family and those in distress who are ready for a new man to rule over them.

Saul has all in the house of Ahimelech slain (by a dog of a man who overheard him helping David), eighty-five priests of the LORD, along with all in the city in which he dwells. Only one of his sons escapes to serve David in the wilderness.

Yes, he from the house of bread must now wander in the wilderness, relying only on the sword God places in his hand and the Word He speaks to his heart. Can this be the king of Israel, with spittle running down his beard? Does a king rule under a night sky? Where are his palace and his royal robes? Where is his sacred throne? To such humility the Father reduces His Son, and so the one who follows Him… yet He gives him all he needs.

YHWH, place your Bread on our table, the sword of the Spirit upon our tongues.

Saul Pursues David

Saul pursues David, but David is faithful to him, for Saul is the king of Israel, the anointed of the LORD. Though on two occasions David finds him at arm's length, easily within range of the thrust of a spear… he leaves his pursuer alone, allowing him to continue his reign.

And though Saul recognizes the righteousness of David, that he has treated him justly and is no enemy to the king – even weeping at the kindness shown to him by his "son"… repeatedly he returns to hunting David down in the mountain crags and caves of the Judean wilderness. He knows and he says that David shall be king, but in his heart he cannot accept the will of God in this. And so he continually pursues David.

David proves himself just not only with Saul but with all men, as he does when he heeds the entreaty of Abigail not to slaughter her husband Nabal and all his sons for the evil done to him and his men. David is ever able to recognize his guilt, to admit his fault and listen to the voice of reason, of truth – and to act upon it. This, Saul cannot do; this just quality in the LORD's chosen one he should rather pursue, instead of seeking to destroy the man who pricks his conscience, who piques his guilt.

O why are our hearts so hardened by jealousy!

The Death of Saul

Seeing that Saul will not cease pursuing him as long as he remains in Judah, David flees to the land of the Philistines, and there pretends to join his enemy's ranks. And Saul indeed stops seeking David's life.

Then the Philistines gather in great number to fight against Israel, and the heart of Saul trembles in fear. And so, against his own decree, he goes to a medium and insists she bring up Samuel from the dead, that he might know what is to become of his life and that of all Israel. Samuel cannot but utter God's curse against the unfaithful King Saul, for the time of his punishment has come, the time for him to lose the throne. Indeed, he will die with Jonathan and his other sons the next day in battle, as the Philistines overtake Israel.

David is asked to leave the army of the Philistines before the battle commences, so he is not among them as they conquer the LORD's chosen people (having rather to rescue all that is taken from him as his city is razed while his back is turned). He does not witness the overcoming of Israel, nor of Saul himself, who unceremoniously falls on his own sword after he is badly wounded by an arrow. It is all that men of Jabesh-gilead can do to recover his headless body from where it has been fastened to the wall of a city. And so the bodies of Saul and his three sons are burned and then properly buried.

O how the mighty have fallen!

2 SAMUEL

David and his men rend their clothes and their hearts as they mourn and weep and fast at the news that Saul and Jonathan have died in battle. David sings a lament for the glory of Israel that is slain. And he has the man killed who slew Saul even as he leaned on his sword in a lingering agony – no man shall raise a hand to the LORD's anointed! It matters not to David that this Amalekite does obeisance to him and brings him the king's crown and armlet... he must die. David has been faithful to Saul all his life, and he is faithful to the end.

Mighty indeed were Saul and Jonathan in war (though none is mightier than David), but now the mighty have fallen; and so, should not all Israel weep at the loss of their king? And does not David weep especially for the loss of his brother Jonathan, whose love was indeed wonderful, "passing the love of women" (1:26). Theirs is a love that lasts beyond the grave, for it is founded on the righteousness of God.

Now Saul is dead, and Jonathan, too. And so, now the crown awaits the head of David. Now the LORD's will shall be fulfilled – now he will be king.

King David

David is instructed by the LORD to go up to Hebron, and there he is welcomed by the men of Judah and anointed king over them. But king over the rest of Israel he does not become for seven years, as Saul's other son is made king by Abner, the leader of Saul's army. During this time there is continual war between the house of Saul and the house of David, David growing ever stronger.

After much intrigue – including Abner killing the brother of Joab (David's army commander) in battle; King Ishbosheth spurning Abner, and so Abner promising to give Israel over to David; David insisting on the return of Michal, his wife; Joab murdering Abner (who had come in peace to David) as revenge for his brother; and the slaying of Ishbosheth by two of his rogue servants... David is called by all the tribes of Israel to rule over them. And so, what had been effected in a hidden way at the hands of Samuel so many years before, now comes to pass in the sight of all: David is anointed king of Israel.

Long live the king and may his rule be blessed! May his Son abide on his throne for ever. O LORD, let your will be accomplished before our eyes.

The Ark in Jerusalem

King David takes Jerusalem and it becomes the city of David. There he builds himself a house of the finest cedar and grows stronger and stronger, repeatedly and thoroughly defeating the Philistines in battle by the grace of God.

And so David thinks to bring the ark of God into Jerusalem, that there it might find its home. But when Uzzah is struck dead by the LORD for reaching out to steady the tottering ark on its way up from the house of Abinadab, David fears the power of God... and so the ark is turned aside into the house of Obededom for three months.

The rejoicing resumes, however, when David sees how Obededom is blessed... indeed, the ark is brought into the city of David with the king leaping and dancing half-naked before it. The ark is placed within its tent and burnt offerings are made to the LORD and shared with all the people of Israel. There is indeed great joy.

But Michal murmurs against David for his uncovering himself like a fool in the sight of the maidens of Israel. For her blindness to the glory due the LORD she shall remain childless, even as David has children with others in great number.

There is but one thing that matters in all our lives – that the presence of God is with us. In this alone let us rejoice! Before the tabernacle of the LORD let us come; in His holy Church we must make our home.

2 Samuel

A House

David is given rest from all his enemies and now thinks to build a house for the ark of God, that the LORD might find a permanent dwelling among His people. It seems a noble thought, and so Nathan the prophet tells him to go forward. But YHWH does not dwell in a house of cedar.

The LORD reveals to Nathan His own plan: He shall build a house for David – the throne of his kingdom will be established for ever; always shall his offspring be seated there… but his son shall build the temple, not him. David humbly rejoices in such surpassing vision and begs the Most High to confirm His word to him.

The Word of the LORD shall indeed prove true, for though the kingship shall not last, though the house in which David dwells shall be torn down… though his sons shall prove unfaithful, a Son shall arise whose kingdom will remain. And in this House, in the flesh of the eternal Son, all of God's children find a home.

David then goes forth into battle to defeat the kingdoms round about him, to extend his reign and gather gold and silver that will be used for God's temple. None can stand before his conquering arm; wherever he turns he is victorious, for justice is with him. But this is not how his house will be established, nor the true House of the LORD be built. Jesus alone is the foundation, the cornerstone of the House of God, and only in Him does the kingship endure.

Bathsheba

In the season when kings go forth into battle, David stays at home, a spirit of sloth upon him. One afternoon on rising from his couch, he spies a woman bathing as he walks on the rooftop. And lust takes hold of him.

And so he takes hold of the woman, who is the wife of another, and thinking he is safe (since she is recently from her time of the month)… he lies with her. But she conceives and so he fears – certainly his sin will be known. Thus a graver sin he adds to this already wicked one, arranging the death of the man whose wife he's stolen.

O how sin can overtake us! O how the LORD's chosen has fallen! O how the king becomes as a worm and no man! How all fall short of the glory of God.

The prophet Nathan discovers what David has done and confronts him with his sin – a sin deserving of death, indeed. He is the one given everything who steals a righteous man's single lamb. David saves his own life by readily confessing his guilt, by his contrition before the LORD... but the child he's conceived must die, though the woman he takes to wife.

Another son is given David by Bathsheba, one of peace, beloved of the LORD; yet the sword shall not pass from David's house for the evil he has done in the sight of God.

Absalom Kills Amnon

Fratricide arises again in the Word of God, between two sons of David. One desires the sister of the other and contrives to force her into submission and so into shame, particularly as he then despises her. Absalom holds his peace for two years, eventually finding opportunity to slay Amnon in the presence of all their brothers.

Absalom flees to the city of refuge to escape the avenger of blood, and there David allows him to stay three years... till a woman of wisdom comes before the king with a tale of fratricide between her sons, and convinces him to call Absalom back to Jerusalem.

At first David does not permit his son under his roof, but later allows Absalom to bow his face to the ground before his throne, and so find forgiveness. But the knave uses his newfound acceptance only to conspire against his father and gather the men of Israel to himself. He soon has himself declared king at Hebron, and David is forced to flee Jerusalem before Absalom enters in.

Has the sword not come into the house of David even as the prophet foretold? Do our sins not come back to haunt us – is there any escape from their bitter fruits? Is this not why the Father sends Jesus to us?

2 Samuel

O Absalom!

David climbs the Mount of Olives, barefoot and weeping for the woes now upon him and his household. As he goes forth from Jerusalem, a man of the house of Saul comes out to curse him and rain stones and dust upon his head, and on those with him. But David seeks not to kill the man or even to stop him – this scourging he takes as from the hand of God.

Absalom enters Jerusalem and seizes David's house, lying with his concubines on the roof, thus fulfilling the LORD's punishment of His king: what he had done in secret is now done by his enemy in the sight of all Israel.

But the men David sends back to the city serve him well as they thwart the counsel of the wise Ahithopel, giving David time to muster his troops to go forth into battle. Victorious they are and, despite David's instructions for mercy, when Absalom gets his hair stuck in a tree, Joab thrusts three darts into his treacherous heart and casts his body into a deep pit... piling a great heap of stones over him.

Messengers bring the good tidings to David at the gate, but all the king can do is weep aloud for his lost son; and so victory is turned to mourning for all his men. David blames himself for the death of Absalom – and a certain guilt he does bear – but in the end each man is responsible for the state of his soul, and the evil he does he must own.

The King Returns

Joab must threaten David to shake him from his mourning Absalom, who sought to take his life, and his thus bringing shame on the men who fought to save the king. David finally takes his seat in the gate and all the people come to him.

Israel call their king back to themselves, and the men of Judah follow and accompany him to Jerusalem. On the way he forgives Shimei, the cursing Benjaminite, and Mephibosheth son of Jonathan, who would have taken David's kingship.

But another Benjaminite summons the men of Israel apart from David as rivalry between Judah and Israel arises on the road to Jerusalem. This pretender to the rule in Israel is pursued by Joab and – after Joab murders the man who is a threat to his own command of the army – the traitor's head is thrown over the wall of his city when it is on the verge of destruction.

The king returns to his throne, but what a heavy heart he has for all the bloodshed that surrounds him. He displays signs of YHWH's merciful love... but how he struggles to realize that call, weighed down as he is by the fruits of his past sin and the vanity of man. It is only his Son who will be perfect in the eyes of God, whose hands are clean of blood. David will die like any man, but his reign shall be fulfilled in Jesus.

The Song of David

David can no longer go into battle, but he sings the praises of God, who has been his protection all these years and who has given him mighty men to fight with him and kill the giants that close in on his kingdom. Mighty are the armies of Israel, but it is always by the might of the LORD they are victorious; and they are only blessed as long as they remain righteous in His sight.

God is indeed the refuge of David – it is He who is his salvation. Yes, as valiantly as David and his army fight, it is always the LORD who delivers them from men of violence. Because of the power of God, foreigners come trembling out of their strongholds to serve David as king.

It is David's fear of God that causes him to be blessed; because he is ever just, he dawns upon the people like the rising sun. And by his justice, famine is averted and fruitful rains pour down on the earth.

The LORD hears the cry of David; He thunders from the heavens and shines forth His brightness, piercing the sky with His arrows to save His king, His servant, from his enemies. All glory be to God! who saves all humble souls but consumes godless men with fire.

The Altar Built

David sins greatly against God and against the people as he determines to take a census of all in his domain. This numbering of his subjects is an offense against the LORD because the king would attribute to himself that which is God's alone – the people of Israel are in His hand and not that of any king. David would know how many souls he has under him that he might lord it over them; and so, many of these are taken away.

The Most High would greatly multiply David's kingdom if he would but trust in Him, but he does not listen to reason, and so must be punished for his deed. He chooses a plague from the hand of God rather than falling into the hands of men, and mercy he does find there... but not before 70,000 men are dead.

David is given vision of the slaughtering angel and cries for mercy upon the people, confessing his sin and calling the punishment (a punishment which shall be realized in Jesus) upon himself. The LORD indeed listens and has pity, stilling the hand of His angel by the threshing floor of Araunah the Jebusite. There David builds an altar for sacrifice that averts the plague... and this will be the site on which the temple of Solomon shall be erected.

Now there will be an era of peace after these days of fighting and bloodshed. Now expiation is made to God for all the sins of Israel's past. Now perhaps she shall be subject to Him.

1 KINGS

David has grown very old and his body become very cold: he is a man nearing death. But before he dies he establishes Solomon as king upon his throne. Though Adonijah tries to usurp the throne – taking Joab and the priest Abiathar with him in declaring himself the new king of Israel – his plans are thwarted by Nathan and Bathsheba, who serve the will of the LORD by recalling to David's mind the promise upon Solomon.

Even as Adonijah and his men wake from their drunkenness after celebrating his false coronation, the city of Jerusalem erupts with shouts of joy that rend the earth: "Long live King Solomon!" On his father's throne Solomon sits, the LORD's anointing upon his head.

And Solomon soon fulfills his father's dying wishes, effecting vengeance on his enemies that they might be justly punished for their sins – Joab for his murder of two great men, and Shimei for his cursing the king. Adonijah, too, Solomon has put to death after he seeks for his wife the young woman who served at their father's bedside.

And so Solomon is settled into his place, the kingdom firmly in his grasp. And so, may David rest in peace, his throne established for ever.

Solomon's Wisdom

The LORD appears to Solomon in a dream after he has made sacrifice to Him on the altar at Gibeon (for the temple in Jerusalem has not yet been built). God says to him: "Ask what I shall give you," and Solomon's response pleases the LORD; for he asks not for riches or honor, long life for himself or the life of his enemies, but for understanding, that though a mere youth he might govern with wisdom the vast people set before him.

YHWH promises to make him the wisest man to walk the earth, with all the earthly blessings besides... and after waking from his dream and offering up burnt offerings and peace offerings in a thanksgiving feast, Solomon is soon confronted with a situation wherein he proves his wisdom.

Two women stand before him, each claiming a baby to be her own and that the other's has died in the night while they slept. The king calls for a sword to divide the child in two, that each might have half of what they both demand so persistently. And when one of the women offers to give the boy to the other to spare his life, Solomon knows this is the mother and grants the woman her son.

O LORD, may your wisdom be with us all that we might discern evil from good and walk ever in your ways.

The Peaceful Kingdom

Solomon is given rest from warfare on every side – he has "neither adversary nor misfortune" (5:4) – and so his expansive kingdom is established in peace. All his needs are provided for by his twelve officers from the various regions; food is abundant on his table and provisions are made for all who serve his house. Horses and chariots and horsemen by the thousands and tens of thousands are at his disposal, and people from every nation come to hear his wisdom, which indeed surpasses that of any other man. His mouth drips with thousands of proverbs and songs… there is nothing of which he cannot speak.

And now that peace has come, it is time for the temple to be built. And so cedar is brought from Lebanon and men of Israel are forced to labor in the building and in the mining of costly stones. All is ordered well in Solomon's domain, and the work is toward the worship of the LORD – but the price Samuel foretold would be paid by the people to support a king is already in evidence.

Yet, indeed, peace does reign and, despite the tribute all must bring to Solomon, Judah and Israel "[eat] and dr[i]nk and [a]re happy" (4:20). And a glorious temple they soon raise.

The Temple

In seven years the glorious temple of Solomon is completed in Jerusalem. It is a house of God most remarkable, most marvelous to behold for its size and craftsmanship, and for the precious wood and metal with which it is constructed.

The cedar and cypress and olivewood are overlaid with the finest gold – and so all is radiant as the sun. Burnished bronze are the pillars and the sea and lavers, and all its simple vessels; but its altar and its table, lampstands and all that is used to serve the sacrifices are of pure gold. And how intricately all is crafted with images of cherubim and palm trees and pomegranates! No expense is spared in erecting this temple of the LORD.

Old Testament

And in the Holy of Holies where the ark of the Covenant shall rest, the wings of the two cherubim guarding the ark span wall to wall (for all is under the watchful eye of God), and all is, of course, overlaid with gold.

O may we enter your courts, O LORD! May we praise your holy NAME in the assembly of the faithful. May we shine like the stars, like the sun at its rising, and may all our works give glory to you. There is no place on earth that can contain your infinite majesty, but let us be covered in your glory, surrounded by your light, held in your mighty hand, O LORD and God!

Solomon's Prayer

The temple of the LORD is consecrated as the ark of the Covenant carrying the two stone tablets of the Law given to Moses on Mount Sinai is brought into the Holy of Holies and there finds its resting place beneath the wings of the two cherubim. And the glory of YHWH in the form of a thick cloud fills the house of God so that none can minister therein, for all are overwhelmed. His presence indeed comes to dwell in this place.

King Solomon declares his blessing before all the assembly of the people of Israel, begging that He who cannot be contained by heaven and earth might remain in this house built to His NAME and so bless the Israelites and all those who come to worship the living God and entreat His intercession in this holy place. The will of the LORD has been fulfilled in the completion of this temple – may Israel be faithful to their God and they shall be blessed for ever.

But if they should sin against Him, if they should turn their backs on the one true God, they will bear their guilt and so be punished with draught and famine, pestilence and infestation, and the attacks of their enemies. Yet when they look to this city and this temple and call on the NAME of the LORD who dwells there, forgiveness they shall find. Even when they are sent into exile for the gravity of their sin, cut off from the land God has given them – even from out of His sight He shall bring them back if their hearts become obedient to His Word again. Amen, the LORD has willed it so.

1 Kings

Six Hundred Sixty-Six Gold Talents

"King Solomon excelled all the kings of the earth in riches and in wisdom. And the whole earth sought the presence of Solomon... Every one of them brought his present" (10:23-25).

They come bearing silver and gold and horses and spices. The Queen of Sheba travels to Jerusalem with a great train of camels carrying gold, abundant spices and precious stones. "And Solomon answer[s] all her questions; there [is] nothing hidden from the king which he [can] not explain to her" (10:3). And she is dazzled by the appointments of his house and table, his officers and his servants, for all are dressed in great finery and gold abounds in the vessels and in his royal throne; indeed, all sparkles with its radiance.

Six hundred sixty-six talents of gold come regularly to Solomon each year, aside from the gifts he receives and the trading he does with the fleet of ships he has built to bring him greater wealth from abroad. By the forced labor of the people of the nations he also builds cities to store his goods, cities for his chariots, cities for his horsemen.... Greater abundance could not be imagined. He is indeed king of all the earth with all its riches at his fingertips.

For nothing more could Solomon ask. But the kingdom of God is not of this world or its shining silver and gold – this is a lesson all must learn to escape the clutches of the evil one. Only from the mouths of babes comes perfect praise, and only perfect praise is known in the YHWH's House.

Solomon's Sin

In his old age Solomon's heart turns away from the LORD his God, and so the loss of the kingdom is prophesied over him. Led astray by his thousand foreign wives and concubines, he embraces the worship of the false gods of the nations. To appease his wives he forgets his God, and so will lose his blessing.

Yes, the kingdom shall be torn from Solomon's hand; the great promise that is upon him as the son of David shall come to naught – all his riches shall die with him. For David's sake the LORD will not despise him in his lifetime, and He will leave his descendants a remnant, the tribe of Judah (and Benjamin); but, again, this is only for the sake of His servant David and the blessing He has placed on the city of Jerusalem.

Upon the death of Solomon, ten tribes shall be given into the hands of Jeroboam. Because of the grave sin of the king, division shall ever exist between Judah and Israel... and enemies shall afflict them from without as well.

How has the peaceful kingdom come to ruin? How has he who was given such great wisdom ended in such utter foolishness? How has he who was blessed with vision of God grown so blind to the truth? Lust of the heart has caused the king to be lost in the flesh, and so the Spirit is taken from him. And so he dies in vain, in sin; and his reign comes to an end.

Division

Upon the death of Solomon the kingdom indeed becomes divided, for his son, Rehoboam, spurns the counsel of the old men and vows to increase the heavy yoke his father laid on the people. And so all Israel return to their houses, spurning the rule of Rehoboam that the will of the LORD might be accomplished and the kingdom be taken from Solomon for his grievous sin.

The foolish pride of Rehoboam is exceeded by the iniquity of Jeroboam, to whom the LORD gives the ten tribes of Israel: he sets up altars in two places apart from Jerusalem and calls on the people to worship golden calves made by his own hands, on feast days he himself devises, served by priests he in his arrogance appoints.

But his hand is stricken by the LORD when he reaches it out against a man of God who declares to him that his altars will be reduced to dust. Still, he does not heed God's word and turn from his evil way; and so his son falls sick and dies... and all his house shall soon be utterly destroyed, reduced to dust with his altars.

O the woe that comes now upon both houses! Judah and Israel, why are your hearts so wayward, straying so easily from the Word of God? How your kings shall betray you! How much punishment you will have to endure! How will you ever find the LORD's promise secured?

Evil

The kingdoms are divided. They remain ever at war with one another, and within themselves. In Judah the treasures are taken from the house of the LORD and from the king's palace – gold shields no longer protect the kingdom. There are evil kings in Judah, though occasionally one who follows in the way of the LORD arises, as with Asa... but in Israel the situation is much bleaker.

It seems the kings of Israel are set on outdoing each other in the evil they perform in the sight of God. The son of Jeroboam is murdered for his kingship, and all in the house of Jeroboam are killed, as the LORD God foretold. Then the son of this murderous Baasha is himself slain in his drunkenness, and all the house of Baasha is destroyed... again as foretold by the LORD.

The next usurper compounds the evil done in Israel, and then comes Ahab, who does "evil in the sight of the LORD more than all that were before him" (16:30), taking Jezebel as his wife and worshiping Baal, building an altar to his name.

Where is the promise of God now? Banished from the hearts of His chosen ones. A bare remnant continues in Jerusalem, but how Israel does sin! No different from the nations are they now. And what hope have the wicked for salvation?

Elijah

Elijah sets himself against King Ahab and all his wickedness: there shall be no rain in Israel except by the word of this great prophet of the LORD. And for three years there is no rain.

But for that time Elijah must escape the wrath of Ahab, who hunts him down in every nation. First he hides by a brook in the wilderness east of the Jordan, and is brought bread and meat by ravens morning and evening. Then he is instructed to go to the land of Sidon, where he meets, and stays with, a poor widow and her son about to die from the famine. She gives the prophet a small cake made from a jar of meal and a cruse of oil, both about to run dry but which by God's blessing do not fail them for all the time of the draught.

Old Testament

Finally, Elijah returns to Israel to confront Ahab and the prophets of Baal that Jezebel has set up. On Mount Carmel he offers a challenge to the hundreds of prophets: Call on your god and I shall call on mine, and we shall see who brings fire on our sacrifice. Baal does not answer even as these false prophets gash themselves – he is not away, nor asleep, but dead. Then, though Elijah covers his sacrifice in pools of water, the LORD consumes it and all around it (and the water) with his fire... and so the hearts of the people are turned to the living God, the prophets of Baal are all killed, and rain now comes upon the land.

O LORD, may all be washed and made clean of iniquity!

A Still Small Voice

An incensed Jezebel vows to kill Elijah as he has killed her prophets, and so for fear of his life the great prophet of God flees again into the wilderness, where he lies down under a tree ready to die. He has had enough. But the angel of the LORD wakes and feeds him (twice) and entreats him on his journey: forty days he walks to Mount Horeb, where YHWH first spoke His NAME to His servant Moses. There he takes refuge in a cave.

From the cave the LORD calls him to go and stand on the mountain; and as He spoke to His servant Moses, YHWH now speaks to Elijah, not in the great wind or in the earthquake or in the fire... but in "a still small voice" (1Kgs.19:12). Is this not again the NAME of God spoken to His holy one? As Moses trembled, does Elijah not hide his face and cower at the entrance of the cave at the sound? Does the Most High God not make Himself present again on this holy ground?

And the prophet is told to anoint two kings as well as the man who will succeed him – the LORD's house must be set in order. And so Elijah throws his cloak over Elisha, on whom a double portion of his spirit shall rest; and Elisha follows him faithfully, leaving his family and even slaughtering the twelve oxen with which he has plowed.

It is the voice of God, His perfect silence, which must guide our hearts in all humility, in all things, and we shall find his blessing. Be with me, O LORD, this day.

Naboth's Vineyard

Ahab is twice victorious in battle against the king of Syria, but in opposition to the will of the LORD he allows the king himself to go free. And so it is prophesied to Ahab that his life shall be taken for the one he has released. And so the king of Israel becomes resentful and sullen.

This sulking mood is compounded when he asks to buy the vineyard of his neighbor but has his request denied. Now he takes to his bed and refuses to eat, like a petulant child. But Jezebel comes to rouse the king with her devious plot to have Naboth stoned to death at the accusation of two scoundrels.

The obstacle removed, Ahab happily sets out to take Naboth's vineyard; but Elijah stands in his path and foretells that Ahab's own blood shall be shed for that which Jezebel has consumed. His house shall come to utter ruin, like that of Jeroboam and Baasha... though not in his own lifetime, for the LORD looks kindly on the repentance he displays in sackcloth and ashes.

But (despite his attempts to hide) the king of Israel is soon killed in battle for his transgressing the Word of God. And the dogs in the city lick up his blood, washed from the chariot in which he dies.

How can the wicked of this world stand before the face of God? They shall always come to utter ruin for all the blood they shed.

2 KINGS

And shall the sons of Ahab be any different from their father; shall there be any lessening of sin in Israel? There shall not. For upon falling and finding himself near death, to whom does Ahaziah send to find answer to his prayer? Does he invoke the NAME of the LORD, the God of Israel? Does he turn to YHWH in a faith borne of troubles? No. He sends to entreat Baalzebub, the god who is no god. He could not choose a worse place to go.

But Elijah stops his men along the way and tells them to turn back – their king shall surely die for his faithlessness, for his denial of the God of Israel. He shall be no more.

Elijah calls down fire on the troops of fifty sent twice by the king to take him to himself, but has pity on the third fifty when their captain begs mercy. Thus, Elijah declares to Ahaziah before his face that he shall surely die. And he does die.

And his brother will be no different than he; his way, too, will be evil. Here is the story of the kings of Israel, whose houses cannot stand before the throne of God.

Why? Why are we so blind, so hard of heart and empty of soul? God is ours, He calls to us, desires our company... and we decline His invitation and go elsewhere for our food, for our wisdom – for our healing. What can we then do but die as the house of Ahab, as Israel?

Chariots of Fire

A double portion of Elijah's spirit indeed rests upon Elisha, for he sees his master carried to Heaven in a whirlwind by a chariot of fire and horses of fire; his own eyes witness the hand of God taking Elijah to Himself.

The great prophet is nowhere to be found on any mountain or in any valley across the Jordan. He is in this place no more. And though Elisha cannot fly away with his master, though he cannot by his word rend the heavens and find passage to the side of God, yet taking the mantle of Elijah, striking the water with it and calling on the NAME of God, he is able to part the Jordan River as has his master... and pass freely back into the Promised Land.

How he stays faithfully with Elijah! How he refuses to leave his side, even as the prophet approaches the gates of Heaven! Will we be so faithful to Jesus, seeking to accompany Him even to the Cross that we too might approach the heavenly kingdom, that He might draw us up with Him to His Father's side?

YHWH, let your Spirit be on us! Let us do your will in this place, making the waters in it wholesome by the salt you give into our hands. Your fire come down and consume all evil in our midst, that all souls might be purified for Heaven.

Elisha

Yes, great power is upon Elisha, the man of God; a most remarkable Spirit is in him. He makes the bitter water sweet, the poisonous pot safe to eat; at his word water fills the empty stream bed for the armies of Judah and Israel, and he causes iron to float. He stretches himself out on the dead body of the son of his benefactor, a boy whose birth he prophesied, and breathes life back into his frame. What is there he cannot do? For the Spirit of God is with him.

And when Naaman the Syrian comes to him to be healed of his leprosy, Elisha proves indeed there is no God except in Israel. Heeding his simple command to wash in the Jordan seven times, Naaman is made clean... and his heart is opened to worship of the one LORD. Then at the prophet's word, his own servant is afflicted with Naaman's leprosy for seeking remuneration for the healing power that comes from God.

Such power, such utter trust in the Word and will of YHWH, in the NAME of the Father of all, seems beyond our comprehension, beyond our ability to grasp. It seems too miraculous. But a greater miracle than this is in our midst even this day, for Jesus comes to us with His Body and Blood to make our water fresh and cleanse our very souls. May our spirits be one with His own, and we shall live again.

Prophecy Fulfilled

On Mount Horeb when YHWH spoke to Elijah with His still, small voice, He called him to anoint Hazael king of Syria, Jehu king of Israel, and Elisha to succeed him as prophet. Elijah threw his cloak over Elisha, and now the rest of the call is accomplished through him who was given a double portion of Elijah's spirit.

After thwarting the king of Syria by informing the king of Israel what he plotted against him in his bedchamber, the great prophet Elisha leads the murderous Syrian army away from his own doorstep into the midst of Samaria without their realizing they are walking into enemy environs. However, Elisha calls not for their destruction, but a feast for the Syrians in Israel.

When the Syrians later return, the sound of the LORD's fiery chariots and horses causes them to flee in fear their camp surrounding Samaria, thus breaking the great famine upon the city and saving Israel.

Elisha then sees before his eyes the servant of the king of Syria, Hazael, and prophesies the kingship over him – with tears for the evil he shall inflict upon Israel. And Hazael kills his king and takes his throne.

Finally, Elisha calls a prophet to go and anoint Jehu king of Israel; and the LORD's Word is fulfilled as Jehu kills the king of Israel and the king of Judah, who has also followed in Ahab's wicked path.

The ways of the LORD are not our own, but His will is ever done.

Jehu

On the property of Naboth, Jehu slays the son of Ahab, king of Israel; and on that plot of ground his body is cast. Jezebel is thrown to her death by her servants at the command of Jehu, and the dogs eat her flesh as it lies on the ground in Jezreel, as the LORD foretold.

The heads of all seventy sons of Ahab are sent to Jehu by the elders of Samaria to show their loyalty to the new king, and Jehu slays all those that remain of the house of Ahab in Jezreel and in Samaria. The whole house of Ahab indeed perishes, as spoken by the mouth of the LORD.

Then all the prophets of Baal and all his worshipers and priests Jehu utterly destroys with the zeal of Elijah, and the house of Baal is demolished, becoming a latrine to this day. But, though Jehu wipes out Baal from Israel, he does not take away the golden calves of Jeroboam; and so, though the LORD promises his children shall reign four generations for all the faithfulness Jehu has shown, already in his time Hazael begins to cut off parts of Israel, defeating them in battle.

All our good deeds the LORD will bless; but if our hearts are not completely with Him, we shall not last in His holy presence.

Joash

Upon seeing that her son, the king, has been killed by Jehu, in her wickedness Athaliah has all the royal family slain that she alone might be left to rule the house of Judah. But her youngest grandson is saved from the sword and hidden in a bedchamber for seven years.

In the seventh year, the priest of the house of Judah, Jehoida, takes Joash from his place of hiding and, thoroughly surrounded and protected by all the guards, brings him into the temple to be anointed king.

Upon hearing the shouts of "Long live the king!" Athaliah comes running into the house of the LORD… but is ushered out to her death. And there is peace in the kingdom. "And Jehoida ma[kes] a covenant between the LORD and the king and people, that they should be the LORD's people" (11:17). And so the house of Baal is torn down and its priest killed, and all rejoice to see Joash on the throne.

Led by Jehoida, the king does what is right in the sight of the LORD, and he sees to it that repairs are made to the house of God. He placates Hazael when he comes with his troops, and so the peace in Judah is maintained. It again becomes the land of the LORD.

More Evil Kings

The sons of Jehu "sit upon the throne of Israel to the fourth generation" (15:12), as the LORD promised, but, as was indicated, they all do evil in His sight... as do those who follow them.

There is indeed another succession of evil kings in Israel, none turning from the golden calves Jeroboam set up, one slaying the other and reigning in his stead. But the LORD has pity on Israel and does not let them disappear. When the king of Syria is about to overrun them completely, when their armies are all but depleted, Elisha (before he dies and contact with his bones causes a dead man to rise) prophesies they will be victorious three times against their enemies. Judah, too, is defeated by Israel, despite the faithfulness of their kings, and land is taken back from them.

But there is no rest for these evil kings, and soon the king of Assyria comes and captures much land from Israel. What hope can there really be for those who continually turn their backs to God? He may have mercy for a time and keep them from utter destruction because they are His chosen, but their lives can only be a misery.

Are there not golden calves in our own lives that need to be uprooted and tossed in the fire? Should we not see that this is done before the Day of the LORD comes?

Ahaz

When Ahaz becomes king of Judah he causes it to sin, to walk in the ways of the evil kings of Israel; he even burns his own son as a sacrificial offering, in line with the abominable practices of the nations. He removes the bronze altar from before the LORD in the house of God and replaces it with one he has made according to the altar in Damascus, so bent is he on copying pagan ways. He seeks to please the king of Assyria, who rescues him in battle, and not the LORD God of Israel. And so he changes the layout of the temple as he wishes, desiring that it reflect not the glory of Heaven but the iniquity of this corrupted earth.

O why do we trust in the might of the nations and not in the LORD of Heaven and earth? Shall such foolishness, such wickedness, not result in death, in utter separation from the Life that is God? For false idols cannot stand; the work of our hands soon turns to dust, and we with it. Only God remains.

YHWH, let us see our blindness to your presence and your will! O may we find salvation by following your Word and your way! Let us not be removed from before you or lose your eternal blessing.

Israel's Exile

The LORD can countenance the unfaithfulness of Israel no more, so great has their wickedness grown, and so first the king of Assyria comes and shuts the king of Israel up in prison; then he besieges and captures Samaria, and carries the Israelites from their land.

There has indeed been no end to the profligacy of the people, as they walk ever in the ways of the nations. Ignoring the LORD's command to worship Him alone, they bow to all the false idols of the land, worshiping golden calves and the sun, and burning their sons and daughters as offerings to demons. They sell themselves to do evil and so provoke the LORD to anger, and to their exile.

Another Jeroboam they set up as king, who even more greatly increases their sin... and so there is no hope left for them to remain in the land. The foreigners from Babylon and elsewhere who occupy the cities of Samaria in place of the Israelites themselves are cursed by the LORD and devoured by lions. And though the Israelites bring in a priest to offer sacrifice to God and elicit His mercy upon them, they continue to worship all their false and empty idols and walk in utter wickedness.

Why do the people not fear the LORD but instead turn to other gods? Why would they be delivered into the hands of their enemies? What makes your children so obstinate, O LORD? And when will we see your face again?

Hezekiah

Hezekiah reigns in Judah in the place of his father Ahaz, but he does not follow in his evil ways: he does what is right in the sight of the LORD as none other. He destroys all the vain images in the land and removes all the high places where the people worship, allowing no false god to remain. Even so, after fourteen years the king of Assyria comes up and lays siege to Jerusalem, threatening to do to it as he has Samaria.

Sennacherib mocks the LORD, boasting that He is unable to deliver Jerusalem out of his hand. His messenger vows the people will eat their own dung if they do not surrender. But Hezekiah prays to God, prostrating himself in the temple, and through the prophet Isaiah the LORD assures him that this day of distress will pass and the king of Assyria return the way he came. Indeed, one hundred and eighty-five thousand of Sennacherib's troops are killed in their camp by the angel of God; and back in his own land, the king himself is soon assassinated by his sons.

Then when Hezekiah falls sick unto death, he turns his face to the wall and begs the LORD in tears for mercy... and God gives him another fifteen years of life. But soon after he's gone, the king of Babylon will come and take all the riches of Jerusalem away.

Manasseh

Though his father does right, Manasseh turns distinctly from the path Hezekiah set out and returns the land of Judah to all the abominable practices of the nations. In his fifty-five year reign he adds iniquity to iniquity, bringing the false idols, the graven images by which all men sin, even into the house of God. In the place YHWH put His NAME for ever, Manasseh builds altars to Baal and Asherah. There he worships the hosts of heaven, sun and moon and stars, and burns his son as an offering to them. He practices soothsaying and augury, consults mediums and wizards... to his evil there is no end. And so for all this wickedness he brings into Judah, the LORD in His anger vows to remove the people from His sight, to give them into their enemies' hands – to cast them off to the nations.

Innocent blood mounts up throughout Manasseh's reign, and his son in his stead does no differently... and so he is soon assassinated by his servants. And though the son who follows shall provide a ray of hope for the remnant of the LORD, how heavy His hand shall yet be upon the land of Judah – "the ears of every one who hears of it will tingle" (21:12).

Josiah

Before the exile to Babylon, a good king arises who "turn[s] to the LORD with all his heart and with all his soul and with all his might, according to all the Law of Moses" (23:25). Indeed, in the midst of his reign the Book of the Law is rediscovered in the house of God. Josiah listens attentively to the words of Moses, tears his garments in repentance for all the disobedience of the LORD's chosen people, and sets about to put into practice all the commands which so pierce his soul.

And though he can only save himself from witnessing the utter destruction coming upon Judah for her forsaking the LORD and burning incense to other gods, though his sons will quickly turn again to evil upon his death and exile will then be imminent... with great zeal Josiah delivers the land from all the false idols that have beset it for so long, even since the death of David. He destroys all the unholy images throughout the country and within the temple, crushing even the idols Solomon had set up, along with those made by Ahaz and Manasseh, and even Jeroboam. The bones of the false prophets he burns, scattering their ashes abroad. No sign of pagan worship does he allow to remain in his reign.

The book of the Covenant he has read in the hearing of all the people, and he leads them in renewing their commitment to the Word of God. For the first time under the kings, the Passover is kept... yet the king of Babylon is on the horizon after the death of this faithful king.

Judah's Exile

Some twenty years after the righteous Josiah's death, the time comes for Judah to be taken into exile. His evil sons become servants to Egypt, then to Babylon. Rebelling against the king of Babylon they are attacked by the Chaldeans, Syrians, Moabites and Ammonites. For all the innocent blood shed in Jerusalem, she has to be destroyed.

First Nebuchadnezzar takes only the king into exile, with all the leading men of the city and the warriors. When the brother of Josiah left in charge rebels as well, the king of Babylon comes and burns the house of the LORD, the king's house, and all the other houses of significance in Jerusalem. He breaks down the walls around the city and takes the rest of its people into exile. And all the treasures of the temple are taken, too – gold as gold, silver as silver, bronze as bronze. O the utter destruction upon the place the LORD had rested His feet! (How He must weep at such a sight.)

As if this were not enough, the few people who are left in the land soon flee to Egypt, finally fulfilling their wish to return to the land of their slavery.

YHWH's will must be done for all the sins of His people. He takes no pleasure in our suffering but cannot countenance our wickedness. But if Jerusalem had to be destroyed for the sins of Manasseh and all its evil kings, perhaps a ray of hope is indeed found in Josiah's reign; maybe there is a remnant of obedience still in God's children.

1 CHRONICLES

Before focusing on the reign of David (about which this book is primarily concerned), a recounting of the genealogy that leads to him is thoroughly drawn. Beginning with Adam, expounding upon Noah, and especially on Abraham, Isaac, and Jacob – detailing the descendants of the twelve tribes of Israel and their lands (particularly the Levites and their service in the house of God) – the account makes its way even to those who return from exile in Babylon, outlining along the way all the descendants of David and Solomon.

Most fascinating, aside from the brief stories that are occasionally offered amid the lines of genealogy, is seeing how territories great and small find their origins, if not their names themselves, in particular individuals. There are Egypt and Canaan and Sidon and so many other names of men that become places on the ancient map, some that exist to this day. One sees the world of man forming, a real history developing, in the flesh and blood of people.

Here indeed are the origins and development of the world as we know it, given in brief in the genealogies of men. Here indeed we see the earth being peopled, and glean a sense of the good and bad characters who have a hand in this development. And so we come to the time of the kings, and to the king of all the kings of Israel, David, the shepherd boy.

King David

After the recounting of the history of men to the return from Babylon, we hear of the death of Saul, whom the Philistines overcome in battle with all his sons for his unfaithfulness to the LORD, and who falls on his own sword when the end is near. Then David is anointed king of Israel in Jerusalem.

David's three and thirty mighty men and the thousands and tens of thousands and hundreds of thousands of warriors from all the tribes of Israel come to Hebron to make David king. For three days they celebrate with a great feast this blessing that has come upon them.

The word of the LORD by Samuel is thus fulfilled. And David's kingdom is "highly exalted for the sake of [God's] people Israel" (14:2). A majestic house is built for him of the cedar of Lebanon; and by his hand the LORD breaks upon his enemies the Philistines "like a bursting flood" (14:11). They abandon their gods in the fields, and David burns them in the fire. Indeed, God goes before His king to smite his foes. "And the fame of David [goes] out into all lands, and the LORD [brings] the fear of him upon all nations" (14:17).

So King David is established in his house by the mighty hand of God. So YHWH's will is done among His chosen people.

Sing to the LORD!

After an unsuccessful attempt at bringing the ark of the LORD into Jerusalem – on this first occasion the man dies who reaches out his hand to steady the ark upon its stumbling cart, and so the rejoicing is quickly ended and the ark left at the nearest house – David calls again for the ark to come up.

And so with great joy the ark of the LORD is brought into its tent in Jerusalem, this time carried with poles upon the shoulders of sanctified Levites, as Moses prescribed. And now there is no limit to the rejoicing; with good cause do the Levites lead all in song with lyres and harps and cymbals, and trumpets blaring, for today the LORD is with them in their mission.

And when the celebration is over, when the ark rests in its tent, David declares the praises of the LORD be sung continually in the house of God. And so, while the priests offer the burnt offerings every morning and evening as commanded by God, and some of the Levites guard the gates, those so appointed for ever sing the praises of the LORD in His holy place. Ever does the music play a sacred song to Him who reigns over all. Alleluia!

The House of David

Though David thinks to build a house of cedar for the LORD, it is the LORD who promises an everlasting house to David. He will make for him a name like the great ones of the earth and subdue all his enemies, that Israel may dwell in peace. A son of his shall sit on his throne for ever.

And what praise David gives to the LORD for the blessing promised him and His people Israel! And how the LORD is with David as he sets forth to conquer all the nations round about: the Philistines and their giants; the king of Zobah with his chariots and shields of gold; the Ammonites and the Syrians, who become his slaves; Edom, Moab, Amalek… all are defeated by David and his army – none can stand before the power of God.

But David sins in seeking to number the people under his rule; he does not listen to Joab, the commander of his army, when he says: "May the LORD add to His people a hundred times as many as they are!" (21:3). Instead, David's pride causes many thousands to die at the hand of God.

Truly it is not the house David builds on the bloodshed of war that shall endure, nor the temple made of gold by Solomon where YHWH dwells for ever. It is the House, the Temple that is Jesus, wherein God remains. He is the Son who sits on the eternal throne.

The House of the LORD

David declares he shall build a house for the living God and His holy ark at the threshing floor where the LORD stays His hand from destroying the people. But since he has shed much blood in war, David is not to build this house himself; he can only gather the gold and silver, bronze and iron, wood and stone (in great abundance) for his son Solomon, a man of peace, to construct the house according to the plan David sets forth (in detail), with the men of great skill he appoints.

All the officials of Israel and the officers that serve the king, with all the commanders and their thousands of warriors who come and go tribe by tribe throughout the twelve months of the year – all these and more David assembles at Jerusalem, calling on them to help Solomon build the house of God in keeping with his word. And freewill offerings David and the leaders of the people add to the sum collected for the building of the temple.

The Levites are to serve the priests within the temple as gatekeepers, and as singers and musicians to give praise to God. These serve the LORD and His house according to their family line and the lots which fall to them. All is to be well ordered in God's house and in the kingdom of Israel, and so all are to keep His commandments with a whole heart – particularly Solomon, who is placed by his father on the throne – that all might be blessed and prosper in the sight of God.

2 CHRONICLES

Solomon and the kings who follow him unto the exile in Babylon are recounted now.

Solomon begins his reign well, getting all Israel together to worship the LORD and call upon His NAME, offering a thousand burnt offerings on His altar. And for his dedication, Solomon is visited by the LORD and asked his heart's desire. And how perfectly he responds in his request for wisdom to rule well the people of God; how humbly he stands before the LORD his God and seeks to do His holy will. (How well would all men do to imitate his faith.)

And so YHWH blesses him beyond his requests, giving him not only wisdom greater than any man has known, but surpassing riches and honor as well. There shall be no other king like the great King Solomon... his fame and glory spread far and wide.

But when he turns from the LORD, how severe will be his fall! How far in the depths he shall find himself. The riches and fame the LORD provides in His NAME and by His grace will become a trap from which he is unable to escape. And so, how vain his life will become – how tragically his glory shall fade like the grass of the fields. And should we not all thus learn to beware the trappings of this earth and keep our hearts fixed on God? There is only one King of kings.

Solomon's Temple

The heavens and the earth cannot contain YHWH, but Solomon builds an exalted house where He deigns to dwell among men. Employing those of greatest skill and using the finest materials, Solomon constructs the house of the LORD using slaves taken from the foreigners among them to do the work.

The temple is covered with gold, and immeasurable amounts of bronze serve the casting of its instruments. Cherubim are carved into its walls and wrought into its purple and scarlet curtains; and two cherubim of gold spread their wings above the ark of the Covenant containing the Ten Commandments, which is brought into the finished house with abundant sacrificial offerings.

Fire comes from Heaven and consumes the sacrifices, and the glory of God fills the temple, for the LORD hears Solomon's prayer to be with His people in this place and listen to all who come there in faith. He will be with Israel and with Solomon as long as they heed His commands and walk before Him in holiness. But when they turn to worship of other gods, their punishment shall be severe; then the royal throne will be vacated and the nation taken into exile. For the LORD remains with us only as long as we remain with Him…. He cannot dwell with those who spurn His glorious presence.

The Kingdom Divided

Glorious is the reign of Solomon; queens and kings come from all around to marvel at his wisdom and the unparalleled riches that adorn his house. He is a king wrought in gold.

But his hand is heavy upon the people of the land, and so when he dies they beg his son to lighten their burden. When in his arrogance Rehoboam refuses, threatening boldly to increase their load, Israel turns away from the sons of David, separating themselves from Judah. Thus for the sins of Solomon there come to be two kingdoms, as the LORD has prophesied.

Now there will be war between the two houses. Now the golden calves of Jeroboam will be a continual source of sin in Israel, and the worship in the temple of Jerusalem will be unstable. Rehoboam soon abandons any semblance of faith in God, and so Judah is nearly overrun by Egypt – the gold in her house becoming bronze. And though Rehoboam's sons defeat Israel in battle, any victory, any display of trust in the LORD, is short-lived.

The kingdom will remain divided until and through the exile. Only Jesus can reconcile this house set against itself; only His blood will make the two nations one. In Him is found union of Gentile and Jew.

(Mostly) Righteous Kings

Judah has kings that walk in the way of the LORD and His commandments and not in the ways of Israel, but none can really fulfill God's will. Though courageous in fighting evil, in removing false worship from the land, and though encouraged when the LORD blesses them in battle for their faithfulness to Him, in the end each strays, much as their father Solomon.

It is said of Asa (son of Abijah, son of Rehoboam) that he does "what [is] good and right in the eyes of the LORD his God" (14:2); and for his zeal the LORD gives him great victory in battle against a multitude of Ethiopians. Then Asa leads Judah in a mighty oath to seek the LORD, and peace round about is granted him by God. Yet when a prophet chastises him for his reliance on another nation instead of the LORD, he becomes angry and cruel, and ends his days in suffering apart from God.

Asa's son Jehoshaphat is more faithful than he, yet he too is deaf to prophecy, entering into league with a wicked king of Israel. Though the LORD still fights for him when he humbly seeks His help before all the assembly in the temple, Jehoshaphat eventually joins again with an evil king of Israel.

It is as if God is teaching us that we never learn, never truly give ourselves to His will, and so will always suffer the limitations of our corrupted nature – at least until Jesus comes.

Evil Reigns

After the death of Jehoshaphat, a period of great evil comes to the house of Judah, for when Jehoshaphat's oldest son takes the throne, he murders all his brothers, as well as other princes who are better than he. The nations round about revolt against Jehoram's rule and come and carry away all he owns, including his children. He himself dies a terrible death, as Elijah prophesies: his bowels come out and he perishes in great agony. His demise is to no one's regret.

But his only remaining son proves no better. Failing to learn from his father's fate, Ahaziah also walks in wickedness, guided by his particularly wicked mother. He is soon killed while fleeing from battle, but his evil mother assumes the throne, destroying all the royal family to keep her hold on the kingdom.

However, the youngest son of Ahaziah is stolen away and hidden in a bedchamber six years. When finally he is revealed to all, the priests and people rejoice to seat him on his throne, and to slay Athaliah.

And so the altars and images of Baal are broken in pieces and the house of the LORD is set in order, the city becoming a quiet place.

Half Reigns

Then come three kings who follow rightly in the way of the LORD for half their reigns, then fall precipitously from serving the living and true God, and so become cursed.... These are perhaps the most tragic of men, for they have the blessing of YHWH strongly upon them as they hold fast to His Word, and lose everything because of their pride.

Jehoida the priest guides the young King Joash all the days he remains with him. But when Jehoida dies, how terribly Joash turns to wickedness. He sees that the house of the LORD is repaired and restored after Athaliah had so broken it down, and the people give willingly and joyfully to such a cause; but after the death of Jehoida, Joash murders the priest's son in the house of God, and is destroyed in battle and murdered himself.

His son Amaziah also sets about to do what is right in the eyes of God, building up his army and listening to the prophecy to trust in the LORD alone. But after great victory he proceeds to worship the gods of those he conquers, and stops the mouth of the prophet. And so Israel destroys Jerusalem, and Amaziah too is slain.

And his son does the same. Uzziah prospers in obedience to God, but when grown strong becomes proud, insisting on burning incense before the LORD, which only a priest may do. And so he is struck with leprosy for the rest of his days and dwells apart from the house of God. O how foolish man can be!

Ahaz and Hezekiah

Here we have father and son, one particularly evil in his reign, the other particularly good: one shuts the doors of the house of the LORD, the other opens them and restores true worship of the living God to the land of Judah.

After the righteous reign of Jotham, Ahaz takes the throne and proceeds to follow the most abominable practices of the nations round about, making molten images for the Baals, burning incense to false gods and even burning his sons as an unholy offering. And so he is attacked and destroyed by the kings of Syria and Israel, by the Edomites and Philistines, and even those to whom he's given tribute for help. Yet he becomes more faithless.

But when Hezekiah comes to power he quickly and forthrightly reverses all the evil his father has done, sanctifying the house of the LORD and returning holy sacrifice and glorious song to the temple, employing priests and Levites to take their rightful place in the sight of God. He keeps the Passover feast for the first time since Solomon, even inviting all of Israel to come and join in united worship in Jerusalem. They celebrate an extra seven days, then go out and destroy all false idols, breaking down their altars throughout the land. Tithes and offerings are made in abundance for the house of the LORD, and so, greatly does every work of Hezekiah prosper. Alleluia!

To Babylon

Hezekiah is threatened by foreign invasion, but he and Isaiah cry unto Heaven and Jerusalem is spared. However, the king is not without sin. Because of his pride he does not thank the LORD for saving him from sickness, and then brings the princes of Babylon into the house of God, showing them all his riches... which they will soon take to their kingdom.

His son Manasseh reverts quickly, and in even greater fashion, to the evil Ahaz had done; but he does humble himself after being temporarily taken captive to Babylon... and his later years reflect his reform. His son has a short, evil reign, and then comes Josiah.

Under the reign of Josiah the glory of the LORD is restored to Judah as it has not been before, for with greater zeal than even Hezekiah he destroys the false idols and rebuilds the house of God. The Law of the LORD is rediscovered in his days, and with tears he consecrates himself and the people to the keeping of the Covenant. Then they celebrate the greatest Passover feast. But nothing can alter the will of the LORD that Judah be taken into exile and the land have its Sabbath rest for all the evil done by her kings.

And so, though Josiah's eyes are kept from seeing it, upon his evil children the wrath of the LORD does come: the temple is burned, the walls of Jerusalem are broken down, and all the people are taken captive to Babylon. Not till the seventy years prophesied by Jeremiah are fulfilled will Cyrus king of Persia call for Judah's return.

EZRA

The time prophesied by Jeremiah comes and so YHWH stirs up the spirit of King Cyrus to proclaim to all the earth that the temple in Jerusalem should be rebuilt and that the Jews among his people should return to their homeland and rebuild it. All they need is to be provided them, and so silver and gold, beasts of burden and freewill offerings, and the thousands of gold and silver vessels Nebuchadnezzar carried away accompany the tens of thousands who journey back to Judah.

And when all the men come to their towns and the priests and Levites occupy Jerusalem, all gather as one to set the altar of the God of Israel in its place and offer sacrifice to the LORD. And so the appointed feasts are kept again and the continual burnt offering made each day.

Then the foundation of the temple is laid with the priests arrayed in their vestments and the Levites singing praise to God. All shout loudly, but the old men weep... for they remember the glory of the former house and see the state of the temple this day.

How shall we ever be as we once were, O LORD? Only you can return us to our glorious state.

Opposition and Completion

The people of the land who were brought to Samaria from Syria desire to join the Jews in their rebuilding of the temple of the mighty God. But the Jews deny this request, for they are not of the people of Israel, but of foreign blood. Thus conflict between Samaritan and Jew is kindled.

The rebuffed Samaritans set about to prevent the rebuilding of the house of God, writing to the new king of Persia that he has much to fear from the Jews, accusing them of being a rebellious race. And so, for a time work on the temple is stopped.

But the prophets Haggai and Zechariah rise up and call the people to do as the LORD commands and finish the house of God. The people heed and recommence the work, unaffected by the threats of the governor of the province. And they again find the blessing of a king of Persia: Cyrus' decree is rediscovered and all encouragement is given to the Jews. The cost in full is to be provided them with all the animals needed for the daily sacrifices.

And so the temple is soon completed and the Passover feast kept with great joy, for YHWH has turned the heart of the king to their cause.

Ezra Arrives

Then Ezra is sent from Babylon by the king himself to bring to Jerusalem gold and silver and bronze, that with this money, animals might be bought to be offered in the name of the king so he might find the blessing of the God of Heaven and be kept from His wrath. He also instructs Ezra the scribe, a man greatly skilled in the Law of Moses, to see that the Israelites are keeping the Law well. How great is the blessing upon Ezra and the priests and Levites and people who go up with him to Jerusalem, for indeed even the decree of the pagan king is with them! The LORD watches over their four-month journey, seeing that they all arrive safely.

But what does the scribe of God find when he enters Jerusalem but that the people have greatly transgressed against the LORD and His Word, marrying with women from the nations of the land and thus worshiping their gods and practicing their abominations?

So Ezra fasts and prays, "weeping and casting himself down before the house of God" (10:1) and confessing the guilt of the people. Praise God, the people join his weeping and vow to put aside their foreign wives and children; and this is done in orderly fashion over a two-month period. As by a heavy rain, they are purged.

How quick we are to fall into sin, how slow of heart to believe. Even a moment of favor meant to revive us in our bondage we easily spurn.

NEHEMIAH

As Ezra has come to rebuild the temple, so Nehemiah comes now to rebuild the wall of Jerusalem. In exile he weeps when he hears of the wall's disrepair and the gates' destruction by fire. He fasts and prays several days, seeking the mercy and favor of the God of Heaven... and he finds it.

As Ezra has been blessed by the king, so Nehemiah, the king's cupbearer, also receives his favor. The king allows his servant to go to Jerusalem to work on the wall and the city, sending him off with a letter and his protection, and providing the wood he needs.

After arriving safely, Nehemiah goes out alone at night to survey the damage to the city's wall before proposing to the priests and leaders of the Jews, as well as the workmen, that they should rise up and rebuild. Their hands are strengthened for this good work, and so, shoulder to shoulder each in his own section all the way around Jerusalem, the men of Judah and Israel begin to repair the wall.

Glory to the LORD of Heaven and earth! that He watches over and cares for the needs of His people, giving them not only a house for worship but a city in which to dwell securely, that their worship might be done freely and with great assurance from their God on high. He does not abandon His people.

Old Testament

Opposition and Completion II

Again there is opposition to the building from the governors of the province. They taunt the Jews who work on the wall, saying it will crumble under the weight of a fox, and they plot together to come and fight against Jerusalem. So a watch is set up in the night to guard the wall in its sections; and during the day half the men work while the other half stand ready for battle – even those who work carry a sword at their side. A trumpet is to be sounded should there be an attack, that all might come to the place… and so the Jews never pause in rebuilding the wall.

But opposition is found within the ranks of the Jews as well, for some are taking a mortgage on the land of their brethren who have no money for the tax imposed by the governors, and are levying their own taxes on them! Nehemiah insists all land be returned and no further taxes be taken, that none might have to struggle or complain as the work of the LORD is being accomplished.

Their enemies also threaten them with letters and try to frighten Nehemiah with false prophecies, but he and the Jews remain strong and finish the wall, to the great consternation of the peoples around them. Fear falls upon all for the power of God at work in the Jews.

The doors are set in place with gatekeepers to guard them… and so nothing can deter the song of the LORD being sung in the city of Jerusalem.

Ezra's Proclamation

All the people gather "as one man" (8:1) and Ezra is called upon to read the Law of Moses before this great assembly. He stands on a wooden platform and proclaims aloud the Word of God as the Levites interpret the Law for the people. All gathered declare their "Amen" as Ezra blesses the LORD, and they bow their heads to the ground in humble worship before their Maker. The people are entreated to rejoice, for they begin to weep when they hear the words of the Law and realize how unfaithful they and their ancestors have been. They do rejoice this day, and for seven days more, as the feast of

Tabernacles is kept and Ezra continues each day to read from the book of Moses.

Afterward, they are led in the confession of their sins as Ezra prays aloud to God, reviewing the history of the Israelites, the blessings the LORD has showered upon them through Abraham and Moses and Joshua, and the repeated disobedience of the chosen people.

How perfectly Ezra reviews this history! And how well the people know the suffering that comes from rebellion against God; for only now do they have their city back, and still they are under foreign rule. But led by Ezra, the Covenant with the LORD they mightily renew, promising to walk according to God's Law and observe all His commandments, keeping themselves free of the nations' evil and remembering the holiness of the Sabbath day. They shall tithe and support the house of God.... May YHWH look with favor on them and their resolve.

The Dedication

One tenth of the people come to live in Jerusalem with the priests and Levites, the gatekeepers and singers, and all who do work in the house of God. Nine-tenths remain on their land in the surrounding towns, but this tithe is blessed to enter the holy city.

The day comes to dedicate the wall of Jerusalem with great joy and singing in praise of the LORD. The Levites purify themselves and the people, as well as the gates and the wall; and upon the wall a procession is held with one half of the assembly going to the right, led by Ezra, and the other half to the left, with Nehemiah. All meet in the temple, and great sacrifices are offered this day with abounding joy even among the women and children. Everyone takes his appointed place and the book of Moses is again read aloud.

But on his return from a journey to the king, Nehemiah finds the city and temple in disarray. (It takes not long for man to forget his God.) A foreign governor has been given a chamber in the courts of the house of the LORD, and he and his things have to be purged. The Levites have not been receiving their tithes and so have left Jerusalem for their lands; they have to be called back and the tithes enforced.

Old Testament

Work and much buying and selling is prevalent on the Sabbath, so the gates of the city are locked from the eve of the holy day, and those who still congregate outside are threatened. And once again the people have taken foreign wives. All things foreign Nehemiah cleanses, but how tenuous indeed is the people's dedication.

TOBIT

Tobit is a good man, a man of charity toward his neighbor and of faithfulness to God. He shares his bread and clothing with his brethren in need and hesitates not to bury the abandoned dead. Most admirably, when his entire tribe turned to worship of the golden calf, he alone among his kinsmen in Naphtali traveled to Jerusalem for the feasts to worship the LORD and offer his tithe. And now as an exile in Nineveh, while the others with him eat the food of the Gentiles sacrificed to idols, he keeps himself clean of such abomination.

Because of his faithfulness in burying those murdered among his kinsmen, Tobit is forced to flee with his wife and son from the wrath of a new king, and so loses everything YHWH has favored him with in his exile. When he is able to return he does not cease his good works, desiring to bring the poor in to feast with him, and still burying his slain brothers.

But when blindness comes upon him, despair soon follows. Though cared for two years by his well-placed nephew, and though his wife is able to support him thereafter, his misplaced anger toward her draws reproaches from her mouth… and so in his distress he prays for death. But the LORD does not answer his prayer as he expects.

Tobit

Raphael

Thinking death is upon him, Tobit calls his son to send him in search of a sum of money he left with a relative in prosperous times. First he gives him instructions: to honor his mother, to be always charitable toward his poor brothers, and to marry a woman from among his people so as not to fall into immorality. In all things he must walk with God.

What neither man knows is that on the same day Tobit prays for death, Sarah, the daughter of a kinsman (whose home is near the place Tobias is being sent), asks the same of the LORD after being reproached by her handmaids – seven men to whom she's been wed have been killed by a demon in her bridal chamber. Her prayer, too, shall be answered in a way not expected.

But that of which the men are most unaware is that the guide they hire to accompany Tobias along the dangerous path to Rages in Media to collect the fortune is the angel of God, Raphael. It is by "this man" that "God who dwells in Heaven will prosper [Tobias'] way" (5:16). The LORD's angel indeed attends him!

And it is by this angel the prayers of Tobit and Sarah shall be answered, for the father of Tobias will find healing for his eyes and the daughter of Raguel freedom from the demon.

Blessed Marriage

On the way to collect the money, Tobias is threatened by a large fish while bathing in a river; but at the command of Raphael he subdues the fish and cuts out its heart and liver and gall, which are to serve for healing. They stop at the house of Raguel, where Raphael tells Tobias he is to marry his kinswoman Sarah. He instructs him to burn the heart and gall of the fish on their wedding night and the demon will flee, and so their union shall be blessed.

Tobias does as he is told and the demon indeed flees at the smoke from the heart and liver; and YHWH hears the prayers of Tobias and Sarah as they rise from their bed to beg His mercy on their chaste union. And so Raguel fills in the grave he prepared in precaution for

Tobias, and calls for a feast of fourteen days to celebrate the holy blessing come from God upon these only children.

Death flees, it vanishes like smoke, and new life comes into the houses of Tobit and Raguel. Raphael quickly sets off to collect the money for which he and Tobias have come, that they might be ready to leave at the feast's end... for Tobit and his wife are counting the days in great distress at Tobias' delay. His mother cannot be consoled as she continually mourns and stares down the road, looking for her son's return.

Praise God!

Tobias returns and his father's eyes are opened when anointed with the gall of the fish at Raphael's word. And what can Tobit do but praise the LORD? For now he sees his son whom he feared dead; now he can celebrate Tobias' marriage to Sarah with a whole heart.

Half of all they have brought back Tobit and Tobias determine to give to Raphael, for truly he deserves it. But the angel reveals himself to father and son, and they are overwhelmed. He entreats them to praise God and give alms, and to write down in a book (which we now hold in our hands) all that the LORD has done for them.

"Blessed is God who lives for ever" (13:1), and blessed is His mercy toward our poor souls. Though He bring us down to the nether world, though He scatter us abroad for our sins against His goodness, when we turn to Him, He lifts our heads, showing us His favor.

Give thanks to Him! All the nations shall know His glory; Jerusalem shall be rebuilt and all generations come streaming to it. "All the Gentiles will turn to fear the LORD God in truth, and will bury their idols" (14:6). All will praise the LORD and give thanks to Him.

Upon the death of his father and mother, Tobias goes to Raguel in Media before the destruction of Nineveh, as Tobit has instructed him. There he buries his mother- and father-in-law well; and there he dies at an advanced age, rejoicing for the justice come upon Nineveh.

JUDITH

Nebuchadnezzar, who has conquered Nineveh and rules over the Assyrians from this great city, goes out to take the fortified city of Ecbatana in Media, and he calls Judea and all the nations round about them in the West to come and fight at his side. But they all spurn the king's command.

In his great anger Nebuchadnezzar vows to destroy all these nations who have shamed his messengers. And so, after he has overthrown the army of Arphaxad and taken his cities, capturing even the great walled city of Ecbatana, and after he and his forces have feasted for one hundred and twenty days... Nebuchadnezzar remembers his vow and calls all his officers together. He recounts all the wickedness of the west region and chooses Holofernes, his chief general, to take a multitude of foot soldiers and cavalry and accomplish the utter destruction of these disobedient nations.

Like a swarm of locusts they come and ravage all in their path, plundering the Ishmaelites and the Midianites and the Syrians... and terror falls upon all who lay before them. Many surrender themselves and their cities and bow down to Nebuchadnezzar; and to the frontier of Judea the army comes.

The Siege

The people of Israel prepare for war by fortifying their towns and storing up food, but especially by humbling themselves with much fasting, crying out to God in sackcloth and ashes, for, as Achior the Ammonite witnesses to Holofernes and his great army, it is in YHWH, Creator of Heaven and earth, that the Israelites take their strength: "the God who hates iniquity is with them" (5:17), and as long as they do not sin against Him, none shall reach them on their mountaintops. He will defend them and they shall prosper.

But Holofernes and his whole army go forth and lay siege to Bethulia, spreading over the breadth of the land and terrifying the people of Israel. They seize the springs that supply their water and

Old Testament

prevent anyone's escape... and in little more than a month the people find themselves in dire straits. Without water even the young men faint in the streets, and so in fear of imminent death all the people call on the elders to surrender the city to their enemies.

"Great and general lamentation ar[ises] throughout the assembly, and they cr[y] out to the LORD God with a loud voice" (7:29). Five days more are given for Him to act on their behalf.

May His mercy be on all who are under siege; may He not utterly forsake those who call out to Him. In you alone we find our hope, O LORD!

Judith's Deception

Judith upbraids the leaders of the people for their attempt to force the hand of God by setting a limited time for Him to act to save them. She is a particularly religious and well-respected woman in the community, a widow with considerable possessions who spends her days fasting in sackcloth, and who is very beautiful and wise. "No one spoke ill of her, for she feared God with great devotion" (8:8). And so they listen to her.

But the leaders can do nothing else to calm the people's fear, and their oath cannot be changed. So Judith contrives a plot to defeat the Assyrians and thwart the destruction they have planned for Judah and the temple in Jerusalem. She determines to stand in the breach and prevent the slaughter of God's Chosen and the desolation of their inheritance, for if Bethulia is taken, all Judea will fall.

And so Judith deceives Holofernes. She prays to the LORD at length, then sets aside her sackcloth and goes to the Assyrian camp at night dressed in all her finery. Her beauty and her wisdom overwhelm Holofernes and his soldiers, and she promises to use her closeness to God for their advantage – she will pray to the LORD and He will tell her when the Israelites have broken the command against eating the food dedicated to God and His service. Then they can attack and destroy all Judah in its spiritual weakness.... And they believe her.

Victory

For three nights Judith goes outside the camp with Holofernes' permission, to cleanse herself at a spring. On the fourth day she is invited to a banquet with him, and she attends arrayed in her finery, with flattery on her tongue. She lies down to eat and drink with this leader of the Assyrian army, and his ravished heart is made quite merry.

When evening comes all withdraw from the bedchamber, leaving the two alone. But Holofernes is overcome with wine, and Judith prays to God for strength to accomplish her mission. She takes down the sword over the bed and cuts off her enemy's head, then goes out of the camp with this trophy in her maid's bag.

When she comes into her city, all wake in praise of God who has conquered their enemies. She instructs them to hang Holofernes' head on the city wall and arrange themselves in battle line so that when the Assyrians see them in the morning light they will raise an alarm. When they find their leader dead, separated from his head, in great fear all the soldiers flee and are pursued by the men of Israel.

A great slaughter is made of the Assyrians, and their camp is plundered. Here and in Jerusalem all honor Judith and sing with her the praise of God, who has saved them by a woman's hand. There is peace in Israel all of Judith's days, and even after she is laid to rest beside her husband, to whom she remains faithful till the end.

ESTHER

Mordecai is a Jew taken from Jerusalem to Susa by Nebuchadnezzar along with the other exiles. He serves in the court of the king, and serves him well, exposing a plot to kill the king made by two other servants who guard the courtyard.

Mordecai has a dream of two dragons that threaten to destroy his people; but the people cry unto God and their cry is a tiny stream which becomes a great river and consumes those held in honor – thus are the lowly exalted by the LORD!

This tiny stream is a symbol for Esther, a beautiful young virgin who was raised by Mordecai, her uncle, after the death of her parents. She it is who becomes queen after the great king of Babylon, who rules one hundred and twenty-seven provinces throughout the world, deposes his queen for her disobedience in refusing to come before him with her royal crown that all his friends might see her beauty.

Of all the virgins in the land, Esther finds the king's favor and has the crown placed upon her head (though at Mordecai's instruction she does not reveal to anyone that she is a Jew). Now when the dragon Haman rises to power as second in the kingdom and seeks by letter sealed with the king's signet ring to destroy all Jews – because of Mordecai's refusal to bow down to him – it is Esther who is called on to save them.

The Cry

The lot is cast and the day is set for the annihilation of all the Jews throughout the Babylonian Empire. And so, in every province a cry goes up among the people of God. In sackcloth and ashes they wail aloud for the terrible fate that has befallen them at the word of the wicked Haman.

In the midst of the city of Susa, Mordecai cries out in sackcloth and ashes even to the gate of the king's palace. Esther sends him clothing that he might put his mourning aside, but he refuses. Rather, he informs her of her people's fate, and entreats her to go to the king.

At first she fears to do so for the death that is decreed on all those who enter the king's presence uncalled; but she soon realizes her responsibility and determines to go: "If I perish, I perish" (4:16).

She calls on all the Jews in Susa to fast and pray for her three days, and she joins them with her maids in garments of distress and mourning. Mordecai prays to the LORD, for whose sake alone he has refused to bow down to Haman, and Esther begs Him without whom she is utterly alone to keep her from danger as she goes before the lion.

YHWH looks upon His lowly ones in their time of affliction. All those persecuted for His NAME, who find their joy only in Him, He saves. His inheritance shall never perish.

Esther

Haman Hanged

Esther sets aside her clothes of mourning and comes before the king arrayed in the most majestic attire, though with great fear in her heart. When the king, dressed in gold with precious stones and most terrifying to behold, looks at Esther in fierce anger, she collapses.

But the king takes pity on his queen, assuring her she shall not be killed and promising to fulfill her petition, however great it might be. She begs him to come with Haman to a dinner she has prepared, and when at that dinner the king again asks her request, she begs him to return with Haman for dinner the next day.

Unable to sleep that night, the king has chronicles read to him, and he hears of the way in which Mordecai saved his life from his servants' plot. The next day he asks Haman, who has just erected a gallows for Mordecai, what should be done for a man the king delights to honor – and when Haman hears that the man is Mordecai (and not himself), he is filled with dread.

Later at dinner Queen Esther reveals Haman's evil plot against Mordecai and all Jews, and the king orders him hung from the gallows his own hands have made.

The proud shall not stand before the justice of God; He will destroy all who dare to shed innocent blood.

The Feast of Purim

Mordecai is given the place of Haman as second in the kingdom, and he writes in a letter to all the provinces of Babylon that the Jews should be helped to destroy their enemies on the very day Haman had set for their annihilation.

And so this day of lamentation for the Jews becomes a day of feasting. Indeed, two days of feasting does it become, for in Susa the queen declares a second day on which the Jews may kill their enemies… and so in the city the feasting is delayed a day beyond the one all in the provinces celebrate the victory of the Jews. But all shall feast both days for all generations that all may remember the great favor the LORD has shown His Chosen in blessing their lot over that of their persecutors.

Seventy-five thousand are killed by the Jews throughout the kingdom of Babylon, eight hundred in Susa over the two days – and the bodies of Haman's ten sons are hung from the gallows like their father. Such is the fate of those who plot against the LORD and His anointed.

But the Chosen of the LORD shall feast for ever before Him; they shall be vindicated and their day of gladness come, and never end.

JOB

Job is a man "blameless and upright, one who fear[s] God, and turn[s] away from evil" (1:1). He is blessed by the LORD with seven sons and three daughters, as well as thousands of sheep and camels, and hundreds of oxen and asses. And he offers burnt offerings for his children whenever they come from feasting, for perhaps they have sinned and cursed God in their hearts.

Though Job never curses the LORD, He allows Satan to tempt him. In a single day his adversary takes or destroys his oxen and sheep and camels, and all his sons and daughters. Bereft of all with which he had been blessed, naked before the LORD, what does Job do? He falls on the ground and worships God, blessing His holy NAME.

Satan cannot cause this man, whom even YHWH Himself calls "blameless and upright" (2:3), to sin. Even when the devil afflicts Job with loathsome sores from head to foot, he refuses to curse God. Though tempted to despair even by his wife, he accepts whatever befalls him as coming from the hand of the LORD.

Job's three friends come to console him, but overwhelmed by his suffering they cannot speak a word. They sit silently on the ground with him seven days and nights.

Curse the Day

"After this Job open[s] his mouth and curse[s] the day of his birth" (3:1). No more can he take of the pain upon him, of the darkness which besets him round about, from which he can see no escape. And so, indeed, he curses his birth and longs for death. For why should suffering be of so long life?

He will not be consoled by his first friend's words; he cannot accept that logic by which he has lived all his days: that the fool is condemned to misery and no man is righteous before God, that His chastising hand is for our good and if we have faith and are patient, a new day will come.

Day after day Job finds only darkness, only misery throughout the night. There is no rest for his weary flesh, and his eyes can see no light. His only consolation would be death… but this escapes him as well.

Who can blame Job for his bitterness; who would question his growing despair? Should he be reproached for crying out to God? What hope can he hold on this empty earth? Only Christ. Only Christ could bear such torments; only He is so pure in the sight of God. And only in Him do we find remedy for our despair. For He alone can consume the enemies that consign us to Sheol – He alone confounds Satan's snares. O Jesus, take away our iniquity!

No Encouragement

His second friend attempts to rouse Job from the depths of despair. What he says is very true: "Though your beginning was small, your latter days will be very great" (8:7). And the logic he uses cannot be contradicted – God indeed blesses the pure and upright; He "will not reject a blameless man" (8:20).

"But how can a man be just before God?" (9:1). This is Job's response; and it is just as true. And so, if no man can be found pure in the sight of the LORD, what hope has Job? What hope has any man?

Job is blameless as any man – the LORD Himself has said so. He has kept the Law with all his strength, yet punishment is upon him; and he can find no escape from the bitterness of soul that afflicts him.

What is it the LORD does to him? Where is the measure on which he could depend? If Job is innocent, why are his wounds multiplied without cause? This blessing Job cannot understand. Regarding this condition he has no words with which to approach God.

He knows that YHWH is His Creator, that he himself is but dust of the earth that has been formed by God's hands. And so he knows, too, that he cannot lift his head to speak with the LORD, even if he is righteous. And so, what can he do but hope for death?

I Will Speak

His third friend loses patience with Job, chastising him for his "multitude of words" (11:2) before the LORD. He tells him of the greatness of God and how far His ways are above those of man… and, again, he speaks the truth. But what he cannot see is that Job knows this, that he has already said the same. And he is also blind to the innocence of Job, instead accusing him of being worthless and even wicked – he must be or the LORD would not be punishing him so, and he would not hope for death.

Job is right to say that his friends "whitewash with lies" (13:4), that they show partiality toward God in their judgment; he is in a manner justified in the case he seeks to present before the LORD: "I will defend my ways to His face" (13:15). But one can understand his friends' revulsion at such pride, at such readiness to speak before God.

Job's friends are utterly blind to the fact that YHWH is doing something new. They cannot go beyond the dictates of the law to see that God is punishing an innocent man. But Job too, though he sees the situation, remains himself in the court of law seeking justice for himself. This is what a good Jew knows of God and His ways. But the LORD is calling him further.

Job cannot be silent as Christ on the Cross, as the Son of God before His accusers. He must speak of his suffering. And so, in this his righteousness falls short.

On the Cross

His first friend speaks again, and now more severely. Job, he says, answers with empty wind, presuming against God and His counselors. And so for his "defiance to the Almighty" (15:25), this "wicked man writhes in pain all his days" (15:20). Job's heart is filled with deceit and so he brings forth evil: this is the judgment against him.

O what "miserable comforters" (16:2) his friends prove to be! as they strike Job "insolently upon the cheek" (16:10). They mock and scorn as the LORD pours out his gall on the ground. He has become a "byword of the peoples" (17:6), and no wise man comes to take his pain away.

Should he make his house in darkness – in this place will he find his hope? Is there not but dust in such death…? How can a man bear this desolation! Should Job be counted among the wicked; should he countenance such a judgment?

It is the call of Christ on the Cross Job hears now. It is the weight of man's sin he is asked to carry. In this darkness he might find his freedom and that of the human race. But Job is unable to meet God's call to perfect love, and so he loses hope. He indeed becomes as one who "mourns only for himself" (14:22) and his own sins (or lack thereof), and not those of others. He cannot bear the blessed weight the LORD places on his shoulders – only Jesus can accomplish the world's salvation.

Pity!

"Have pity on me, have pity on me!" (19:21), Job begs of his friends, for "brimstone is scattered upon his habitation" (18:15) by those who should console him. Mercilessly they censure their "wicked" friend, saying that his are "the dwellings of the ungodly" (18:21), that indeed he "knows not God" (ibid); and thus, "by disease his skin is consumed" (18:13)… thus "he will perish for ever like his own dung" (20:7). "Crushed and abandoned" (20:19), their bronze arrows piercing him through, "the glittering point comes out of his gall" (20:25) – what can poor Job do but beg their mercy?

Can they not see that "the hand of God has touched [him]" (19:21), that his "hope He has pulled up like a tree" (19:10), that "the root of the matter is [not] found in him" (19:28) but in the LORD and in His will? They should indeed fear the wrath of the LORD that brings punishment on those who judge unjustly, who condemn others without remorse. For indeed Job's "Redeemer lives, and at last He will stand upon the earth" (19:25). The LORD will hear his words and have pity on this innocent soul... but what shall become of those who have falsely accused him, who have driven him further into the dust? The judgment on them will be fearful.

The Wicked and the Just

The wicked are punished and the just blessed – but is wisdom as simple as this? In the kingdom of Heaven it is so, but what of life on this corrupted earth, where Satan still walks freely? Can we judge a man's righteousness by his material wealth, by his social status and physical health?

Job's plight reveals the foolishness of such thought, for, again, YHWH Himself has called Job a blameless and upright man – yet he suffers great misery. In Jesus, of course, the plight of the innocent victim is fulfilled, but throughout Scripture we see it at work. Who of the prophets is not persecuted for speaking God's Word? Was Elijah not pursued by Jezebel; will Jeremiah not be thrown into a muddy cistern? Did not Moses groan under the weight of the people of Israel and David speak in the voice of Christ of the suffering of the just?

It cannot be denied, as Job says, that it is often the case that the wicked prosper while the just languish. But in their self-righteousness his friends hold blindly to their narrow view of justice, going so far as to invent false accusations of wickedness against Job – that he has oppressed the naked and the hungry, the widow and the orphan – to justify themselves. Unable or unwilling to see past this life, that reward and punishment come beyond the grave, they condemn an innocent man... thus supporting Satan's plans.

Sometimes riches are a blessing and sometimes a curse, and it is the cry of the poor the LORD hears; he who relies on Him alone finds salvation.

Wisdom

"Where shall wisdom be found? And where is the place of understanding?" (28:12). That "man does not know the way to it" (28:13), Job makes evident. That it is hidden from earthly eyes, we can clearly see. For having come from stating how the wicked often prosper till death in this world, Job now declares the portion of the wicked man with God. How fleeting are the riches he amasses! How quickly terrors overtake him! He cannot stand long before his Maker.

Indeed, man is as a maggot or a worm before the majesty and power of the Almighty God. (And so, why do Job's friends not help "him who has no power" (26:2) before the LORD?) Though he mine the deep recesses of the earth for its gold and precious stones, man cannot find the way to wisdom. For it is with God alone. Even Death cannot know it, for it is beyond the realm of this dark place.

Then how shall we discover wisdom? How shall Job ever understand the throes in which he finds himself? How can any of us be kept from despair? We must simply admit we do not know the ways of God, that we are as nothing before Him; and in such fear of the LORD, in such utter awe of His glory, evil shall depart from us and our eyes be opened to see what is beyond our vision, beyond our corrupted hearts to comprehend. It is indeed only with God all things are understood.

Justice!

Job bemoans his lost favor with the LORD, and cries out for answer to his plight. He longs for the days when God watched over him and His light shone upon him. How blessed he was! And how righteous. How good he was to the poor, to the blind and the lame, to the widow and orphan, to the wayfarer and all those in need. He was their help, their salvation from the world's oppression; and for such goodness he had the respect of all. But now the most vile of men mock him.

And so he cries to the LORD, but no answer comes. He pleads his cause, but gets no response. "Let me be weighed in a just balance, and let God know my integrity!" (31:6). This is all he desires, to know why such calamity has befallen him.

His goodness cannot be gainsaid; we must believe what he tells us of his keeping from all sin. We must believe him because the LORD has confirmed it – Job speaks the truth and not his friends. If he has sinned in any way against God, His punishment he would accept... he calls it down on himself. But all he can do is repeat his innocence, as if writing it in stone, and hope for answer from the LORD.

Who can comprehend the ways of YHWH? He is beyond human understanding. So, what can one do but wait on His Word?

Elihu's Response

Then a youth who has been standing by opens his mouth to teach his elders. Job and his friends have again embraced silence, have come to the end of their words... and so, unable to restrain his tongue any longer, this young man feels compelled to enter into the argument. Without compunction he declares his opinion: "Be silent, and I will teach you wisdom" (33:33).

And does his speech not show the foolishness of youth? For does he not simply recount, and repeatedly, what has already been said by Job and his friends? And all this without realizing it. Does this speech not show most of all how Job must endure the contumely of those who before would have remained silent in his presence? (And does he not suffer now in silence himself?)

Elihu tells us again of the might of God and how no man can speak of his majesty, none can know Him – yet he hesitates not to open his mouth: "he multiplies words without knowledge" (35:16). And he adds unjust accusation to his empty words, saying Job "adds rebellion to his sin" (34:37), that he has declared that serving God is useless.

Indeed, Job (with his friends) endures the pride of this young man's empty cry; he does not defend himself against the injustice shown him. And by some paradox of God's will, the young man seems at the end of his lengthy speech to touch upon the truth of the LORD's transcendence.

God Speaks

The LORD speaks. "Out of the whirlwind" (38:1) come His words... and who can answer Him? He says nothing very different than Job and his friends have said, but now the words have meaning. They have meaning because YHWH is present to make them known, to make them so.

Indeed, God is Almighty, the LORD of earth and sea and sky and stars. In His hand alone is all Creation. The lightning and the rain are at His command, as is all that moves below the heavens. From the depths of the sea to the highest heavens, He rules all that is.

"Have you an arm like God, and can you thunder with a voice like His?" (40:9). Then how is it you dare speak, you who know nothing of the LORD? Would you presume to be His equal, O proud soul! How can you open your mouth before Him?

He will bring you low, for He "tread[s] down the wicked where they stand" (40:12). Though He may deign to reveal Himself to the eyes of man, never His essence do we see – His being we cannot comprehend. What will you say when He stands before you?

If you fear the monsters of the sea, if you tremble at the fire from the dragon's mouth, should you not thus revere Him who made these, who made you?

Job Repents

"I lay my hand on my mouth."
40:4

What a blessed gift Job now finds: a silent tongue before the LORD of all. Now in the Almighty's presence, what can he say? He can but "repent in dust and ashes" (42:6) and seek His mercy.

What a wonder this silence is! A true sense of our nothingness in God's sight. Job had "spoken of [the LORD] what is right" (42:8); his words were not false (as were his friends'), but he knew not what he was saying... for he knew not really whom he addressed.

Old Testament

But now Job knows, now he sees the LORD as He stands before him. He hears well what God says to him, showing his attention by repeating in his two responses the first words the Almighty utters. And Job answers them well, in the only way they can be answered – with perfect humility.

And Job answers without question the LORD's call for him to intercede for his friends; and by Job's prayer they are forgiven their folly, their persecution of God's righteous one. (How like Christ Job now is in loving his enemies, in pleading his persecutors' ignorance before the Father of all.)

And in this silent understanding of God and His ways, remembering ever His NAME, Job will live out the rest of his days in the blessing of YHWH, which extends beyond his many years, and the grave.

THE PSALMS

1

O let us meditate day and night on your Law
that we might avoid the way of the wicked
and walk always with you.

2

Your King you set on Zion,
and so the plots of the nations are cast asunder –
may all serve you alone!

3

Though we are surrounded by fear,
in you we find our safety;
you are our deliverance, O LORD.

4

You hear us when we call to you,
you shine the light of your face upon us –
in you we are ever free from distress.

5

Our sacrifices you accept, O LORD,
and so we sing for joy
even as the wicked fall.

6

In death we do not know you, LORD…
O let my tears come unto you
and my troubled soul be healed!

7

You are a righteous judge:
and so the wicked falls into the pit he makes,
while the righteous man trusts in your NAME.

8

Great is your NAME and your glory, LORD,
and in your glory we do share –
all things are beneath the feet of your Son.

9

We praise your NAME, O righteous Judge,
for the wicked you destroy for ever –
you deliver the poor who cry to you.

10

Do not stand afar off, YHWH,
as the wicked man curses your NAME,
but deliver the innocent from his hands.

11

Your eyes behold the children of men:
on the wicked you rain down coals,
while the righteous you save from their bow.

12

Silence the proud tongue, O LORD;
arise and save the needy who groan…
your promise is as refined gold.

13

How long will you hide your face from me? –
do not let my enemy prevail,
for I trust in your steadfast love.

14

All men have gone astray;
they eat up your people like bread…
but you strike terror in their souls.

15

Let us walk blamelessly before you
and speak the truth from our heart,
that we might dwell on your holy mountain.

16

You are our chosen portion, no other,
and so we are blessed with your instruction
and rejoice in your presence for ever.

17

There is no wickedness in me, LORD,
and so, hide me in the shadow of your wings –
save me from the teeth of my enemies.

18

David you saved from his foes
by the fire from your mouth;
give all your holy ones strength in battle.

19

Your Word speaks day and night;
the sun sets forth by its grace –
how sweet you are to our taste!

20

You help your anointed, LORD:
the king finds victory
in your holy NAME.

21

David trusts in your steadfast love,
and so a glorious crown is on his head…
but fire consumes your enemies.

22

Though we seem forsaken, LORD,
pierced in hands and feet,
we will praise your deliverance of our poor souls.

23

YHWH, you restore my soul;
I have no fear even of death,
for I shall dwell with you for ever.

24

With clean hands and pure soul
let us seek your glorious face,
that with the King we might enter your gates.

25

May your mercy be known by the humble soul
who waits in repentance for you –
O let us not be put to shame!

26

Vindicate those who walk in faith,
who turn from every evil way;
in your House may we ever sing your praise.

27

Hide not your face, YHWH;
above our enemies let us lift our heads…
in the land of the living we shall praise your NAME.

28

You requite the evil for their deeds
but keep your anointed from the Pit;
thank you, LORD, for hearing our cry.

29

The God of glory thunders,
His voice shakes the wilderness –
give the LORD the glory of His NAME.

30

Our life you bring up from the Pit,
our weeping you turn to dancing…
and so we praise you in your Temple, LORD.

Old Testament

31

My eye is wasted away with grief,
but I trust my spirit into your hands
and you deliver me from the plots of men.

32

I confess my sins to you, LORD,
and you take away my guilt –
blessed is he who trusts in your mercy!

33

Praise YHWH with all your skill!
for by His Word the world was made;
from Heaven He looks kindly upon us.

34

Let us exalt the NAME of the LORD,
for the poor man He saves from all troubles –
not one of his bones shall be broken.

35

The malicious persecute the just;
raise your spear against them, LORD,
and let them be put to shame and confusion.

36

You are the fountain of life, O God;
your steadfast love rises to the heavens –
thrust down the wicked and their evil plots.

37

Trust in the LORD and wait on His word,
for the wicked wilt and die like the grass
but the poor man shall possess the land.

38

My iniquities are a burden too heavy to bear,
my wounds are foul and festering...
hear my sighing and save me from evil.

39

I cannot hold my peace, LORD:
my life is as nothing in your sight;
chastise me not overmuch.

40

How wondrous are your deeds, O LORD! –
you raised me from the desolate pit,
and so I delight to do your will.

41

My enemies wait to see my death;
my friend lifts his heel against me...
but you raise me up from my sickbed.

42

My forsaken soul longs for you, YHWH,
as men taunt me continually:
you are my song in the night.

Old Testament

43

My soul is cast down in mourning;
send forth your light and your truth
and I will praise you at your altar.

44

Your right hand gives victory to your people,
yet, though we have not forgotten your NAME,
we are made now as sheep for the slaughter.

45

The anointed One rides forth victoriously,
His Queen beside Him in golden robes
praised through all generations.

46

Though mountains shake and nations rage,
the LORD God is our refuge and our strength;
His River flows through the Holy City.

47

Sing praise to YHWH with the sound of the trumpet,
for our God is King over all the earth –
O let us clap our hands and shout for joy!

48

Mount Zion is the City of our God,
causing all the nations to tremble and fall…
praise His NAME to the ends of the earth!

49

Do not fear the boasts of the ungodly,
for like the beasts they shall perish;
they and their riches soon come to the grave.

50

God comes forth like a burning fire
to consume those who hate His discipline,
to save those who offer Him a sacrifice of praise.

51

I have done what is evil in your sight:
cleanse me from my sin, O God! –
accept my contrite spirit.

52

The LORD will uproot the evil man,
silencing his deceitful tongue
but blessing those who trust in Him.

53

All have fallen away,
all are alike depraved –
O LORD, save your people!

54

Ruthless men rise against the just,
but you are the Savior of our life;
for your faithfulness we praise your NAME.

55

Hear my prayer and keep me safe,
for violence and strife surround the city
and my friend has become my adversary.

56

My foes trample upon me
but I trust in you without fear,
for you look kindly on my tears.

57

I lie in the midst of vengeful lions
yet I will awake the dawn with praise,
for great is your steadfast love and faithfulness.

58

O LORD, break the teeth of the liar;
let the wicked be trodden down like the grass
that the righteous may rejoice in your justice.

59

Save me, LORD, from these howling dogs
who seek my life for no fault of mine –
against the bloodthirsty show your might.

60

Though the earth quake and we be rejected,
your right hand shall bring us victory…
it is you who trample down our foes.

61

Lead me, YHWH, from the ends of the earth
to your shelter on high,
where I may dwell for ever.

62

My soul waits in silence for God,
and so I shall not be shaken
by the vain threats of the wicked.

63

From the wilderness I behold your face,
and so I praise your holy NAME;
all my enemies you cast down.

64

They conceive evil plots in their hearts,
they aim bitter words like arrows…
but the LORD brings the wicked to utter ruin.

65

Your mercy pours upon us, LORD,
even as your waters nourish the earth…
and so all creation praises you in your Temple.

66

You test us in fire and in water,
but we pass through the sea on dry land
and so offer you our sacrifice of praise.

Old Testament

67

May your way be known upon the earth;
make your face shine on all nations…
let all the peoples praise you, LORD!

68

Kings perish before the Almighty God,
but the widow and orphan He blesses;
all the righteous enter His House with song.

69

For your sake I suffer reproach:
they give me poison to eat, vinegar to drink,
but you will save me from sinking in the mire.

70

YHWH, make haste to help me!
and put my foes to shame –
let all poor souls proclaim your salvation.

71

In you I have trusted from my youth
and you will not forsake me in my old age,
so I sing your glory all the day.

72

May peace abound on the earth,
all kings bow down before your Son,
for He redeems the life of the poor.

Psalms

73

The proud increase in riches on the earth,
but it is not in vain we keep our heart clean;
for they will fall to ruin as we rise to Heaven.

74

The enemy has destroyed everything in your sanctuary,
but you will not long forsake your poor ones –
arise, O LORD, and crush your foes!

75

You alone are the Judge, O LORD:
you put down the insolent soul
but raise up those who praise your NAME.

76

Both rider and horse lay stunned;
by you all weapons of war are destroyed –
let all the earth fear your glorious NAME!

77

Your mighty arm led Israel through the sea,
but now we moan and our spirit faints…
will you no longer have compassion on your people?

78

How often they rebelled in the wilderness,
testing YHWH despite His wonders in their midst…
when will we be as His sheep?

79

Jerusalem is laid in ruins,
the blood of your saints is poured out like water…
and so we groan for your avenging hand.

80

Tears we have drunk in full measure;
our enemies laugh us to scorn –
restore the vine your right hand has planted!

81

Raise a song to the LORD our God,
who alone frees us from the burden of sin:
open wide your mouth and He will fill it.

82

God calls us to save the weak and the needy,
but we walk about in ignorance;
though we be gods, we fall like men.

83

Your enemies conspire to destroy your people –
O reduce them to utter shame!
that they might seek to know your NAME.

84

Blessed are those who dwell in your House,
for it is lovely, the desire of souls…
let us but stand at the doorstep!

85

As once you forgave us our sins,
so speak peace to your people again,
that your glory may dwell in our land.

86

I cry to you all the day:
save me, O LORD, from ruthless men
that all souls may glorify your NAME.

87

How glorious is the City of God!
for all the redeemed are born in her –
on His holy mountain all nations find their home.

88

Your wrath sweeps over me like a flood;
I am as one in the depths of the Pit…
yet I cry out that I might rise and praise you.

89

Your steadfast love is with your Son,
for though He be mocked and scorned,
you establish His throne for ever.

90

Man is turned back to dust,
but you are from everlasting to everlasting –
teach us to number our days aright!

Old Testament

91

Under your wings we find refuge, LORD,
safe from all terrors and snares,
for your angels guard our ways.

92

We sing praise to your NAME, YHWH,
for the wicked are doomed to be destroyed
but we ever flourish in your House.

93

Robed in majesty, you reign above all,
and the world is established as your throne:
you are mightier than any flood, O holy LORD!

94

Rise up and take your vengeance
on those who condemn innocent blood;
give respite to your people who are crushed.

95

O let us sing praise to our God!
who holds our rest in His hand –
harden not your hearts against Him.

96

Declare the LORD's glory to all nations,
He is to be feared above all gods;
let all the earth sing praise to His NAME.

97

From darkness, fire goes out before Him,
burning up those who worship empty idols…
while the saints rejoice in the Most High God.

98

Sing praise to the LORD with the lyre;
let the flood waters clap their hands!
for the victory of our God is made known to all.

99

YHWH sits enthroned on the cherubim:
praise His awesome and holy NAME
with Moses and Aaron and Samuel.

100

The LORD is God and we are His people;
enter His courts with thanksgiving and praise,
for His love endures for ever upon us.

101

I will walk blamelessly with you, my God;
the haughty and the arrogant I will silence,
but the faithful will be welcome in my house.

102

My bones cleave to my flesh,
I wither away like the grass…
but you, eternal LORD, will build up Zion again.

Old Testament

103

Bless the LORD, all holy souls!
for He forgives our iniquity –
surpassing is His love for us.

104

YHWH, you are robed in light;
all the earth is in your hand...
you give food to all your creatures.

105

Praise the LORD! for by His mighty hand
He brought His people from the slavery of Egypt
into the land He promised Abraham.

106

O how your people for ever rebel against you!
and so deserve your punishment;
yet you save us when we call on your NAME.

107

Though we sit in darkness and in chains,
you save us from the waves of death
and feed us by your holy hand.

108

Let us awake the dawn
with praises sung to our glorious LORD
and He will make us strong against our enemies.

109

I am an object of scorn to my accusers,
those who repay me evil for good...
may their curses fall on their own heads.

110

Jesus is high priest for ever:
He is David's LORD and our own,
and He rules in the midst of all His foes.

111

Great are the works of the LORD,
faithful and just and enduring for ever;
fear Him, and so find wisdom.

112

It is well for the man who is generous to all;
his heart is firm, trusting in the LORD –
the generation of the upright will be blessed.

113

Praise the NAME of YHWH!
for He whose glory is above the heavens
raises the poor man from the dust.

114

The sea fled and the Jordan turned back;
the earth trembles at the presence of the God
who makes His sanctuary in Jerusalem.

115

No sound is in the throat of idols,
and their makers are as dumb as they –
let Israel praise the living God!

116

YHWH has delivered my soul from death;
He brought hope where there was only darkness,
and so I raise His cup of salvation day to day.

117

Let all the nations praise the LORD
for His steadfast love –
His faithfulness endures for ever.

118

With the LORD at our side, we do not fear,
for the rejected stone is now head of the corner:
we shall look in triumph on our foes.

119

Your Word is a lamp to my feet, O LORD;
I meditate night and day on your Law
and I am saved from all affliction.

120

In my distress I cry to the LORD:
save me from the deceitful tongue! –
help me find peace in this place of war.

121

Our help comes from the LORD;
He keeps us safe night and day,
guarding always our going out and coming in.

122

Let us go up to the House of the LORD
to give thanks to His holy NAME –
peace be ever in Jerusalem!

123

Our eyes look up to you, O LORD,
waiting for your mercy
to relieve us from the contempt of the proud.

124

Over us would have gone the raging waters
if the LORD had not been on our side;
by His grace we have escaped the fowler's snare.

125

As the mountains surround Jerusalem,
so YHWH abides for ever in His City –
cast all evil from our midst, dear God.

126

The LORD has done great things for us,
for our mouth is filled with laughter;
though we sow in tears, we shall reap rejoicing.

Old Testament

127

If the LORD does not build the house,
we indeed labor in vain;
only He makes us fruitful in His sight.

128

Blessed is the man who fears the LORD:
his wife will be a fruitful vine,
his children like olive shoots around his table.

129

Israel has been afflicted from her youth,
her back plowed with furrows…
but the LORD puts the wicked to shame.

130

I cry out to you, O LORD:
my soul waits on your Word
to redeem me from iniquity.

131

My eyes are not haughty, LORD;
like a child quieted is my soul…
in you alone I place my hope.

132

YHWH has come into His dwelling,
and so His saints shout for joy;
upon the Son of David His crown does shine.

133

When brothers dwell in unity,
it is like the anointing upon the high priest,
like the dew on the mountains of Zion.

134

O may the LORD bless you
who pray by night in His holy place –
lift up your hands to Heaven!

135

Praise the LORD of Heaven and earth!
who smote many nations and slew mighty kings
that Israel might stand in His House.

136

Give thanks to Him who made the heavens,
who brought Israel into their land,
for His steadfast love endures for ever.

137

Exiled in a foreign land,
how can we sing the song of YHWH? –
O may Jerusalem be avenged!

138

Though your NAME is exalted above all,
you bow down to hear our voice;
you preserve the life of your lowly ones.

Old Testament

139

You know me inside and out, O LORD,
for it was your hand that made me
and your Spirit is present even in the grave.

140

Let burning coals fall on violent men;
save us, LORD, from their evil plots –
execute justice for all the oppressed.

141

O LORD, make haste to help me;
incline not my heart to evil,
for all the wicked shall be condemned.

142

I cry out to you, O LORD,
for my persecutors are too strong
and there is no one else to help me.

143

My enemy has crushed my life to the ground,
and so my spirit faints within me –
O let me hear of your steadfast love!

144

You who strengthen our hands for war,
rescue us from the cruel sword;
let our storehouses be filled with your blessings.

145

Let all flesh bless your holy NAME
and speak of the glory of your kingdom,
for you open your hand and feed every creature.

146

Praise the LORD who made Heaven and earth,
who upholds the widow and the orphan;
trust in Him and not in man.

147

Sing praise to our gracious God
who heals the brokenhearted,
who made the wind and the clouds and the stars.

148

Praise Him, sun and moon,
mountains and hills, kings and princes…
all in earth and Heaven, praise the NAME
    of the LORD.

149

Israel, rejoice in your glorious King!
the high praises of God in your throat,
His sword of justice in your hand.

150

Praise YHWH, exalted in Heaven;
praise Him with trumpet and cymbals and harp –
let everything that breathes praise the LORD!

PROVERBS

1

Solomon seeks to teach us as a son
to avoid the ways of evil men,
lest calamity come like a whirlwind.
Wisdom calls, making known her words:
will you not choose the fear of the LORD?

2

From the mouth of YHWH comes knowledge:
incline your heart to understanding
and you will endure in the land with His saints –
wisdom will save you from the loose woman
whose house sinks down to death.

3

Give freely to God and neighbor;
your faithfulness will mean length of days,
healing and refreshment for your bones.
The LORD reproves him whom He loves…
treasure His words which drip down like dew.

4

David taught Solomon to hold to wisdom,
above all, to gain insight;
and we should be attentive to these words
that we might run in the way of the righteous,
never stumbling with the wicked in darkness.

5

The lips of a loose woman drip honey,
but how bitter she is in the end;
do not go near the door of her house.
Delight rather in the wife of your youth,
and your flesh shall not be consumed.

6

Quickly beg release from your debt;
do not lie like a sluggard in your bed.
An adulteress stalks a man's very life –
by the fire in your loins you shall be burned,
for a jealous man does not spare revenge.

7

The senseless man passes along the street,
taking the road to the harlot's house.
She seizes him on the way,
speaking of her perfumed bed...
and he follows her to his slaughter.

8

Wisdom calls the simple to her gates:
her mouth utters only truth;
her fruit is better than gold.
In the beginning she was made,
before earth or sea or sky.

9

Wisdom has set her table well
and sent her maids to invite souls in;
the righteous welcome her instruction
and in it multiply their days,
while the wanton woman leads the wicked astray.

10

The righteous are fed while the wicked starve;
do not sleep in harvest time.
The mouth of the righteous speaks only wisdom:
accept the reproof of the LORD....
The wicked are removed but the righteous remain.

11

A just weight is the delight of the LORD
and a city rejoices at the blessing of the upright,
for righteousness delivers from death.
He who gives freely grows the richer,
but a curse is on him who holds back his hand.

12

Whoever loves discipline, loves knowledge,
but the counsels of the wicked lead to ruin;
lying lips are an abomination to the LORD,
for there is no mercy in them.
The work of a man's hand comes back to him.

13

He who guards his mouth preserves his life,
but the fool flaunts his folly.
The soul of the sluggard craves and gets nothing;
poverty comes to him who ignores instruction –
his heart is made sick by unfulfilled desire.

14

There is a way which seems right to a man,
but its end is death itself –
a scoffer seeks wisdom in vain.
He who is slow to anger has great understanding;
he who is kind to the needy honors the LORD.

15

The eyes of YHWH are in every place,
and so the hearts of men lie open to Him:
the prayer of the upright is His delight.
It is fear of the LORD that brings honor…
the wise man's path leads upward to life.

16

Commit your work to the LORD,
for only by Him is anything accomplished;
better to rule your spirit than take a city.
Inspired decisions are on the lips of our King,
His throne is established in righteousness.

17

A foolish son is a grief to his father;
a man of crooked mind does not prosper.
The LORD tries hearts in His crucible –
never return evil for good
(keep silent and you will show wisdom).

18

Do not be partial to the wicked
or give answer before hearing,
for a fool's lips bring strife
but the NAME of the LORD is a strong tower.
Death and life are in the tongue.

19

A poor man's brothers may hate him,
but better is a poor man who walks in integrity
than a man perverse in speech.
For he who is kind to the poor lends to the LORD,
but a false witness will not go unpunished.

20

The King winnows evil with His eyes:
a faithful man He cannot find.
So avoid strong drink and excess sleep,
keep aloof from strife and deceit,
and let your steps be ordered by the LORD.

21

The scoffer acts with arrogant pride,
but the wicked are cast down to ruin –
justice is a joy to the righteous.
Gain by lying is a fleeting vapor;
better life in a desert than with a contentious woman.

22

A good name is better than riches;
humility and fear of the LORD have their reward.
Train up a child in the way he should go,
and in purity of heart he will be blessed....
Listen to the words of admonition and knowledge.

23

Desist from toil to acquire wealth;
it will fly like an eagle from you,
and the sparkling wine bite like a serpent.
Buy truth and do not sell it –
a wise son is the joy of his father.

24

Be not envious of evil men,
and do not rejoice when your enemy falls;
rather, rescue those being taken to death.
The wise are mightier than the strong –
be not partial in your judgment.

Proverbs

25

The mind of our King is unsearchable,
so do not put yourself forward in His presence
but wait for His call to come up.
A faithful messenger refreshes his Master's spirit,
and he who feeds his enemy, YHWH will reward.

26

Like a dog that returns to its vomit
is a fool who repeats his folly;
as a door turns on its hinges,
so does a sluggard in his bed.
Be not wise in your own eyes, lest you die.

27

Faithful are the wounds of a friend,
profuse the kisses of an enemy,
for iron sharpens iron and one man another.
The mind of a man reflects the man:
know well the condition of your flocks.

28

When the wicked rise, men hide themselves...
those who keep the Law strive against them.
He who gives to the poor will not want;
the blameless will have a Godly inheritance –
confess and forsake sin to obtain mercy.

29

A man's pride will bring him low,
but the lowly in spirit will obtain honor –
it is from the LORD justice comes.
Bloodthirsty men hate one who is blameless;
do not stiffen your neck against reproof.

30

How shall I stand before the eternal God?
Remove from me falsehood and lying;
give me neither poverty nor riches.
Some have teeth like swords to devour the poor –
put your hand over your prideful tongue!

31

Give not your strength to women, my son;
a good wife is more precious than jewels...
her lamp does not go out at night.
It is not for kings to drink wine –
open your mouth to defend the poor.

ECCLESIASTES

Vanity of vanities, all is vanity for the aged King Solomon, whose life has become a pursuit of the empty things of this earth, who because of his sin, because of his turning his heart away from the LORD, is now utterly blind to the goodness of God and His Creation.

How can a man so blessed with wisdom, upon whom the LORD's Breath had come, be so filled now with a darkened spirit that he has lost all hope and courts despair? Is his plight not that of a soul who does not open himself to the mercy of God, who cannot see the Messiah standing before him? For under this Son all things are made new; in Him the glory of YHWH does shine... and even the trials and sufferings of these difficult days are cause for rejoicing, for by the Cross we are brought closer to eternal life.

But eternal life escapes the Preacher; the Word of God has become dead weight to the dissipated king and he cannot see beyond the nose of his face – all he knows is the emptiness around him, because there is nothing but emptiness within him. Darkened eyes see no light. And so it is no surprise that he leads a toilsome life, that he finds himself bound upon the wheel, spinning out of place... for he cannot take a step forward into the LORD's presence.

Ecclesiastes

Fruitless Labor

The gathering and heaping Solomon does is indeed an empty striving after wind, for he sets his heart on what is vain, seeking his joy in the pleasures of the flesh and lasting glory in the possessions of this earth – and so he comes only to despair. He imagines in drinking wine and having many concubines he will discover happiness, and so he keeps his heart from no pleasure, taking hold of whatever he desires. He builds houses and plants vineyards for himself, all for himself and only for himself, and so he hates life: "What is done under the sun [is] grievous to me" (2:17). He especially cannot bear the thought that another will have these passing things after he is gone, one who is not worthy as he.

Yet he says he still has wisdom. But what wisdom is this? A wisdom of selfishness, a wisdom of profligacy... what wise soul would seek his purpose in sin? There is no wonder "all his days are full of pain" (2:23) and he finds no joy in his toil, for in vanity what can one find but vanity? And his lack of wisdom is most evident in his saying both the wise man and the fool come to the same end, for here he demonstrates his utter inability to see beyond this life. And so, what wisdom can he have?

You are wrong, O pitiful king, to say there is no remembrance of men, for even now we read your witness to the darkness of the soul that strives after wind; and we are quite sure you have found there is something beyond the grave.

A Time to Die

It is true that man goes from dust to dust, that as with beasts, so men too must die. But that "the spirit of man goes upward" (3:21), why do you not know, O wise king? And it is true that all things have their time, but this does not mean they are all in vain; because things repeat themselves does not therefore make them void of purpose, or goodness. For indeed, as you say, God "has made everything beautiful in its time" (3:11), and so long as in His light you stand, His beauty shining in all things you shall recognize. "Also, He has put eternity into man's mind" (ibid), and the fact that you are unable to put your finger on it does not demean its importance or its relevance for your days – you are thus called to faith! that you might come to see the invisible God.

Do not be afraid to die, to let your possessions go to another; nothing of this world has any significance except that it bring you to the eternal kingdom. And even if wickedness stand in the place of righteousness and the poor be oppressed, it would not be better for them not to have been – God forbid! For indeed, judgment is in the LORD's hands and all shall find their just reward when they stand before Him. Take joy in your labor, yes, and know it will bring you to YHWH's presence.

Pay Your Vow to God

"Guard your steps when you go to the house of God" (5:1). Listen to His voice. What you promise to the LORD fulfill – why should you speak in vain? Do not seek to make excuses for your failing to love God with all your heart, mind, and soul. This will only dig your grave deeper; rather, admit your fault and do as you must.

In many words there is but pride; "therefore let your words be few" (5:2). How can you presume to speak with YHWH or know His ways when He is so far above you who crawl beneath the heavens? Rather, bow down humbly before Him and hear His voice speaking in the depths of your soul, and you will find the way you must tread in this world.

Sorrow is indeed better than laughter; should you not then be sorry for all your sins before the LORD? Better to go to the house of mourning than continue your feasting with fools, for where shall that lead you? Will you preserve your life by wallowing in corruption? No, you will come to a bitter end, naked in soul as well as body, with nothing to show for your days on this earth.

Your very self should be given to the LORD and to His work; all your spirit should praise His favor to you. If you would avoid the darkness, you must worship God alone.

Ecclesiastes

One Fate Comes to All

Why do you insist, O Preacher, O Gatherer of emptiness, on "adding one thing to another to find the sum" (7:27) but finding yourself in the end with nothing; why do you repeat the blithe statement: "One fate comes to all" (9:3), declaring that all "the sons of men are snared at an evil time" (9:12) – why do you so glorify death as if it were all powerful? You tell us that "it will be well with those who fear God" (8:12) but "it will not be well with the wicked" (8:13); you seem to exhibit the wisdom that penetrates the ways of YHWH, who passes our understanding, whose reach extends beyond the bounds of this dark earth... yet to this dark earth you remain bound, unable to fathom any blessing or curse beyond the ones men know on this plane.

Why? How can it be the wisest of men has become so blind? Could it be "the woman whose heart is snares and nets, and whose hands are fetters" (7:26); could it be she whose grasp you cannot escape, who has led you so astray? Is it this fall from which you cannot rise? Riches and a woman's allure – you speak better than any of the dangers therein, yet find yourself trapped by them and wallowing in despair.

You see well the death that comes to all men, but the light of the transcendent God is hidden from your eyes. Will you come to the Christ?

Remember Your Creator

Though sun and moon and stars be darkened, though "the clouds return after the rain" (12:2); though our eyes be dimmed and our teeth few, though "the daughters of song are brought low" (12:4); though "mourners go about the streets" (12:5) and "the golden bowl is broken" (12:6)... though all the earth fall to pieces, the Spirit of God does not die – nothing can dim the LORD's eternal light. His "Spirit comes to the bones in the womb" (11:5) and does not leave them: the soul of man is immortal. Upon the Spirit of God within us, we must set our hearts.

Old Testament

And so, "cast your bread upon the waters" (11:1), for it shall come back to you. What good you can do, do now, "for God will bring every deed into judgment" (12:14) and repay a man good or evil thereby.

O how pleasant is the light of the LORD! O how holy His call to man! Do not fear the death of this world and all the vanity it holds; rather, find the wisdom that comes from God and sustains a man through all his days, even unto eternity. The end of the matter is indeed this: "Fear God, and keep His commandments; for this is the whole duty of man" (12:13). Those who turn their hearts away from Him will find themselves in darkness, but blessed are those who heed His Word.

THE SONG OF SOLOMON

"The Song of Songs, which is Solomon's."
1:1

Now shall we sing of the glory of the love of YHWH and our walking in His ways and finding His hand upon us, His breath on our lips. Indeed, He kisses us with the Holy Spirit and we are joined to Him as bride to Bridegroom. Jesus, His Son, washes away our sins, takes the darkness from our souls that we might be wed to Him, that we might become one with our God.

Why should we wander anywhere else? Why should we be any place but in His vineyard, drinking His holy Blood, the Blood of His most fair Son? O let us "follow in the tracks of the flock" (1:8) and so find ourselves pastured among His blessed sheep. Then we shall be filled with His fragrance, His Spirit anointing our very souls; then "ornaments of gold, studded with silver" (1:11) will be our own and we shall be pleasing to Him and come to make our home in His House of cedar.

With great delight we shall sit in His shadow and be fed with the sweet fruits of His holy love. We shall take our place at His banquet table and be for ever sustained by the kisses of His mouth.... O LORD, with your right hand, embrace us!

Song of Solomon

Arise, My Love

"Arise, my love, my fair one, and come away" (2:10), whispers my Beloved's voice in my ear. He comes to me "leaping upon the mountains" (2:8) and gazes in at me through the windows; through the blinds He sees me and calls me to join Him now that "the winter is past" (2:11) and "the flowers appear on the earth" (2:12). O let Him cover me with His hand in the cleft of the rock, like Moses, but at least let me see His back (cf. Ex.33:18-23)!

I seek Him in the night and do not find Him; I call to Him, but He gives me no answer. So I rise in darkness and "go about the city, in the streets and in the squares" (3:2), searching for Him whom my soul loves. Leaving the watchmen behind, I find Him, and hold Him fast.

O let my soul be wed to the King! who comes up from the wilderness surrounded by His angels and carried by His saints. Behold the King on His wedding day, clothed in majesty and glory! He calls to His bride in her beauty to be joined to Him, that His heart might rejoice in her.

Are we not your Church, O LORD? Do we not find you when we heed your voice and leave all of this world behind? Does your glory not await our souls; does your Son not come to us this day? O let us seek Him with all our hearts! To Him let our senses be conformed.

You Are Beautiful

How beautiful we are to the LORD! Our "cheeks are like halves of a pomegranate" (4:3) and our "neck is like the tower of David" (4:4) – He takes great delight in us. How can it be that He who is Love takes pleasure in our poor love? How is it that we lowly creatures could ravish the heart of our Maker "with a glance of [our] eyes" (4:9)?

He calls us from Lebanon, from the lion's den and from all our sin, and by His grace alone makes us favorable in His sight, finding no flaw in us. And so, as He took great joy in the Virgin Mary, whom He made without stain and who thus could give birth to His only Son, so He takes delight in us whom He has cleansed of sin by the blood of this Lamb and enables us to bring forth His grace to the ends of the earth.

We become "a garden fountain, a well of living water" overflowing with the Spirit... channels of grace as is our Blessed Mother. And though the guards beat us, though the world try hard to hide from us the face of YHWH, yet our "fragrance [is] wafted abroad" (4:16), yet we remain servants of the LORD, ever seeking Him with all our souls and calling on His saints to aid us in our search. For He has made us beautiful, He has made us fruitful, and as the apple of His eye we shall remain.

Strong as Death

Yes, "love is strong as death.... Many waters cannot quench love" (8:6,7). Our Beloved is "all radiant and ruddy.... His head is the finest gold" (5:10,11), and our only desire is to see Him bounding upon the mountain, "His legs...alabaster columns" (5:15). O that He would be by our side! O that He would "pasture His flock among the lilies" (6:3)! that in our hearts He might make His home.

"I am my Beloved's and my Beloved is mine" (ibid). What a wonderful exchange of love there is between God and His creatures, between YHWH and the soul on fire with His love. For she becomes as His own, as the sheep of His flock, His Spirit breathing in the depths of her being.... Who could tell one from the other? Such blessing is upon us that we become one with our God.

And as we look upon the LORD with great love, with great admiration for His beauty and grace, so He looks upon us, so He is enrapt by the beauty in us. For there He lives, in the depths of our soul.

O let us be one, dearest LORD! "Your kisses [are] like the best wine that goes down smoothly" (7:9). "Let us go forth into the fields... let us go out early to the vineyards.... There I will give you my love" (7:11,12). Let us join together in the chamber of the House of our Mother – let us dwell for ever in the New Jerusalem, drinking the Blood of Christ.

THE WISDOM OF SOLOMON

1

The LORD does not desire the death of the living,
but He hears and punishes ungodly thoughts –
wisdom will not enter a deceitful soul.

2

Thinking death the end even of spiritual reason,
the wicked give themselves over to revelry
and persecute the righteous man.

3

The hope of the righteous is full of immortality;
they will shine forth in the LORD's kingdom…
but the ungodly will end in misery.

4

The prolific brood of the ungodly is of no use;
the LORD will dash them to the ground speechless –
but the virtuous He takes up in His grace.

5

The One derided wears a glorious crown:
amazed are the arrogant at His eternal favor,
even as they are driven away.

6

Listen to instruction, O kings of the earth;
a strict inquiry is in store for the mighty –
desire for wisdom is what leads to God's kingdom.

7

Solomon is mortal but God gave him wisdom,
she whose radiance penetrates all things,
she who reflects the glory of the Almighty.

8

From his youth Solomon sought wisdom;
for wealth and virtue, understanding and renown,
honor and immortality are with her.

9

YHWH, send your Holy Spirit from on high
to correct the king and his worthless reasoning
that he might rule in wisdom and in justice.

10

The righteous men of ancient times
had wisdom as their strength and guide
to save them from flood, fire and slavery.

11

LORD, you would have mercy on all souls;
but while the Israelites you bless as they repent,
the Egyptians who persist in sin you can but condemn.

12

Yes, little by little you correct with kindness,
seeking to spare even those who slaughter children...
but failing repentance they will know your judgment.

13

How foolish to worship creation rather than the Creator! –
but miserable above all are those
who worship lifeless things, the work of men's hands.

14

What woe to souls who call upon a piece of wood!
bowing down to images of men and kings –
worship of idols is the beginning and end of every evil.

15

Desiring the lifeless form of a dead image,
made of clay by one who himself is made of earth,
they are blind to the God who breathes spirit into them.

Old Testament

16

Your Word preserves and heals and feeds us well,
even as our enemies suffer inexorable want;
all your creation serves the purpose you intend.

17

Their sins bind the lawless in chains of darkness,
driven by monstrous specters they do not understand…
paralyzed with terror by every sound.

18

Moses intercedes to save Israel from wrath,
but all the firstborn of Egypt the angel destroys…
for they heed not even their dreadful dreams.

19

O LORD, you have exalted and glorified your people;
on dry ground they make their way through the sea,
but yawning darkness awaits those who pursue them
    relentlessly.

SIRACH

Prologue

There is great wisdom in the Law and the prophets,
so Sirach studied well and wrote about them
that you might make progress in God's way.

1

YHWH pours wisdom on all his works.
Fear of the LORD is the beginning of wisdom,
bringing eternal blessing to men of undivided heart.

2

My son, prepare yourself for temptation;
be patient and humble, and wait for God's mercy.
Trust in the LORD and you will be saved.

3

Honor your father and your mother always
and you will ever be forgiven and blessed,
for the LORD is glorified by the humble soul.

4

Do not avert your eyes from the needy;
show no partiality in anything you do,
but speak when wisdom demands the truth.

5

Do not trust in your own wealth and strength,
nor presume on the mercy of the LORD;
severe condemnation comes to the double-tongued.

6

Listen well to the counsel of the intelligent;
under wisdom's yoke you will find glory –
keep from your enemies and be sure of your friends.

7

Do not despise a good wife or friend or servant;
honor the priest and give to the poor...
for fire and worms await the ungodly.

8

Do not contend with the rich or consort with fools;
do not reproach the repentant or disdain the aged....
Do not walk with a wrathful man, lest you die.

9

By a woman's beauty, passion is kindled;
turn your eyes from what is not your own.
Let your conversation be of the LORD and His Law.

10

Arrogance is hateful before God and men;
only those who fear the LORD are worthy of honor.
The king of today will die tomorrow.

11

It is Godliness YHWH blesses,
not looks or clothes, riches or power –
trust in the LORD and humbly keep to His work.

12

Give to the good man, but do not help the sinner;
never trust your enemy or his false tears,
for he will overthrow you and rejoice at your fall.

13

Do not associate with the rich and the proud:
though he smile, he will forsake you.
What fellowship has a wolf with a lamb?

14

Evil is the man with a grudging eye;
he is not generous to himself, nor to others.
Give as much as you can before you die.

15

The LORD sets before you life and death,
but He wishes no man to sin:
drink the water of wisdom and rejoice for ever.

16

Better one good child than a thousand ungodly,
for wrath is kindled in the disobedient nation…
the deeds of men are not hidden from God's eyes.

17

Though man has few days upon this earth,
the LORD gives understanding and dominion to him –
turn from iniquity and sing praise to God.

18

No one can trace the works of YHWH,
yet He is compassionate toward all living beings.
Promptly pay your vows to Him.

19

Do not repeat a conversation,
and believe not everything you hear –
death and worms await the reckless.

20

There is a gift that profits you nothing,
and good fortune may come in adversity…
know when to be silent and when to reprove.

21

The mind of a fool is like a broken jar,
but to the sensible, education is a golden ornament:
flee from sin as from a snake.

22

Chastising and discipline are always wisdom;
the mind fixed on reasonable counsel has no fear.
Do not revile a friend or speak with a fool.

23

O LORD, let whips be set over my thoughts,
allow no sinful speech to pass my lips…
and keep me from the dark deeds of adultery.

24

Wisdom came forth from the mouth of the Most High
and found a resting place in Jerusalem…
the Law of Moses fills the earth with understanding.

25

How attractive is wisdom in the aged!
The fear of the LORD surpasses every good,
but a garrulous wife is a sandy ascent.

26

A loyal wife is the joy of her husband –
how precious her silence and modesty!
But the yoke of an imprudent wife chafes the soul.

27

Sin is wedged between selling and buying;
whoever winks his eye plans evil deeds,
but he who digs a pit will fall into it.

28

A blow of the tongue crushes the bones:
make a door and a bolt for your mouth.
Refrain from anger and strife, and forgive.

29

Assist your neighbor as you are able,
store up almsgiving in your treasury…
but take heed lest you fall into want.

30

He who disciplines his son will glory in him,
but a spoiled child brings only sorrow.
Gladness of heart is the life of man.

31

A little food is ample for a well-disciplined man,
and wine drunk temperately rejoices the heart –
but he who loves gold will not find rest.

32

Speak concisely and with accurate knowledge,
and leave a party in good time.
Do nothing without deliberation.

33

Men are as clay in the hand of the Potter:
some the LORD blesses, others He curses.
Distribute your inheritance at the end of your days.

34

He who heeds dreams pursues the wind….
The LORD is not pleased with the offerings
    of the ungodly,
but to those who love Him, He is a strong shelter
    and support.

Sirach

35

The prayer of the poor man pierces the clouds;
he who gives alms offers a holy sacrifice…
but the LORD crushes the loins of the unmerciful.

36

Let the nations know there is no God but Thee;
crush them and bring us back into your House –
a man without a wife wanders and sighs.

37

Beware false friends and selfish counselors;
rather, find a soul in accord with your own,
one set on the LORD and following His ways.

38

The workmen keep stable the fabric of the world,
but the proverbs of the scribe require leisure:
honor the physician, and mourn the dead in measure.

39

Study the Law of the Most High God;
send forth His fragrance in hymns of praise.
All things prove good in their season.

40

Man's anxious thought is the day of death:
all bribery and injustice will then be blotted out,
but fear of the LORD will bring a garden of blessings.

41

Do not fear the sentence of death:
the ungodly go from curse to destruction,
but a good name endures for ever.

42

The work of the LORD is full of His glory;
do not be ashamed of accurate scales and weights.
Keep strict watch over a headstrong daughter.

43

Sun and moon and stars shining in glory,
thunder and snow and the depths of the sea…
how shall we praise Him who has made all things?

44

Praise great men blessed with wisdom and power,
Enoch and Noah, Father Abraham, Isaac and Jacob –
their names live to all generations.

45

God gave Moses the commandments face to face
and Aaron the priesthood in glorious robes of holiness;
in his zeal Phinehas made atonement for Israel.

46

Joshua, its savior, gave Israel its inheritance –
even the sun was held back by his prayer.
Samuel prophesied faithfully and established
    the kingdom.

47

David killed the giant and his ten thousands;
he made the sanctuary resound with God's praise…
but the lust of Solomon divided the kingdom.

48

The word of Elijah burned like a fire,
and Elisha prophesied even from the dead…
while Isaiah revealed what will occur in the end.

49

Josiah took away Judah's abominations;
Jeremiah saw her downfall, Ezekial vision of glory –
Zerubbabel, Joshua and Nehemiah rebuilt God's house.

50

Simon fortified the city and the temple;
he made the court of the sanctuary glorious,
and all praised and worshiped the Most High God.

51

Jesus, son of Sirach, thanks and praises the LORD
for hearing his prayer and saving him from destruction:
He has given him a tongue and wisdom.

ISAIAH

The prophets, and what they saw.... The vision of Isaiah and what he saw concerning Judah and Jerusalem. The LORD speaks to His people.

The people of God are laden with iniquity; they have despised the Holy One of Israel and become utterly estranged from Him. And so, from head to foot they are smitten with sores – their country lies desolate. Like Sodom and Gomorrah they now are, except that the LORD has left a remnant.

He has had enough of their vain offerings. What good are their sacrifices when they have blood on their hands, while they do evil in the sight of God, oppressing the fatherless and the widow? She who was full of justice has become a harlot, a city inhabited by murderers and thieves.

The LORD will vent His wrath against His enemies; He will devour the rebel by the sword. But those who repent shall become white as snow. Those who are obedient will have their sins of scarlet cleansed and dwell again in His holy land.

YHWH greatly desires the redemption of His wayward children, and so He sends the prophets – and so He sends Isaiah to call souls back to Himself.

Burning Judgment

The pride of men shall be brought low and they will hide themselves in caves and holes from the terror of the LORD, casting forth their idols of silver and gold.

It has been silver and gold the house of Jacob has pursued, and she has bowed down to the work of her own hands, becoming like the wicked nations round about. But the LORD will take away her anklets and bracelets and all her finery; her perfumes will turn to rottenness and she will be girded with sackcloth instead of festal robes. Her mighty men shall fall by the sword and all will weep and mourn. None will wish to rule in this heap of ruins.

But the survivors in Jerusalem shall be called holy, beautiful and glorious in the sight of God. The city cleansed by the burning judgment of the LORD, the righteous shall then shine. In the latter days the mountain of the House of the LORD shall be established as the highest mountain, and all the nations shall stream to it and seek the ways of the Most High God. They shall beat their swords into plowshares and their spears into pruning hooks. No more will there be war. No more will the face of the poor be ground into the dust. A cloud shall again shade His people by day and the shining of flaming fire watch over them by night.

The Desolate Vineyard

Jerusalem shall go down to Sheol, Judah into exile, and the land become a desolate waste. A conquering nation will come from afar, roaring like a lion, and carry them off. For all their blindness and deafness to the Word of God, this people shall be forsaken.

What more could the LORD do for His vineyard? How well she was planted in the midst of the land, but how rotten she has indeed become. These wild grapes know only how to run after wine and strong drink, and to shed innocent blood. The LORD and His works they do not know nor care to know, standing in arrogance against Him. And so His anger is not appeased – His hand is stretched out against them.

They do not see what Isaiah sees, "the LORD sitting upon a throne, high and lifted up" (6:1), for their hearts are lifted up in pride: they are wise in their own eyes. They do not find the temple filled with His glory, nor with the seraphim declare Him holy.... They glorify themselves instead. They do not confess their guilt, that they are men of unclean lips, and so no angel comes with a burning coal to purify their souls.

And they will not listen to the prophet who speaks this truth to them; and so, no understanding or healing will they find. YHWH's vineyard will be devoured, a bare few remaining in the land.

Old Testament

A Child Will Be Born

Israel threatens to conquer Judah with the aid of the king of Syria, but the LORD calms the hearts of His people and calls on Assyria to serve as the rod of His anger. Israel shall be turned back in its arrogance; thrust into utter darkness, fire shall consume even its briers and thorns. Yes, Samaria is carried away by the king of Assyria.

But for Isaiah and those who have not walked in the way of this wicked people but fear the LORD instead, prophecy is given of the birth of a Child to sit upon the throne of David: "A young woman shall conceive and bear a Son, and shall call His Name Immanuel" (7:14). He indeed is the Root of Jesse, the Prince of Peace upon whom all nations rest their hopes for an eternal kingdom blessed by God.

A remnant shall return even from Israel when Assyria has finished with its destruction. For Assyria itself shall be destroyed for trusting in its own strength and vaunting itself above the LORD who called them, for seeking to conquer even the holy city of Jerusalem.

The LORD will "assemble the outcasts of Israel, and gather the dispersed of Judah from the four corners of the earth" (11:12), and there shall be peace on His holy mountain. None will again hurt or destroy, but filled with knowledge of the LORD all will praise Him and find in Him their salvation. Alleluia!

Fallen Is Babylon

The earth will be shaken out of its place and the haughtiness of the ruthless be laid to the dust: Babylon shall rest among the worms and maggots. She who would have exalted herself above the heavens like the Most High shall be brought down to Sheol. Like the Day Star she has fallen, and nothing will be left of her anymore.

She who oppressed the nations with insolent fury has herself been thrust through and trampled underfoot, her infants dashed to pieces and her wives ravished by a nation without mercy. Her young men are slaughtered and her land becomes uninhabited, save by the wild beasts that howl from the hilltops.

The LORD has called mighty men from the north, from a distant land, from the end of the heavens, to destroy the whole earth with the weapons of His indignation. The day of the LORD is indeed near when the oppressors will be in anguish like a woman in travail, their faces aghast in the flames.

But YHWH will have compassion on Jacob: "They will take captive those who were their captors, and rule over those who oppressed them" (14:2). And they shall taunt the king of Babylon even as he is cast into the depths of the Pit.

The LORD's purpose will not be turned back – the yoke shall be broken from the shoulder of His people.

Weep for Moab

"The nations roar like the roaring of many waters, but He will rebuke them, and they will flee far away" (17:13). Like chaff before the wind they will be chased away, left a desolate waste for their plundering of the people of God.

The Philistines will melt in fear and famine overtake them – and O how Moab shall weep and cry aloud for the punishment come upon them! "In the streets they gird on sackcloth; on the housetops and in the squares every one wails and melts in tears" (15:3). Their grass is withered, their "verdure is no more" (15:6)... in a night Moab is laid waste.

And the LORD calls on all those round about, and especially Jerusalem, to weep and mourn with Moab that they might show the compassion of God for His wayward children, that they might say with Him: "My soul moans like a lyre for Moab" (16:11). Thus the throne of David will be established in steadfast love (a love even for one's enemies), and the LORD "will sit in faithfulness" (16:5) in his tent.

Damascus, too, will become a heap of ruins and Jacob itself be brought low, only gleanings left in it, that men might again "regard their Maker and their eyes...look to the Holy One of Israel" and not "to what their own fingers have made" (17:7,8). Let all souls remember the God of their salvation.

Egypt and Ethiopia

"In that day there will be an altar to the LORD in the midst of the land of Egypt" (19:19); and from the Ethiopians, too, "gifts will be brought to the LORD of hosts" (18:7). There will indeed come a time when Egyptian and Assyrian will be at peace with one another in their worship of YHWH. But before that day they will both be led away captive by the Assyrians. They shall go into exile naked and barefoot as Isaiah has been in his prophecy against them.

The tall and smooth people of Ethiopia, "a people feared near and far" (18:7), a mighty and conquering nation, will themselves be conquered, will be left as food for the birds of prey. And "the Egyptians will be like women, and tremble with fear before the hand which the LORD of hosts shakes over them" (19:16); the idols of Egypt will tremble at His presence as their emptiness is revealed.

And in whom will the nations trust then, when the mighty of the earth have fallen, when all other gods are shown to be worthless and their boasts and their hope come to nothing? Yes, Babylon and all the nations who have plundered and destroyed will know the wrath of the LORD. Who stands on watch with Isaiah to see the shattering of all vain images before the one true God? And who will be shattered with them?

The Steward

And there shall be the battering down of walls in Jerusalem, "a day of tumult and trampling and confusion in the valley of vision" (22:5)... the destruction of the daughter of God's people. The covering shall be taken away from Judah and all his iniquity be revealed, for the LORD calls His Chosen "to weeping and mourning, to baldness and girding with sackcloth" (22:12), and they feast instead, fatting themselves for the day of slaughter.

The steward of the house of God shall be thrown down. The whitewashed tomb he built for himself will not be his resting place; rather he will be cast out into the open field with all his splendid chariots – there he shall die. And another shall take his place.

Yes, Peter shall be the chosen head of the New Jerusalem, fastened "like a peg in a sure place" (22:23). The LORD "will place on his shoulder the key of the house of David; he shall open, and none shall shut; and he shall shut, and none shall open" (22:22). The whole weight of the Church shall hang upon him, the Rock the Father has chosen (cf. Mt.16:18-19). Those who have led God's children astray will be removed from their place and all power be taken from them.

Bitter tears the prophet sheds for the loss upon his people.

A Curse Devours the Earth

"The earth lies polluted under its inhabitants" (24:5), and so it is scorched and few men are left. There is no wine or strong drink, no music or mirth to be heard, for "all joy has reached its eventide; the gladness of the earth is banished" (24:11). "Utterly laid waste and utterly despoiled… the earth mourns and withers" (24:3,4), for men have transgressed the Law of God.

The strongholds of the sea are laid waste: Tyre and Sidon, who were the merchants of the nations honored by all of the earth, are brought to ruin. The ships of Tarshish no longer sail, for the LORD has shaken the kingdoms of the sea and defiled their pride and glory.

These shall be in desolation seventy years; then Tyre will "play the harlot with all the kingdoms of the world" (23:17)… but her work and her wares will serve the LORD and His people. Indeed, from the ends of the earth there shall be songs of praise as from east to west strong peoples give glory to God: "ruthless nations will fear [Him]" (25:3).

The LORD of hosts will reign on Mount Zion; "He will swallow up death for ever" (25:8). Even as He tears down to the dust the high fortifications of the princes and peoples and powers of this world, He will take away the reproach of His people and wipe every tear from their eyes.

Old Testament

A Pleasant Vineyard

Let us sing of the pleasant vineyard Judah shall be when the LORD slays the dragon, the twisting serpent that has oppressed them (and us), when the feet of the poor trample down the lofty city. His hand is lifted up for the zeal of His people and He will enlarge the borders of their nation. They cry out to Him, writhing like a woman with child, and He raises them from the dust of death to live in His holy light.

And so, should we not sing for the redemption upon us, for the expiation of the guilt of Jacob, "the full fruit of the removal of his sin" (27:9)? This is what Jesus has wrought in our midst by His blood. He is Himself the great feast celebrated on the LORD's holy mountain – He is our food and our drink. "This is the LORD; we have waited for Him; let us be glad and rejoice in His salvation" (25:9)!

The way of the righteous is made level and smooth for "like chalkstones crushed to pieces" (27:9) are all the false idols that held sway over our souls. The gates are thrown open for the one who keeps faith in God's holy NAME, and He keeps "in perfect peace, [the one] whose mind is stayed on [Him]" (26:3).

YHWH guards and keeps us night and day; He waters us with His love. And should we not thus sing for joy?

Drunkards of Ephraim

Woe to those in Jerusalem who reel with strong drink, who are confused with wine; even prophet and priest stagger and err in vision – "all tables are full of vomit, no place is without filthiness" (28:8). And so an overwhelming scourge the LORD becomes to His people, morning by morning, in unending fashion pursuing them in their sins. In earthquake and whirlwind and devouring fire He comes, and they collapse like a bulging wall, like a potter's vessel "smashed so ruthlessly that among its fragments not a sherd is found" (30:14). For they rebel against Him who made them, and His Word becomes but "…precept upon precept, line upon line…" (28:13) in a rote repetition of phrases empty as their souls. They "honor [Him] with their lips, while their hearts are far from [Him]" (29:13).

O how blind they have become! They do not know the LORD and cannot see the things He does in their midst. They despise His Word and His ways and command the prophets not to speak what is right but rather to prophesy illusions. They seek refuge in Pharaoh and his chariots and desire to race upon horses rather than rest in the Holy One of Israel; and so they shall be sped away into exile. Trusting in men and flesh and not in the Spirit of God, they can but perish.

Woe to those whose deeds are in darkness, who take refuge in falsehood, for their deal with death shall not stand – the drunkards will stumble and fall to the dust.

Now I Will Arise

Though the wicked and complacent in Jerusalem are consumed by the everlasting fire of the LORD, for the righteous He comes with salvation, making for them a holy way in the wilderness: "everlasting joy shall be upon their heads" (35:10).

His Spirit will be poured forth from on high and everyone shall cast away his idols of silver and gold; indeed, "all the host of heaven shall rot away" (34:4) – all false gods will fall to the ground before the wrath of the Almighty One. His sword, "a sword not of man" (31:8), shall devour the treacherous knaves of this earth who ruin the poor with their lying words.

Then ears will be opened to hear and eyes opened to see, and the lame man shall leap like a stag for the glory of the LORD in our midst, for the recompense come to His ransomed sons. The insolent shall no more oppress God's people but Jerusalem will again be "a quiet habitation, an immovable tent... a place of broad rivers and streams" (33:20,21).

O may the Spirit of the LORD pour upon His holy ones! Though the lands of their enemies become the dwelling place of wild beasts, His redeemed shall walk in safety for ever under the protecting hand of their God – "and sorrow and sighing shall flee away" (35:10).

YHWH, arise and save us!

Respite for Jerusalem

The king of Assyria has conquered many nations, including Israel and much of Judah, and he now lays siege to Jerusalem, openly threatening to do the same to the city of God: haughtily he lifts up his eyes against the LORD and wags his head toward His sanctuary. He boasts of the great destruction wrought by his chariots, failing to recognize it is by the LORD's will he has made "fortified cities crash into heaps of ruins" (37:26). Because of his pride he shall be turned back and Jerusalem be spared for a time.

Hezekiah seeks the intercession of Isaiah, who prophesies the protection of Jerusalem, but it is not until the king himself prays to the LORD, prostrate in the temple, that an angel goes forth and slays a hundred and eighty-five thousand in the Assyrian camp. And the king of Assyria is killed upon his return home.

Hezekiah's own life is spared from a deadly sickness; after he begs the LORD in tears, he is granted an extra fifteen years. But because of his foolishness in revealing all his treasures to envoys from Babylon, this kingdom is prophesied to conquer Jerusalem and take Hezekiah's sons into exile.

Though God in His mercy turns back the clock a short while, though He listens to the cry of a repentant heart, those who merit condemnation shall be condemned.

I AM HE

"The LORD is the everlasting God, the Creator of the ends of the earth" (40:28). He comes with great might to save His people, to "open rivers on the bare heights" (41:18), to pour out His Spirit on those who have burdened Him with their sins... that we might be renewed, that we might be drawn from the ends of the earth back into His fold – that we might be called by His NAME.

We know not the former things or the latter things, for we know not Him who is the first and the last – we know not our Creator and Redeemer. Bowing down before pieces of rotting wood, our eyes become blind and our ears deaf to His presence in our midst. And so John the Baptist cries out Jesus' way in the wilderness of this world that the LORD might make the rough places into level ground, that He might bring us out of our prisons and turn our darkness into light.

Do we hear the voice of the LORD calling us to righteousness, calling us to Himself? Do we recognize the Servant upon whom His Spirit rests as He walks among us? He will save us from the consuming fire if we are witnesses to the One "before [whom] no god was formed" (43:10). O let us not weary Him with our iniquities any longer! but worship the God who blots out our transgressions.

Fear not! Judah shall be inhabited again: "I will raise up their ruins" (44:26), says the LORD. Let earth and Heaven sing of His salvation.

Cyrus

A day of salvation is prophesied upon Jerusalem, upon Jacob, upon the people of God… and that salvation shall reach to the ends of the earth. For the LORD calls by name a pagan king who does not know Him to deliver Israel from their captivity in Babylon; and so, from the rising of the sun to its setting all men shall know that He is LORD of Heaven and earth, and all shall bow down to Him.

"Come down and sit in the dust, O virgin daughter of Babylon…. Sit in silence, and go into darkness" (47:1,5). She who put herself in the place of God will learn how empty are all her boasts – how the LORD will crush the idols on which she depends! For her lack of mercy toward His Chosen, He will bring her to sudden ruin.

The LORD declares "before they c[o]me to pass" (48:5) the things that shall be hereafter. By Him all is made new. The Spirit of the LORD is strongly upon Isaiah and he prophesies, even before they have gone into exile, the Jews' liberation by Cyrus. He sees the transcendent hand of God at work and declares openly the salvation YHWH prepares. He calls even now for Jacob to go forth from Babylon, for all whom the Father formed in the womb to come from the ends of the earth and be gathered into His loving arms.

"The prey of the tyrant [will] be rescued" (49:25). All shall know that God alone is LORD and Savior. Alleluia!

The Servant

The LORD will redeem the righteous. As He made a way for the Israelites through the Red Sea and sends Cyrus to free them from their captivity, so He sends His Servant to loose our neck from the bonds of sin. Though He has made us drink the cup of His wrath and caused us to stagger like drunken men, though He has cast us off like a wife forsaken, His compassion comes to us in the grace of His Son, and we are vindicated. And His "deliverance will be for ever... [His] salvation to all generations" (51:8).

Though the Servant be despised and rejected, He sets His face like flint and gives His "back to the smiters, and [His] cheeks to those who pull out the beard" (50:6). His appearance is marred beyond human semblance, and like a lamb led to slaughter He is silent before His oppressors; He freely accepts this severe chastisement from the hand of God – but why? Why is He given a grave with the wicked but to save those who torment Him from the punishment we deserve? Indeed, He is "wounded for our transgressions... bruised for our iniquities" (53:5). He makes Himself an offering for our sins that we might be kept from the Pit of death. "The LORD has laid on Him the iniquity of us all" (53:6).

Because of the suffering Christ endures for our sakes, we may now sing and praise the LORD and "spread abroad to the right and to the left" (54:3). O may Jesus see the sinful souls He has died to save prosper now in His holy Name!

House of Prayer

YHWH calls all peoples into His House to share in His feast; without money and without price, all may receive the gracious gifts He offers to any righteous soul who follows in His way.

The heavens are indeed higher than the earth and the LORD's thoughts and ways far above our own, yet to His presence, to His holy mountain with its peaks in the clouds, He calls us that we might share in His eternal glory.

His Word comes down from Heaven to nourish the earth, and it shall achieve its purpose; and all souls who seek His justice will be blessed with surpassing peace and joy. Yes, the mountains and hills "shall break forth into singing, and all the trees of the field shall clap their hands" (55:12) – there is none that is kept from knowing God's salvation.

O let the wicked forsake his way! for the LORD has mercy on all who turn to Him; all who seek Him, He will abundantly pardon. Even the eunuch and the foreigner are welcomed into His gates and given "an everlasting name which shall not be cut off" (56:5). He accepts the sacrifices of anyone who loves Him and ministers to Him – contrite and humble hearts will rejoice for ever in His House of prayer. Let us be gathered into the arms of God.

Children of Transgression

What shall become of those who wag their heads at the righteous, those who "burn with lust...under every green tree; who slay [their] children in the valleys" (57:5)? What shall the LORD do with His people who turn to the idols of the nations and set themselves in wickedness? Though He has patience with those who transgress His laws, though He heals whoever turns to Him, His wrath is for His adversaries who harden their hearts against Him.

Do not come before God with false and empty worship. Do not pretend holiness, going through the motions of fasting and prayer. He knows your heart and sees your actions, and by vanity He is not appeased. Rather, loose the bonds of wickedness and let the oppressed go free; feed the hungry and care for the homeless and the naked, and He shall hear you and bring healing and refreshment. But as long as there is innocent blood on your hands and a lying tongue in your mouth, His salvation will be far from you.

Where there is no justice, there is no peace; where there is no truth, the LORD is not present. Where transgressions are multiplied, where souls engage continually in "speaking oppression and revolt, conceiving and uttering from the heart lying words" (59:13), the vengeance of the LORD shall fall like a rushing wind from on high. And those who commit iniquity shall not stand.

Light Has Come

The glory of the LORD rises upon His people like a light in the darkness, and to this light all nations are drawn. Seeing the radiance of God's holy City, peoples come from afar bearing gifts of gold and frankincense and proclaiming the praises of YHWH. All the wealth of the nations pours into Jerusalem, into the sanctuary of the Most High God – into His Church – and she is made "majestic for ever, a joy from age to age" (60:15).

O let all hear the glad tidings the Spirit declares to His afflicted ones! Liberty comes to the captives, for the prison gates are flung open at the Word of God. His year of favor is upon us! Jerusalem is covered with the robe of salvation like a bride adorned with her jewels, for the LORD delights in His Church and rejoices over her as a bridegroom over his bride.

Watchmen are set over the House of God all the day and night, and so Zion shall not again be broken into. All the redeemed of the LORD now enter through her gates; all His holy people praise Him in His sanctuary. And no more do we need sun and moon, for the LORD God is our everlasting light, a sun that no longer sets. And so all mourning flees away as His vindication dawns upon our souls and praise springs up from our hearts even unto Heaven.

New Heavens

The LORD's garments are soaked in blood, for His day of vengeance is at hand. How long He looked for a faithful soul, but not one was to be found among His rebellious people. And so His wrath is let loose upon them.

"Where is He who put in the midst of them His Holy Spirit?" (63:11). "In our sins we have been a long time, and shall we be saved?" (64:5). Will the LORD who brought up His people from the depths of the sea into freedom remember His own… or will He be angry for ever?

"In all their affliction He was afflicted" (63:9), and is afflicted even now. Though His sword must come to destroy all those who persist in their iniquity, His compassion is poured out in the blood of His Son for the man "that is humble and contrite in spirit, and trembles at [His] Word" (66:2). For this one He creates new heavens and a new earth. God our Father redeems His children and gives them long life in His House.

To His holy mountain shall all stream who have mourned over Jerusalem. There God comforts us as a mother comforts her infant. On His holy mountain "the wolf and the lamb shall feed together" (65:25), for there no destruction shall be found. There our hearts will rejoice and our bones flourish like the grass. O what blessing shall be upon the LORD's servants, gathered from every land! Even as the rebellious lie in the dust, the redeemed will worship before Him.

JEREMIAH

"Before I formed you in the womb I knew you,
and before you were born I consecrated you;
I appointed you a prophet to the nations."
1:5

The LORD calls Jeremiah from his youth to speak in His NAME, saying, "Behold, I have put my words in your mouth" (1:9). At the time of the Babylonian exile He commands this poor soul to prophesy against the iniquity of Judah, to destroy and overthrow their sin by the power of the Word upon him. Great strength the LORD gives to this weak child, making him "a fortified city, an iron pillar, and bronze walls, against the whole land" (1:18). None shall stand before him or prevail against him, for the LORD God is indeed with him. Out of the north shall Judah's destruction come: YHWH is watching over His word to see that it is accomplished.

O why do we not see the power of God working through those whom He calls? Why are we so deaf and blind to prophecy, thinking it is the words of men and not the LORD? Why can we not believe that the hand of God has indeed reached out and touched the mouth of Jeremiah and all His prophets? And if we do not believe this, how can and why should we listen to them (or His Son)... and so, to what end shall we come?

The Harlot

"By the waysides you have sat awaiting lovers."
3:2

Faithless Israel and false Judah follow one another in mounting iniquity; "committing adultery with stone and tree" (3:9), forsaking God to go after the empty idols of the nations, they burn with lust on every high hill and under every green tree. And they refuse to be ashamed, hardening their brow against the call of the LORD to return to Him. "I will not serve" (2:20), they insist, and so make their lands an abominable waste.

O how can it be that the people of God, those whom He brought up from Egypt and led through the wilderness to give it blessings, so readily embrace worthless lovers, becoming worthless themselves? Why have they forsaken "the fountain of living waters, and hewn out cisterns for themselves, broken cisterns, that can hold no water" (2:13)? How can they be so foolish?

And how can we? How can we reject the grace offered freely to us by a loving God who would make us His holy Bride, by saying, "I am innocent... I have not sinned" (2:35), thus arrogantly declaring we have no need of Him or the blood of His Son? Are we any different than those "who say to a tree, 'You are my father,' and to a stone, 'You gave me birth'" (2:27)? Are we not just as devoid of the glory of the LORD?

Return

"Return, O faithless children, says the LORD" (3:14). YHWH is calling you back, back to your land, back to your blessings – back to His love. "Circumcise yourselves to the LORD, remove the foreskin of your hearts" (4:4), for He desires again to be your Father and make His home among you, to fill you with knowledge and understanding... to pour out His grace and mercy upon you. And so, "wash your heart from wickedness, that you may be saved" (4:14)!

O there is a lion coming out of the north to lay waste the land, and will you continue with your delusions? God's wrath will not be turned back but will make the earth desolate and void. The heavens will give no light and the mountains quake and fall; "acknowledge your guilt, that you rebelled against the LORD your God" (3:13), or you will not know His mercy and love – only disaster will be your lot.

In anguish God's people writhe in pain at the doom come upon them. Their hearts beat wildly at "the sound of the trumpet, the alarm of war" (4:19). Will they be consumed by their fear, "gasping for breath, stretching out [their] hands" to emptiness and "fainting before [their] murderers" (4:31), or will they turn to the LORD? And what about you?

Refuse

"In vain the refining goes on" (6:29), for Judah has become a "foolish and senseless people, who have eyes, but see not, who have ears, but hear not" (5:21); they are utterly faithless, readily scorning the Word of the LORD, and so He in His turn rejects them – and they become as refuse in an abandoned wasteland.

Though Jeremiah searches the squares of Jerusalem, he cannot find a single man who seeks the truth, who sets his heart on the justice of God... O when shall Jesus come with His blood! All have broken the yoke the LORD placed lightly on their shoulders, and so, only the freedom found in death will they know. Torn in pieces by the might of the nation descending upon them, all they have is eaten up, devoured as by a beast of the field... but still they know no shame, and so, still they suffer apart from their God.

The roaring waves know the bounds set for them by the hand of the LORD, but the people of Judah have made their faces harder than stone in their refusal to obey the Law of God or heed His warning. Since they have no fear of the LORD, no desire to walk in His righteous ways, "the shadows of evening lengthen" (6:4) upon them. They do not heed the sound of the trumpet, and so the terrors of war overtake them and their empty worship.

Lament

A lamentation must be raised over Jerusalem, a cry for the vanity of their worship. Abomination has come into the temple of the LORD, into the house which is called by His NAME, and profaned His blessing. The sons of Judah even burn their sons and daughters in unholy fire as sacrifice to their false gods, and so, what can God do but vent His fury upon them? His Word is far from them; His voice they do not obey – against His prophets they stiffen their necks. "Truth has perished; it is cut off from their lips" (7:28), and so there is no place for them in the LORD's presence anymore. Their bones shall be removed from the tombs and spread out before the sun and moon to which they bow down.

"Everyone is greedy for unjust gain" (8:10) – even prophet and priest deal falsely. But their own peace they cannot make; it is the terrors of war they sow instead. The LORD "will feed this people with wormwood, and give them poisonous water to drink" (9:15), for oppression and deceit are all they know.

Weep and wail for the mountains that fall, for the ruin come upon Jerusalem. O "that our eyes may run down with tears, and our eyelids gush with water" (9:18)! A lament, a dirge, let all be taught – what should we know but mourning for the healing that does not come to our troubled, forsaken souls, to our uncircumcised hearts? To wood we come with our prayers, and find no answer.

A Lamb Led to Slaughter

Jeremiah cries for his people, but they do not heed his voice. He entreats the LORD for their good, but the LORD will not listen to him – for they must be punished. It is the false prophets to whom the people choose to listen, and so they bring destruction on themselves.

Jeremiah is pursued for the truth he speaks to Jerusalem. They devise schemes against him, seeking to "cut him off from the land of the living" (11:19). But it is they who will be destroyed. Though they were like a green olive tree before the LORD, He will set them aflame and consume all their branches. For their adulteries and their neighings, the sword shall come upon them, along with famine and pestilence... and captivity. "I will dash them one against another" (13:14), says the LORD. No pity, no compassion has He anymore.

"Do not pray for the welfare of this people" (14:11), YHWH insists of His prophet. Though they curse him, still his tears fall for their sakes. What woe is upon Jeremiah! He is "a man of strife and contention to the whole land" (15:10), yet he remains faithful to the words the LORD feeds him. But he does call for vengeance on those who would slay him – in this he is not like the Christ, uttering only what is precious. The true Lamb led to slaughter for the sins of the people is still to come.

A Pen of Iron

"The sin of Judah is written with a pen of iron; with a point of diamond it is engraved on the tablet of their heart" (17:1). To their sin they stubbornly cling, and so a fire is kindled against them that shall burn the gates of Jerusalem.

Indeed, "the heart is deceitful above all things, and desperately corrupt" (17:9), but the LORD sees what is written on the heart and judges every man according to his deeds. He sees that Israel has forsaken its sanctuary, that they place no trust in Him but relentlessly pursue their idols; and so "their dead bodies shall be food for the birds of the air and for the beasts of the earth" (16:4). No mirth, no gladness, no rejoicing of bride and groom shall be known in her midst, and the mourner shall not be consoled. Though God will bring them back from all the lands to which He scatters them, their fate is sealed, written in stone – they will pay double for all their crimes.

And what of you? Will you keep holy the Sabbath day? Will you worship the LORD alone? Will you give all over to Him who holds your life in His hands? If not, you will be punished, too. If not, the same fate awaits your soul. If you persist in your sin, what can you be but cast from His presence for ever?

YHWH, may all peoples stream to your House to praise your might and power! Let your NAME be written on our hearts.

The Potter

At the potter's house Jeremiah sees the craftsman at his trade, doing what seems good to him with his clay: when a vessel becomes spoiled, he reworks it as he sees fit.

So are we in the LORD's hands. If upon an evil nation He declares destruction and that nation repents, He, too, will repent of the evil he intends. But if a people on whom His favor rests turns from Him to wickedness, all their blessings shall disappear. Such is Jerusalem in the sight of her God – His highly-favored one shall become a curse.

O what horror it is to see one filled with the grace of God abandon the righteous ways of the LORD! O how cursed shall be Jerusalem for all its sins! It shall be smashed into pieces like the potter's jar, "so that it can never be mended" (19:11). Greatly defiled shall the city be – consuming the flesh of their sons and daughters when under siege – and to Babylon the people shall be taken, and live in captivity. The LORD "will show them [His] back, not [His] face, in the day of their calamity" (18:17).

The Word of God cannot be turned back by persecution of His prophet, and His prophet must speak however naked and beaten he may be. The "violence and destruction," the "terror...on every side" (20:8,10), must be proclaimed to them that opportunity be given for their repentance. But it is only revenge they shall know for hardening their hearts in the unholy fires of this world.

Jeremiah

The Burden of the LORD

The LORD is against the evil king and the false prophets that defile Jerusalem and lead His people astray; against all those who "have eyes and heart only for [their] dishonest gain, for shedding innocent blood, and for practicing oppression and violence" (22:17), He shall come in His great wrath with outstretched hand and leave them a desolation. The king shall have no one to succeed him but shall be hurled out of Judah by the LORD's mighty arm and be buried with "the burial of an ass" (22:19). The land shall be cursed for the sin of the evil shepherds who scatter the people of God... until His righteous Branch shall come.

O the woe upon the prophets who strengthen the hands of evildoers, causing Judah to become as Sodom and Gomorrah in the sight of the LORD, who presume to speak for Him but instead dream dreams and conceive lies. He is against those who prophesy lying dreams and will bring "everlasting reproach and perpetual shame" (23:40) on them and any who call the liberating Word of God a burden to be borne with indignation.

The LORD is good and His Word is good; it is only out of love for His children He speaks at all. Yet those who take refuge in their sin and not in Him and His righteous ways spurn His holy Word. They refuse to repent of their wickedness, and so like a hammer His Word shall break them in pieces. The LORD is against all that evil men conceive. Only those who do justice for the poor and needy will bear the light yoke of the Christ.

The Cup of Wrath

> "I begin to work evil at the city which is called by my NAME, and shall you go unpunished?"
> 25:29

The LORD will punish His people mightily. Though those taken into exile shall be blessed and protected and built up in the land to which they come (as good figs in God's hand), those who remain in Judah and Jerusalem will be made "a reproach, a byword, a taunt, and a curse" (24:9) among all kingdoms; and these nations shall soon follow in their steps and be just as devastated.

For twenty-three years the people have refused to listen to the words of warning Jeremiah has persistently spoken to them in the NAME of the LORD. And so the anger of the LORD is provoked. And so Nebuchadnezzar shall utterly destroy them – all light will be banished from Jerusalem.

But the nations round about shall not escape the almighty hand of God. He shall make them drink to the dregs His cup of wrath. Drunk with His anger they shall vomit and fall, "and rise no more" (25:27). None shall be spared. None shall be spared, from the Egyptians to the Philistines, to Edom and Moab and all the kings of Tyre and Sidon, Arabia and Media. And finally, Babylon will fall.

"The LORD will roar from on high... entering into judgment with all flesh" (25:30,31). From one end of the earth to the other, there will be no refuge for shepherd or lord – all shall wail and be slaughtered, utterly despoiled. Nothing will turn back the fierce anger of God.

The Yoke

There is a war of prophets, false and true. And to which shall we listen? To what word are our hearts inclined? Is it the will of God we seek, or stubbornly to follow our own desires?

Jeremiah continues to prophesy doom upon the nations and upon Judah. He exhorts them to serve the king of Babylon, and not to rebel. The LORD places a wooden yoke on his prophet's neck to symbolize the subjection to which all are called. For God has made Nebuchadnezzar king over every land; even the beasts of the field He has given into his hands. Those obedient to him will remain in peace on their land – but great desolation will come upon all who rebel.

The false prophets would have the life of Jeremiah, would silence the voice that contradicts their lies. But YHWH's mouthpiece is kept from their snares, and he who breaks the yoke from Jeremiah's neck soon dies – as Jeremiah foretells – and an iron yoke awaits every soul who would throw off the wooden one the LORD lays on our backs.

Jeremiah encourages the exiles to "build houses and live in them" (29:5), to multiply in the land to which they are brought... but the lying prophets who speak of an early return they prefer to hear, accepting not the LORD's sentence of seventy years. And so a curse they and the king who remains shall become.

His Cross is easy and His burden light; embrace the chastisement of your God.

The New Covenant

The LORD promises the return of the exiles of Israel: "I will break the yoke from off their neck, and I will burst their bonds" (30:8). He will have compassion on them and restore their fortunes; the city of God shall be rebuilt from end to end and extend further, and all will be sacred to Him.

"A voice is heard in Ramah, lamentation and bitter weeping. Rachel is weeping for her children" (31:15). YHWH will hear her cry and comfort her and all her children: they shall be brought back from foreign lands. Though Ephraim has been chastened for his great guilt and flagrant sin, the LORD "will surely have mercy on him" (31:20). He will heal his incurable wound and ease all his pain. "Out of them shall come songs of thanksgiving, and the voices of those who make merry" (30:19) will again be heard in their house. They will again be His people and He their God.

And the Covenant He makes with them will not be like the one written on stone, which they broke so readily. Thus says the LORD: "I will put my Law within them, and I will write it upon their hearts" (31:33). All from least to greatest will know Him when He has forgiven their iniquity, and each shall be responsible for his own soul. As long as the sun is in the sky, they will remain blessed before Him.

"The LORD bless you, O habitation of righteousness, O holy hill!" (31:23) and all who dwell within you. Make us your Temple, dear God!

Old Testament

The Deed

Even as the Word of the LORD comes to pass, as siege mounds are cast up against Jerusalem and "because of sword and famine and pestilence the city is given into the hands of the Chaldeans" (32:24); even as Jeremiah is shut up in prison by the king for speaking this truth... the LORD calls the prophet to buy a field from his cousin. Why? Why at this time when the Chaldeans are about to make the land an utter desolation should he purchase a piece of that waste? Is this not done in vain?

This word comes to Jeremiah to reveal quite clearly to all that though Judah and all Israel be overrun by Nebuchadnezzar, the time shall come when the LORD will indeed forgive His people and all their disobedience and return them to their homeland, where they will dwell in safety. They will be His joy again.

The Righteous Branch shall spring from David and the promise that he shall always have a son on his throne will be fulfilled in Jesus. Even now Zedekiah is to be spared from the sword and die a peaceful death, lamented and mourned as the kings of old.

O let us set free the slaves among us! Let us heed the LORD's call to liberty. Let us imitate the faithfulness of the Gentile peoples who keep the word their fathers hand down. If we are faithful to our God, He will have mercy on us. Let us praise His NAME, "for His steadfast love endures for ever!" (33:11).

The Scroll and the Mire

YHWH commands Jeremiah to write on a scroll all the words He has spoken to him; and so, at the prophet's dictation, Baruch inscribes the Word of God. Jeremiah then tells Baruch to read all the words in the temple on a day of fasting, that the people might have opportunity to repent and so be spared the LORD's wrath.

The princes of the king are filled with fear when Baruch proclaims the scroll to them at their request; but the king himself does nothing but mock the LORD God, cutting off pieces of the scroll as it is read in his presence and throwing them into the fire. Another scroll

Jeremiah dictates to Baruch, and he prophesies a desolate death upon Jehoiakim.

No son of Jehoiakim sits on the throne, but rather a brother, who seeks word from Jeremiah when Pharaoh comes and the Chaldeans retreat temporarily. But Zedekiah is more afraid of his fellow Jews than of the hand of God, and so fails to obey the LORD's command to surrender to Nebuchadnezzar. He does prevent Jeremiah's being returned to a dismal prison – keeping him instead in the court of the guard – but he does not stop his being cast into the mire of an empty cistern, only later permitting Ebedmelech to fish him out. And Zedekiah himself falls into a great mire as Nebuchadnezzar indeed takes and razes Jerusalem: his sons are killed before his eyes, which are then put out... and he is carried off to Babylon. But Jeremiah is treated well by the conquering Chaldeans. Released from his prison and given freedom to go with them or stay, he remains with the poor of the land who are left in Judah.

To Egypt

Jeremiah dwells with Gedaliah, whom Nebuchadnezzar has left as governor of Judah and who is faithful to the king and to the LORD, encouraging all to dwell in the land and serve the Chaldeans. As long as they do so, it shall go well with them.

But Gedaliah and the Jews with him are soon slain by a certain Ishmael and his wicked men. A great slaughter they make, piling the bodies in a large cistern. The renegades are stopped from carrying away captives to the Ammonites, as Ishmael flees from Johanan and his men... but these rescuers of the Jews are not obedient to the Word of the LORD come through Jeremiah.

They beg the prophet to pray to God that they might know His will for them, vowing to obey His voice "whether it is good or evil" (42:6); but they refuse to remain in Judah as commanded, insisting on fleeing for protection to Egypt, that land of their slavery... and in this place they shall die. They shall become "an execration, a horror, a curse, and a taunt" (42:18) when the king of Babylon sets his throne in Tahpanhes – no more will they see Jerusalem.

How obstinately the people and their wives vow to continue burning incense to the queen of heaven and the other false gods of Egypt, foolishly thinking it is by these idols they are blessed. They cannot see that because of this wickedness Jerusalem has become a desolation, nor that they shall soon be consumed by sword and famine and pestilence in this foreign land.

Egypt, the Philistines, and Moab

Jeremiah prophesies the conquering of many nations, beginning with the land of Israel's slavery. O how Egypt shall be destroyed by the mighty arm of Nebuchadnezzar! She has lifted herself up before the LORD, rising like the surging waters of the Nile in her pride, but she shall know "terror on every side" (46:5) and flee in haste at the horsemen and spears come against her, her warriors beaten down to the dust.

A day of vengeance has the LORD for Egypt; she shall become a ruin, a waste. There is no healing for her. More numerous than locusts are those who descend upon her from the north country – nothing shall stand in their way. Her gods and her kings will be no more.

All the nations round about Jacob shall know like destruction, but His servant YHWH will save. He will not make a full end of them, only those from whom they return.

The Philistines will be stamped down by the rushing hooves of stallions and chariots; those who gash themselves before their gods will be run through by the sword. And Moab shall also be put to shame, its god going into exile, its great pride likewise broken down. Those who follow in her ways "sit on the parched ground" (48:18) and bemoan her slaughter. O how they wail for the derision and horror she becomes! Yet though the LORD set pit and snare for her and she be taken captive, her fortunes He shall later restore.

The Other Nations

The LORD indeed will destroy all the nations round about Israel; none shall be spared His fury. Against the Ammonites He prophesies desolation for their dispossession of the Israelites. He calls them to wail and cry and lament for the terrors come upon them as they go into exile. But He promises to restore the fortunes of this people.

The fortunes of Elam, too, the LORD promises to restore after He has scattered them to the four winds and destroyed their kings and princes; but of Edom and Hazor He declares, "No man shall dwell there" (49:33). The camels and cattle of Hazor will be taken as spoil as they too are scattered to every wind and calamity falls on them from every side. An everlasting waste shall they be. Edom the LORD will strip entirely bare, destroying even his children and all his neighbors as He makes him drink the cup of His wrath. O the calamity of Esau, brother of Jacob! "All [his] cities shall be perpetual wastes" (49:13). Like Sodom and Gomorrah shall he be as he is brought down from his heights. How the earth will tremble at his fall!

And Damascus and Kedar shall not fare better, for they will also be forsaken as the LORD brings terrors on them from every side. His fire burns against every evil and none shall be spared its purging flames. Who can stand before YHWH? Not even Babylon.

The Fall of Babylon

"How Babylon is taken, the praise of the whole earth seized!" (51:41). "How the hammer of the whole earth is cut down and broken!" (50:23). "Babylon was a golden cup in the LORD's hand, making all the earth drunken" (51:7); she was the instrument of His vengeance against all the nations. But now she herself shall know the vengeance of the LORD – now she herself will be suddenly broken... for the slain of Israel, Babylon must fall. The blood she shed in violence against Zion shall come upon her own head, and a heap of ruins she shall for ever be.

Let all flee from the midst of Babylon; let all save themselves from the destruction that God is about to inflict on the Chaldeans. A sword from the north is advancing with great power to run through her diviners and warriors, her horses and chariots and all her treasures. The vain idols shall be destroyed and all their madness with them. For none is like the LORD God; none can stand before the Maker of Heaven and earth – every man shall perish with his worthless images.

"The broad wall of Babylon shall be leveled to the ground and her high gates shall be burned with fire" (51:58). She shall sink like a stone in the midst of the sea. For the sins of others do not excuse one's own sin, and so she must be punished for her sins against the LORD and His people: Israel shall be restored once more.

Captive to Babylon

After Jeremiah's final prophecy against Babylon, the exile of Judah is recounted and completed: "Because of the anger of the LORD things came to such a pass in Jerusalem and Judah that He cast them out from His presence" (52:3).

Yes, Zedekiah is taken to Babylon as siege is again laid against Jerusalem. His sons are slain before him, then his eyes are put out by the king… and he is imprisoned in Babylon the rest of his days.

Yes, the house of the LORD is burned to the ground with the king's house and all the houses of Jerusalem, and the walls round about are broken down. Even the poorest of the people are now carried away – only a very few remain.

The temple is pillaged of all its gold and silver and bronze, all its vessels and tools and accouterments – the house of God is stripped bare. And those taken in the final of three attacks are put to death. The total number of persons carried away captive to Babylon is four thousand and six hundred.

Yes, Jerusalem is left a desolate waste; but the head of Jehoiachim a succeeding Assyrian king later lifts up, bringing him from prison to sit at his table in a place above the other kings captive in Babylon. Perhaps this is a sign of the future restoration of the people of God, of their release from captivity and return to Jerusalem when their seventy years is complete.

THE LAMENTATIONS
of Jeremiah

"How lonely sits the city" (1:1), like a widow weeping bitterly in the night with none to comfort her. Even "the roads to Zion mourn, for none come to the appointed feasts" (1:4). Her enemies prosper as her prisoners flee, for Jerusalem has grievously transgressed against the LORD her God. And so her sanctuary is invaded, and so fire is sent into her bones and her sins become like a yoke upon her neck. The LORD is in the right in what He does, for she has rebelled against His Word.

"My eyes flow with tears" (1:16) for the desolation of Jerusalem – "my heart is wrung within me" (1:20). Her enemies rejoice over her as she is cast down to the ground, all her splendor utterly despoiled. In His fury, God "has slain all the pride of our eyes" (2:4) and left us nothing but mourning and lamentation.

"The LORD has scorned His altar, disowned His sanctuary" (2:7), putting an end to the vain sacrifices. Prophets see only false and lying visions as infants cry to their mothers and die in the streets. The LORD slays without mercy even priest and prophet – none escape or survive His day of anger. All peoples "hiss and wag their heads" (2:15) at Jerusalem, as her enemies gnash their teeth and exult at their victory. O cry aloud to God for the misery upon her! "Let tears stream down like a torrent day and night!" (2:18).

Hope

O how Jeremiah presents the affliction of Jerusalem! taking it upon himself: "He has made my flesh and my skin waste away, and broken my bones" (3:4). Besieged and enveloped "with bitterness and tribulation," he dwells in darkness "like the dead of long ago" (3:5,6). Heavy chains the LORD places upon him and walls him in round about – even his prayers are shut out from the presence of God. He is torn to pieces as by a lion or a bear, and his teeth "grind on gravel" as he "cower[s] in ashes" (3:16). There is no happiness left to him; bereft is he of the LORD's glory.

Yet he has hope as he calls to mind the steadfast love of YHWH, His unending mercies that rise anew every morning. In God there is always hope! We must but wait quietly for His coming, enduring all the hardships placed upon us for our sins and the sins of man. Remember this, that the LORD wishes to afflict no one, that though He must cause us grief for our grieving Him by our oppression of the weakest of His children, His compassion awaits all who turn to Him, who seek His forgiveness and grace.

"Let us test and examine our ways, and return to the LORD!" (3:40). Though He slay without pity, though panic and pitfall come upon us, He sees our eyes flowing with tears. When we call on Him from the depths of the pit, He says: "Do not fear!" (3:57). He will save us from our enemies – redemption is in His hands.

Distress

The LORD has utterly rejected His people. When will He restore them and renew their days? Will they be forgotten for ever? The children beg for food but are themselves eaten by desperate mothers in the midst of "the burning heat of famine" (5:10). The priests and prophets have blood on their hands and wander blindly through the city's streets, avoided by all like lepers.

Great is the disgrace upon Jerusalem; her people are as orphans and widows. "The holy stones lie scattered at the head of every street" (4:1) – what has become of her temple? Her pursuers are "swifter than the vultures in the heavens" (4:19), consuming with fire even the city's foundations. The crown has fallen from the head of God's holy ones, and they are now slaves, slaves to slaves who rule over them without mercy. The yoke of sin is upon their necks and they are hard-driven.... Vainly do they wait for help, for vainly have they trusted in the nations that enslave them.

There is no relief for you now, Jerusalem, cry as you will to the LORD, for He is exceedingly angry and will not be easily appeased by empty words and promises. The load upon you must be borne until your time has come, until you are redeemed by God's only Son.

BARUCH

Baruch writes the words of this book while in exile in Babylon, and reads it in the hearing of all the people, low and high. They then send the book to those remaining in Jerusalem, along with vessels taken from the house of the LORD and a collection they have made after fasting and prayer. They ask that offerings be made for themselves and prayers be raised for Nebuchadnezzar and his son, that they might dwell securely in Babylon. They thus come to an obedience of the LORD's command to accept their exile and serve the king set over them.

Baruch clearly recognizes and confesses the sins of his people against the LORD from the time they left Egypt to this day: for their disobedience the curse laid down in the Covenant has come upon them. Because they have followed their own wicked hearts and worshiped other gods, they become a reproach and a desolation, left few in number and scattered far and wide.

Righteousness is with God and confusion with those who sin against Him. Calamity awaits all who turn from His voice. But in our distress let us cry out to the LORD, for it is the feeble and weary who will ascribe glory to Him. Make your prayer for mercy, in your exile turn to God, and He shall hear your anguished cry. Your heart must fear the LORD for all your iniquity and He will remember His compassion. Come to your senses like the Prodigal Son.

Take Courage

Because Israel has "forsaken the fountain of wisdom" (3:12), she herself is forsaken by YHWH. To her alone He has revealed the wisdom that is known to Him alone, but she spurns the Law that brings life and walks toward darkness rather than light. Though they know what is pleasing to God, they provoke Him by sacrificing to demons. And so Jerusalem is grieved, a widow whose sons and daughters have been sent away.

To no other nation has the LORD shown the way to knowledge; His wisdom has not been heard in foreign lands. The princes of this world who hoard silver and gold "have vanished and gone down to Hades" (3:19), yet the LORD's Chosen follow in their path. The stars gladly shine at the command of God, declaring His glory... but His children refuse to obey. And so, only sorrow do they know.

And so a nation without respect or pity comes from afar bringing ruin; and so Jerusalem lies desolate. But take courage, children of the Most High: put on sackcloth and cry to the Everlasting One! He will deliver you from your enemy – His mercy will soon come to you. "Return with tenfold zeal to seek Him" (4:28), and you will see your sons and daughters gathered from east and west into His House. "Arise, O Jerusalem, stand upon the height" (5:5); God is filling in the valley before you that you might travel safely to His side.

They Are Not Gods

Jeremiah writes a letter to the exiles telling them that for all their sins they will remain in Babylon a long time, and warning them especially against the false gods worshiped in this foreign nation.

"You will see gods made of silver and gold and wood" (6:4) followed by a multitude and inspiring great fear in foolish souls. But on the LORD must your hearts be kept, for only He is able to protect and bless you. Why should they be called gods that are decked out in silver and gold and purple robes but cannot keep themselves from rust and corrosion? Their eyes fill with dust and their faces become black with smoke, and so must be wiped clean by the hands of men. It is the hands of vain craftsmen that have made them, and so they are inferior even to sun and moon, wind and flame... or the beasts of the field, which at least can move and so flee when danger is near. Indeed, "there is no work of God in them" (6:51).

These sticks of wood must be locked behind doors and hidden from war, and will burn to ashes when fire comes. Better to be a household utensil or a door than these useless images which inspire only greed in their priests and lust in the hearts of the women who serve them. They cannot save a man from death or restore sight to the blind; they do not pity widow or orphan but are as stone from the mountain... and so how can they be gods? Do not fear these vain idols: there is no breath in them.

EZEKIEL

While sitting among the exiles by the river Chebar, Ezekiel is touched by the hand of the LORD: the heavens are opened before his eyes and he is given vision of God.... And YHWH speaks to him His mighty Word.

Out of flashing fire as of gleaming bronze appear four living creatures, each with four faces and four wings. The four faces are of a man, a lion, an ox, and an eagle, looking out in the four directions. Two of their wings are spread out above and touching the wings of the creatures beside; the other two cover their bodies. Their legs are straight and they do not turn as they move in whatever direction the Spirit leads, darting to and fro like torches in the midst of burning coals.

A wheel of gleaming chrysolite is beside each living creature, and they move and stand and rise with the creatures, also going in the four directions without turning. "The spirit of the living creatures [is] in the wheels" (1:20); their rims are full of eyes and each appears like a wheel within a wheel.

A crystal firmament is over the heads of the living creatures. Under the firmament the creatures move, their wings thundering like the sound of many waters.... When they stand still, they let down their wings. Above the firmament is a sapphire throne upon which sits "the likeness of the glory of the LORD" (1:28) in human form, gleaming like bronze and bright fire, shining like the bow in the clouds on a day of rain. Ezekiel falls on his face before such a vision.

The Scroll

Ezekiel hears a voice and Spirit enters into him and sets him on his feet. He is sent by YHWH to speak His words to the exiles of Israel. Such is the prophet. Such is he who says, "Thus says the LORD God" (2:4), who speaks for the LORD.

It could not be made clearer that Ezekiel, as with all the prophets, speaks the Word of God and not his own, for the LORD hands him a written scroll with words of "lamentation and mourning and woe" (2:10), and tells him to eat it. The scroll is from God's hand, it contains His words, and Ezekiel takes them into his very self and is ordered to go forth and speak.

The prophet is overwhelmed by the call upon his soul. When the Spirit of God brings him back to the exiles at the river Chebar, he sits there in a dazed silence seven days. Then the LORD calls this watchman of Israel, telling him again in words that make clear the role of the prophet: "Whenever you hear a word from my mouth, you shall give them warning from me" (3:17). It is the LORD's words of warning he must deliver, whether the people listen or not.

The people harden their hearts and their foreheads against the Word of God, but the LORD makes Ezekiel's forehead harder still. He speaks faithfully to this rebellious house, and so saves his life by this faithfulness to his call. Though the people die in their sin for ignoring his warning, he shall not die. Though they shut the prophet's mouth and tie him with cords inside his house, he must speak again to reprove them. "He that will hear, let him hear" (3:27).

Siege of Jerusalem

Ezekiel is instructed to take a brick and portray Jerusalem upon it, to raise a siege wall against it with battering rams, and place an iron wall between himself and the city. "Press the siege against it" (4:3), he is commanded, thus to act as a sign.

He is also told to lie on his left side 390 days, taking the punishment of Israel on himself, then on his right 40 days for the sins of Judah. And he is tied with cords so he cannot move till he has completed the days of his siege and his prophesying over Jerusalem.

While lying on his side he must eat but once a day, and only the measure of bread allotted him; likewise, only a limited amount of water once a day the LORD allows him... and he must cook the bread over dung.

O how unclean Jerusalem has become! How the people have defiled themselves with the idols of the nations, bringing abominations into God's sanctuary. And so, how they must be punished. How the LORD will vent His fury upon them! They will lack bread and water as they come under siege; father will eat son and son father as they "waste away under their punishment" (4:17). A third of Jerusalem shall be consumed by the fire of hunger, a third fall by the sword, and a third be scattered to the four winds. The holy city will indeed become a desolation, "a reproach and a taunt, a warning and a horror" (5:15) for having rebelled so grievously against the LORD, for acting more wickedly than the nations round about.

The End of Israel

The prophet sets his face against Israel, against its mountains and hills, "wherever they offer pleasing odor to all their idols" (6:13). All these high places will be destroyed and all their idols broken down, and the people shall fall by the sword, famine and pestilence, and their bones lay strewn around their altars. All their works will be wiped out and the land become a desolate waste. The LORD will have no pity as He punishes Israel for its wickedness.

The end has come for Israel: their day of doom is upon them for all the injustice and pride and violence in their midst. The LORD pours out His wrath on His people, and "their silver and gold are not able to deliver them" (7:19). These they have used for vainglory and to make their abominable images – but their idols cannot save them. And so they moan in their weakness and are covered with shame for all their evil deeds, as the basest of nations comes and puts an end to their pride and their sacred places are profaned.

"I AM the LORD" (7:27). All men must know that YHWH is God and there is no other. All will be struck with terror as disaster comes upon those who spurn the Most High and turn their hearts to bloody crimes made in the name of idols. The end of all evil is upon the land.

Vision of Abominations

Vision of the LORD comes again to Ezekiel, and the Spirit lifts him up from where he sits before the elders in their exile and takes him by a lock of his hair to Jerusalem, to the temple. The glory of

God he sees at the temple, where he is also shown the great abominations the elders commit.

He first sees the image of jealousy, which provokes the LORD to jealousy for His house. There also in the dark, seventy elders hide themselves and worship images of beasts and creeping things they have drawn on the walls, each standing before his idols with censer in hand. And he sees women crying for vegetation gods and men turning their backs to the temple to worship the sun.

For all their abominations and for the blood on their hands and the injustice they invoke, God will not spare their lives. He calls in a loud voice for the executioners to come. First a mark is put on the foreheads of those who mourn over the fate of the city, that they might be preserved; then all others are slain without pity. The courts of the LORD are thus filled with blood.

The living creatures, who are now revealed as cherubim, rise and go forward without turning, the four wheels filled with eyes beside them… and the glory of the LORD over them goes and fills the inner court. From the midst of the cherubim coals are taken and cast over the forsaken city. Those who have devised iniquity fall by the sword outside the city, but YHWH gathers the exiles and places a new heart within them – they will return and remove the detestable things from Jerusalem.

Useless Vine

A useless vine has Jerusalem and the house of Israel become. Good for nothing when whole, it shall be burned, and then burned again in the fire of the LORD. What else but a desolate waste can the people of God become?

They shall go into exile. Ezekiel will be a sign for them: as he has done in taking his baggage and digging through the wall at night at the Word of the LORD, so shall the prince and all the people shoulder their burdens and seek to escape the horrors upon Jerusalem. But they shall not find safety. A few will escape the pursuing sword and confess their abominations among the nations, but the rest will be scattered by God's avenging hand and die in their sin in Babylon.

They shall eat their bread with quaking and drink water with trembling as their land is stripped bare for all its violence. No longer will the LORD delay His judgment upon them – His vision will be fulfilled, and they shall see it.

No longer will they be able to blind their eyes with the lies of false prophets who presume to speak in God's NAME. Their delusions of peace and magical divinations will fall to the sword with the wall in which they pretend protection. A great deluge of rain and strong wind will come and lay bare their foundations.

"Repent and turn away from your idols" (14:6), the LORD entreats His people Himself, for both the lying prophet and the one who inquires of him will be destroyed by famine, sword, pestilence and beasts… and not even Noah, Daniel, and Job will be able to save them from the wrath to come.

The Outcast

When Jerusalem was born no eye pitied her; she was cast out into an open field weltering in her blood, unwashed, unclothed. But the LORD passed by and called her to live and grow up before Him. When she reached the age of love He covered her with His cloak and brought her in to Himself, making her His own. He washed her clean and clothed her in fine linen, silk and ornaments, and placed a crown on her head. She ate fine flour and oil and honey from His hand.

O how beautiful was Jerusalem! blessed with every gift from God… but O how she prostitutes herself! giving her beauty to the nations. She takes the gold and silver the LORD lavishes on her and makes for herself images to worship in His place, even sacrificing her sons and daughters to them in the flames. A harlot to all the nations' idols she has become, freely giving herself to every passerby, an "adulterous wife, who receives strangers instead of her husband!" (16:32).

And so the LORD will strip off her clothes and take her jewels and leave her naked and bare again. Worse she has become than Samaria and Sodom, whom she indeed makes seem righteous; more corrupt in her abominations is she than any nation. And so she shall bear her disgrace.

And how she shall be confounded and ashamed when the LORD restores her fortunes and places her above her sisters, when He makes high this lowly one, though she deserves it not. She will be silenced by His grace, by the New Covenant He makes with her by His Word alone. Even after a remnant refuses to stay in the land, attempting fruitlessly to transplant itself to Egypt; even after all are judged for their treason and fall by the sword or die in Babylon... even then He will make this dry tree flourish by the sending of His Son to them.

Turn and Live

God takes no pleasure in the death of the wicked, and so He calls all men to turn from their sins that they might not die but live and receive the reward of the righteous. By one's own deeds is each man judged, not by those of father or son; and what a man has done in the past, good or bad, shall not be remembered, but only what is on his soul today. So, embrace what is right and just and walk now in the way of the LORD. A new heart and a new Spirit He wishes to give you.

Why should a lamentation be raised over you as it is over Israel, whom the LORD blesses and makes strong as a lion but who repeatedly rebels against Him and His ways? Would you be a slave in Egypt, a captive in Babylon – would you treasure detestable idols rather than YHWH's holy NAME? Cast these abominations from you!

How often the LORD thought to pour out His wrath on wayward Israel. How they rebelled against Him in the wilderness and in every land to which He brought them. He would have made a full end of them, but withheld His hand. This day, too, He refrains from punishment, from the annihilation of His people, for the sake of His NAME and those few who turn to Him, who will not worship wood and stone.

Be ashamed of your blasphemy, of all the iniquity on your hands; "loathe yourselves for all the evils that you have committed" (20:43), and the LORD will look with favor on your repentance and spare your life when He purges the rebels from among us. You will enter His righteous reign.

Ezekiel

Into the Cauldron

The LORD is unsheathing His sword against Jerusalem and all Israel. The sword is polished and sharpened for slaughter; flashing like lightning in the hand of the king of Babylon, it bears the wrath of God against His bloody city – He thunders against it for all its abominable deeds. All Israel is gathered like dross into the cauldron of Jerusalem, there to be consumed in the fire of the LORD's fury.

O the brazen harlotry of these two sisters! Judah outdoing Israel in her lewdness with the nations and their mighty warriors. Her princes roar like lions, devouring human lives, like wolves tearing at their prey... and the prophets whitewash their deeds with lies. They oppress the widow and the orphan and the stranger, and profane the holy things of God. To their lust they give free rein, uncovering even their fathers' nakedness and taking bribes to shed innocent blood. They sacrifice their children to their idols and come into the LORD's sanctuary on the same day! And so the time of the LORD's vengeance comes, even by the hands of their adulterous lovers, whose issue now disgusts them.

The appointed hour is here – "Heap on the logs, kindle the fire, boil well the flesh, and empty out the broth, and let the bones be burned up" (24:10). Let the pot itself be heated in the fire, yet still their filth is not consumed! There is not one man the LORD can find, and so His sword comes upon all, and so Jerusalem is destroyed... and none even mourn her passing.

The Nations' Ruin

The sword of destruction in the hand of the king of Babylon will come upon the Ammonites as well; because they have rejoiced with malice over the desolation of Israel and the exile of Judah, they too will be taken as a possession and perish from the earth. With them shall be destroyed Moab and Edom and the Philistines: since they have acted with vengeance against the LORD's Chosen, His great vengeance will fall upon them.

And O the woe upon the royal nation of Tyre! who sits in the midst of the sea in perfect beauty, with whom all the nations trade and whose great wealth is beyond compare. Mighty is she, imposing terms on all, making herself a god in her pride. But her towers shall be broken down; Nebuchadnezzar will come with horse and chariot, battering ram and axe, and trample her streets and slay her people… and she shall sink in the heart of the sea, descend into the Pit, and no more be known or seen.

And the merchants round about will cast dust on their heads and weep bitterly at her ruin, for all her riches are gone. O how she profaned the gifts God gave her! And so this beauteous mountain is thrust to the ground.

Upon Sidon, too, the LORD will send His sword of judgment, that there shall be no thorn to harm the house of Israel among all her neighbors. He will manifest His holiness and bring them back to dwell securely in their own land.

Egypt's Fall

And Egypt shall come to ruin with all the nations. The LORD shall take from the sea by His hook this great dragon that troubles the waters and cast her down on the bare ground. How she exalts herself, towering high above the peoples who dwell in her shadow! How she prides herself in her might! But a mightier one than she God calls forth to slay her with His sword: Babylon shall despoil Egypt and carry off all its wealth as recompense for a job well done.

Egypt shall be desolate. It shall go down to the Pit with all those who shudder at its passing. And though the LORD restore its fortunes in forty years, it shall then be the lowliest of nations, one in which no people, especially not the Chosen, will trust again for protection.

A day of darkness is indeed coming upon Egypt and all her multitude. The arm of Pharaoh will be broken and all his idols destroyed. The LORD will set fire to Egypt and her great cities, and O how the king shall groan! All in league with her will keep her company as she lies with the uncircumcised in the Pit of hell. The daughters of the nations will raise a lamentation over her as her carcass lies in the valley, her blood drenching the land. Though "no tree in the garden of God was like it in beauty" (31:8), its light shall shine no more.

Ezekiel

The Watchman

The LORD reminds Ezekiel, and so us all, that He takes no pleasure in the death of the wicked but desires that they should turn to Him and be saved – and that the righteous shall be condemned if they leave the path they tread. The prophet must warn them as called, that at least he will save his own soul.

And Ezekiel is a faithful watchman. His tongue is loosed and he speaks as he hears of the fall of Jerusalem. The Word of the LORD, a word of destruction and desolation for all Israel's abominations, he makes known. But they listen to him as a man would a singer of a song: they hear his words but do not act, do not change their ways. And so for a love only on their lips they shall not be spared the sword, wild beasts, and pestilence – their empty pride shall come to an end.

For the shepherds of His sheep the LORD has the harshest words, for what kind of watchmen have they been? They do not seek the lost or strengthen the weak but feed on their flesh and make themselves fat. And so the sheep wander to idols on every hill over all the earth.

And so YHWH Himself will be the Shepherd of His flock; He will judge the fat ones who trample upon His lean sheep. David He will set up over them and He will be their God. The land shall again know His blessing and His faithful ones dwell secure under His watchful eye.

Dry Bones Renewed

Because the nations have plundered Israel with great contempt, thinking to take the LORD's land as their own; because Israel suffers the reproach of the nations, who accuse her of devouring her inhabitants and bereaving herself of children; because when they were scattered among the nations they profaned the NAME of God (for men said: "These are the people of the LORD, and yet they had to go out of His land" (36:20))... YHWH now swears that He shall rebuild Israel and multiply men within her, even as the nations themselves suffer reproach.

For all their uncleanness the LORD punishes His people; because they defile it, He takes them from their land and makes it desolate.

Old Testament

But for the sake of His holy NAME, He will again make Israel like the Garden of Eden and shower His blessings on her as never before.

A new Spirit He will place within them, that they might do His will. Their dry bones, which lie hopeless in the midst of the valley, He shall bring together with sinew and flesh and skin... and He shall breathe new life into them. Israel and Judah shall be as one nation with David ruling over them, and His sanctuary will be set in their midst for ever. Cleansed of all iniquity, an eternal covenant of peace with Him they will know.

Not for our sake does He redeem our souls, for we stand ashamed and confounded for our sins. It is that all nations might know He is God that the LORD works such grace through men.

Gog

Gog will come with all the hordes from the uttermost parts of the north; the LORD will put hooks into their jaws and bring them forth wielding swords with all their horses and armies. They shall advance like a storm against the mountains of Israel, an evil scheme in their hearts to plunder those who live quietly in unwalled villages. O how they would seize the spoils of those "who dwell at the center of the earth" (38:12)!

On that day when His people dwell securely, when the LORD has brought them back from the nations to their inheritance, then will this great army come forth to shake the land of Israel. But it will be all the men of the earth, all the fish of the sea, every bird of the air and beast of the field that will quake at the presence of God; for He will rain terror upon Gog, pouring fire and brimstone upon them and making the mountains of Israel their burial place. The bow shall be struck from their hand and they shall be no more.

Birds of prey and beasts of the field will feast on the sacrifice of the flesh and blood of their mighty warriors. Men of Israel will go through the land seven months, burning the dead and so cleansing the land; for seven years they will burn their weapons in place of wood. The despoilers will be utterly despoiled as YHWH has mercy on His people – though they sinned against Him, He now showers His Spirit upon them. Let all the earth know He is the LORD!

Ezekiel

Vision of the Temple

Ezekiel is given vision of the temple by the LORD that he might describe its grandeur to the exiles and they might be ashamed for all the abominations that have led to its destruction. In vision the prophet is taken to Israel, where a man with the appearance of bronze stands with a measuring line in his hand. As Ezekiel looks on and listens carefully, the dimensions of the temple are shown to him in detail.

The man measures the wall around the temple, which is perfectly square, and the gates that lead to the outer and inner courts, which are all the same size in general as well as in their side rooms, jambs, vestibules, etc. Gates are in the east, north, and south sides of either court; the inner court and its three stories of chambers are for the priests and are to be preserved in holiness, whereas the outer courts are for the common people. At the center is the most holy place with its images of cherubim and palm trees filling the walls. In front of the holy place facing east is the altar of the LORD. The priests shall make atonement for the altar seven days; then their sacrifice will be acceptable to Him.

Ezekiel next sees the glory of God come from the east with a sound like many waters... in vision like his previous ones. As the glory of the LORD enters the east gate, Spirit lifts the prophet up and brings him to the inner court, where he sees YHWH's glory fill the temple. This is the place of His throne and of the soles of His feet, where He dwells in the midst of Israel for ever.

Put away the abominations by which you have defiled His NAME! if you would dwell in God's presence.

Ordinances of the Temple

The outer gate facing east shall remain always shut, for it is the way by which the LORD God entered the temple: no one may enter there. The prince may sit in the gate, but only by entering and exiting through the vestibule.

No uncircumcised foreigner may enter the LORD's temple at all; and when the people of Israel enter, by the north or south gate, they must leave by the gate opposite, going straight through (never

Old Testament

returning the way they came). The inner gate facing east is to be opened on Sabbaths and new moons, but only the prince may enter there, and he through the vestibule. All others worship at the threshold.

The Levites who served other gods shall not come before the LORD but only wait on the people and tend the gates. They shall bear their shame. The priests who remained faithful, however, shall enter the inner court and minister in the sanctuary. They shall wear linen garments when they enter the gates of the inner court, and put them off when they leave. They shall keep God's laws regarding the feasts, marry only a virgin, and not defile themselves for the dead. By them shall be shown the difference between the holy and the common, the clean and the unclean.

They shall have no inheritance in Israel, for the LORD is their inheritance. They shall eat what is offered to Him and live in a holy district surrounding the land set aside for His sanctuary. And the prince is called to be especially just and fair. He must not dispossess anyone of his inheritance and must provide the offerings of the temple from all that is required of the people.

Morning by morning and on all the feasts, let there be holy offerings unto God!

The River and the Land

The angel then reveals to Ezekiel the water coming from the south side of the temple and flowing east. He goes eastward with a measuring line in his hand. After a thousand cubits the water is ankle-deep; after another thousand it is knee-deep; next it becomes waist-deep; and finally a river through which Ezekiel cannot pass except by swimming.

The river flows into the sea, making it fresh. There will be very many fish thriving in the sea, and all kinds of trees along the banks of either side, watered by the flow from the sanctuary. The trees will bear fresh fruit every month: the fruit will be good for food and the leaves for healing. "Everything will live where the river goes" (47:9)... even as everything lives where the Spirit of Christ passes.

Finally, YHWH tells Ezekiel of the boundaries of the land of Israel and each of the twelve tribes' inheritance therein. Joseph shall have his two portions, and the aliens who live and bear children among the tribes shall have their inheritance, too.

Beginning in the north, first shall come Dan, adjoined by Asher, then Naphtali, Manasseh, Ephraim, Reuben, and Judah. Next shall be set apart a holy portion where the priests shall dwell, with the LORD's sanctuary in the midst of them. Within the holy portion the Levites also have their allotment; and there shall be a smaller area for use of the city, surrounded by open land tilled by workers from all the tribes and supplying the city with food. The prince shall have an area either side of the holy portion; then will come Benjamin, Simeon, Issachar, Zebulun, and Gad. And around the city there shall be twelve gates, as exits for each tribe: for Reuben, Judah, and Levi to the north; Joseph, Benjamin, and Dan to the east; Simeon, Issachar, and Zebulun to the south; and Gad, Asher, and Naphtali to the west. And the city shall be called, "The LORD is there" (48:35).

DANIEL

With the vessels of the temple, the king of Judah and the leading Jews are taken captive to Babylon by Nebuchadnezzar. The king of Babylon asks that certain youths who are especially handsome and wise be taught the language and culture of the Chaldeans, that they might serve in his court. Daniel, Hananiah, Mishael, and Azariah are among the young men.

These young Jews are very concerned not to eat and drink from the table of the king, as he has prescribed for all the youths, for they do not wish to defile themselves with meat and wine sacrificed to idols. So they request of the eunuch caring for them that they be given only vegetables and water. He allows it for ten days as a test, and afterward finds them healthier in appearance than all the rest. So they are kept from defilement by the grace of God.

Old Testament

YHWH also blesses them with great skill for learning, as well as understanding of visions and dreams; and so at the end of their three years of training they prove to be wiser than all the other youths, and indeed "ten times better than all the magicians and enchanters" (1:20) in Chaldea.

O LORD, thank you for the blessing of wisdom which comes only from you and which you give to those who are faithful to your Word.

The Dream

Nebuchadnezzar has a dream that greatly troubles him and keeps him from sleep. So he summons all his wise men – magicians, enchanters, sorcerers – and insists they tell him not only the dream's interpretation, but the dream itself, lest they all be put to death. "There is not a man on earth who can meet the king's demand" (2:10), they respond; and so, in his fury, Nebuchadnezzar decrees that they be slain.

But Daniel steps into the breach and speaks with prudence, requesting audience with the king before he kills him and all the other wise men. He and his three companions then seek the mercy of God… and the LORD answers their prayers.

The God of Heaven reveals to Daniel in a vision in the night the dream the king had of a terrifying, shining image with a head of gold, chest and arms of silver, belly and thighs of bronze, legs of iron and feet of iron mixed with clay. A stone cut from a mountain by no human hand smites the figure on its divided feet… and the whole image is crushed into dust that utterly disappears in the wind.

Though Nebuchadnezzar is a great king, a head of gold appointed by the LORD, and though other mighty kingdoms shall follow him, all the kingdoms of this earth shall come to naught, shall be overcome by the King of kings and Lord of lords, Jesus Christ, and His rule shall last for ever.

For the wisdom Daniel imparts, the humbled king gives him rule over all of Babylon. Daniel transfers this power to his friends so he can remain at the court.

The Fiery Furnace

Nebuchadnezzar sets up a magnificent image of gold, sixty cubits high and six cubits wide, and orders all his officials of whatever nation or tongue to bow down and worship it, or be cast into the fiery furnace. Shadrach, Meshach and Abednego, Daniel's three friends, refuse to obey the king's command, even to his face. And so they are bound and thrown into the furnace, which is heated seven times more than usual… so hot that it kills the men who carry them.

But in the LORD they trust and their prayer for mercy He hears. They confess their sins and the sins of Jerusalem, for which exile has come upon them, and their "contrite heart and humble spirit" (3:16b) is acceptable to God as if it were a sacrifice of thousands of rams and bulls and lambs.

By a moist wind YHWH protects them from the flames, and so with one voice these three faithful souls praise Him and all His Creation. By the heavens above and all the elements of wind and rain, cold and heat; by all the earth's mountains and seas and all the creatures that swim or crawl or fly; and by man himself and Israel, His humble servant, the LORD is blessed… for His mercy endures for ever!

The three just men come out of the furnace without even the smell of smoke upon them, and Nebuchadnezzar is astonished, himself brought to bless God and declare His glory and the wonders He has done, even by a letter to all nations.

The king is then put into a furnace of his own, cast down from his pride and out from among men to crawl on the ground and eat grass like a beast, as his hair grows long and his nails become as bird's claws. But from this forsaken state he is raised to greater glory when he comes to his senses and extols the LORD of all, whose kingdom lasts for ever.

The Handwriting and the Den of Lions

Though he has witnessed the humiliation of his father, Belshazzar does not learn from it, but acts with great pride in the sight of God. At a feast he and his friends drink wine from the vessels

Nebuchadnezzar took from the temple in Jerusalem, praising the false gods of silver and gold.

And so a hand is sent from the LORD to write on the wall before his eyes. The king is greatly alarmed, and more so do his knees knock when his magicians cannot read the writing for him. But Daniel is called in and declares to the king his vain pride and the seriousness of his offense. He reads the writing on the wall, telling Belshazzar his days are numbered and he has been found wanting – the kingdom will be torn from him and the Chaldeans. That very night he is slain and Darius the Mede takes his throne.

Darius appoints Daniel one of the three men to preside over his kingdom, and soon decides to set him alone over all. The other leaders take offense but cannot find any fault in Daniel, and so have no grounds for complaint. They must therefore invent one, devising a law that for a month no man shall pray to any god or man but the king. They then have cause to cast Daniel into the lion's den for worshiping the LORD with his windows open to Jerusalem.

Darius is very distressed and seeks to make excuse for Daniel, but the law he has signed is irrevocable… so he can but fast all night for the great prophet's deliverance. At dawn the king rejoices to find Daniel alive, preserved from the mouths of the lions by the Most High. His accusers are then made to take his place, and the living God is praised by Darius in decree to all the earth.

Kings come and go but indeed the wise and blameless Daniel remains in the court till the end of the exile.

Four Beasts and a Ram

Daniel is given two visions in the night. The first one is of four great beasts: one like a lion that becomes like a man; another like a bear that devours much flesh; a third like a leopard given dominion; and a fourth most terrible and exceedingly strong, with iron teeth, stomping feet, and bronze claws. From the fourth comes a little horn displacing three of its ten, with eyes and a mouth speaking arrogantly. This is a king of greater terror than the rest who will seek even to change the Law of God as he makes terrible war against His saints. He will prevail until the Ancient One – who appears in the midst of

Daniel's vision – comes on a throne of burning fire and destroys him in the flames. Then will the saints receive the everlasting kingdom.

Daniel's second vision is of a ram with two horns (the kings of Media and Persia) charging west and north and south, destroying all in its path and exalting itself till a he-goat from the west (Greece) comes and runs it into the ground. A little horn rises from one of the he-goat's four and magnifies itself even up to the Prince of Heaven, overthrowing His sanctuary and its burnt offering and casting truth itself to the ground. But after 2,300 days the sanctuary is restored, as by no human hand this king of bold countenance is utterly broken.

But the vision is for many days hence (when the Son of God is on the horizon), so Gabriel instructs Daniel to seal it up for now. Afterward the prophet lays sick for days, not able to understand what he has seen, despite the angel's interpretation.

The End Times

As Israel returns from Babylonian exile, an aged Daniel seeks to understand his visions and what will become of his people. He fasts and mourns three full weeks and word is sent to him in vision of a terrifying figure with a face like lightning, eyes like flaming torches, and arms and legs like burnished bronze. All strength departs from Daniel, and on hearing the sound of this great One's voice… he falls on his face to the ground, asleep.

The prophet must be touched once, again, and a third time to raise him first to his knees, then trembling to his feet, and finally that he might speak, and hear the word of the vision. He is told of the kings that will rise in Persia, Egypt, Greece, and Rome, and the wars that will be fought between the kings of north and south… and how these kings will exalt themselves. Most importantly, he is told of the time of the temple's profanation, when the continual burnt offering will be taken away and the desolating abomination set up. Then Michael shall arise in a time of great trouble and the end will be upon all, and the final judgment as well.

Daniel cannot comprehend the time prescribed for the end (and would you presume to do so, my friend?), even though the number of days (3½ years) is spelled out for him – he cannot see Jesus though

He stands before him. (This is the span of our Savior's life, but who can say whence He comes or whither He goes? Who can know the Son without seeing the Father, and who is there that sees the Father?)

So the words of the vision are sealed up and Daniel goes to his rest; for those whose names are written in the Book of Life shall awaken to everlasting glory, but others to everlasting contempt. (And even the faithful and wise must be purified by suffering, that they may be made white for the kingdom of God.)

Susanna

We now go from an aged, dying Daniel watching the return of the exiles, to the very beginning of his call, when he is first infused with wisdom by the Holy Spirit, even as a boy. (Since this incident occurs before Daniel's training in the Babylonian court, it might be more appropriately placed at the beginning of the book, to give proper context.)

Should not Daniel's reputation for great wisdom go forth from this day? For he saves the innocent blood of a particularly righteous woman even as she is being led away to death. Susanna is indeed a woman in whom nothing shameful has ever been found, the wife and daughter of most honored men who follow well the Law of Moses.

But two elders who serve as judges here in Babylon are filled with lust for her beauty. They hide in her garden and one day find her alone as she prepares to bathe. But she does not relent to their wicked demands to lie with them, despite their threats of condemnation – better to fall into their hands than God's.

Because of the elders' standing as judges, all the people believe their testimony that they discovered Susanna in the embrace of a young man. But the Spirit stirs up young Daniel to call everyone back to court, where he uncovers their lie. He asks each separately under what tree they saw Susanna committing adultery. The two contradict each other and are thus led off to their death, as all rejoice at the exoneration of an innocent woman and Daniel's remarkable wisdom.

Bel and the Dragon

The Book of Daniel ends with stories of the great prophet exposing the false nature of two idols of Babylon. Cyrus has come to power, and he comes to know, too, by Daniel's wisdom, that there is no other god but the living God of the Jews.

First, Bel, a statue of clay covered in brass – which the king and his subjects earnestly believe consumes the mounds of food and wine they place before it each night – is shown by Daniel to be quite empty of life.

The prophet laughs when asked by the king to worship Bel as a living god. He accepts the king's challenge to prove it does not eat the food it's given by spreading ashes on the temple floor before the king seals the door. The next morning when Daniel and the king return, footprints of the seventy priests and their families are visible all around. And so these deceivers are all killed, and Bel and his temple destroyed.

Then Daniel bursts open a dragon the Babylonians worship (which, though living, certainly is not a god) by feeding it fat mixed with pitch. The king and the people then see what they have been worshiping! But the Babylonians are not happy about having their false gods destroyed, and so they force the king, whom they accuse of being a Jew, to throw Daniel into the lions' den for six days. Though the lions are not given their daily portion of two humans and two sheep, Daniel they do not eat... and the prophet Habakkuk is transported from Judea by the Spirit to feed Daniel with bread and pottage.

Upon finding Daniel alive on the seventh day, the king casts to the lions those who conspired against him, and praises the living God. This is the same Cyrus who calls for the return of the Jews from Babylon (and was prophesied by the mighty Isaiah).

Praised be God for His wisdom! and for His remaining with Daniel until his old age.

# HOSEA

In the time before the exile, the LORD calls Hosea not only to speak His Word but to live it, particularly in marriage, first to a harlot and then to an adulteress. For such is the people of Israel to their God, turning from Him who is their husband to sell themselves in worship to Baal.

With his first wife Hosea has three children, whose names reveal YHWH's relationship to wayward Israel: though they are the seed of God, them He will Not Pity, for they are Not His People. Yet in virtually the same breath the LORD declares that in the end He will gather together Israel and Judah – which does not yet lose God's favor, but shall – as His sons under one King, Jesus Christ.

But that day is still far away; now the LORD God is about to uncover the lewdness of His people. There shall come a day when Jezreel will say to his brother, "'My people,' and to his sister, 'She has obtained pity'" (2:1)… but now let their mother cry out to her forsaken husband; let her turn from her lovers in whom she trusted. Let her put away her harlotry and her adultery and realize whose hand feeds her.

Yes, the LORD will "put an end to all her mirth… lay waste her vines" (2:11,12), and wall up her way to her lovers; but after many days He will allure her to the wilderness and speak tenderly to her, and she shall again call Him "My husband" and lie down in safety for ever. She shall return and seek her God, and He will again have pity and make her as His own.

Sowing the Wind

How worthless Israel has become, how corrupt in faithlessness, in wickedness… in their harlotry. And Judah joins them in such vanity. And so the LORD's people "are destroyed for lack of knowledge" (4:6) of Him and His ways.

The priests lead the people in their lawlessness, in their greed for iniquity; and so the land is filled with murderers and thieves, with men who "go aside with harlots, and sacrifice with cult prostitutes" (4:14). And so the land shall become a desolation, void of even bird or beast or fish – and the earth shall yield no grain. O the emptiness that encompasses Israel for her sins!

Neither Israel nor Judah shall find healing, for they cry out not in repentance for their transgressions against the living God, for their worshiping idols of wood and gold, but for the food that is missing from their bellies now. Their hearts are not with the LORD; their love is not steadfast but passes like a morning cloud. Still they murder, still they commit great horrors in the sight of God. Like a dove without sense they seek their help from Egypt and Assyria rather than YHWH – still they break His Covenant with them.

And so, since "they sow the wind... they shall reap the whirlwind" (8:7) of the LORD's anger. They burn with lust and drunkenness, but He burns with a chastising justice that shall not depart from them. His fire shall come upon their cities and leave them barren.

Days of Punishment

Israel shall be punished for all her sins; she shall bear her guilt. She shall not remain in the land of the LORD but eat unclean food under the yoke of foreign rule. Because they consecrate themselves to Baal, because they turn from Him who holds them in His arms of compassion and kiss calves rather than His holy face... He who loves them will become as a roaring lion to them, and mothers with their children will be dashed to pieces by His chastising hand.

O how it troubles the LORD to destroy His people! O how His heart recoils to see them abandoned of His love and suffering in the dust. But His great compassion He must hide from His eyes – Death and Sheol must have their day of plague and destruction.

How faithful was Jacob to YHWH, weeping and seeking His favor without pause... and so, he was blessed to know His holy NAME. But now God speaks to Israel only to condemn their wicked deeds, to break down the altars they have multiplied in their arrogance and vanity. Like chaff they shall be blown away.

Hear the LORD's call to return to His love; know that in His arms the orphan indeed finds mercy. Confess your guilt, turn from your idols... beg Him to take away your iniquity and you shall blossom like the lily and flourish as a garden in His sight. Be wise and understand the ways of God – do not stumble in them. And in His arms with Israel He shall hold you once more.

JOEL

"The day of the LORD is coming; it is near, a day of darkness and gloom, a day of clouds and thick darkness" (2:1-2). A powerful army descends upon the land with the rumbling of chariots. Running like war horses they leap upon the city, the earth quaking and fire devouring before them. A nation powerful and without number, whose teeth are lions' teeth, destroys the grain like swarming locusts and lays waste the vines.

O how the priests mourn! For all offerings are cut off from the temple. The tillers of the earth are utterly confounded, for the trees of the field are all withered to their roots – there is no fruit of gladness in the land. Even the wild beasts cry out, for their brooks are dried up.

Gird on sackcloth and proclaim a fast; lament and cry unto the LORD. Return to Him rending your hearts and weeping aloud, and perhaps He may have mercy on you. Perhaps the crackling of the flame you shall avoid and the stubble will not be consumed before your eyes.

"Spare thy people, O LORD, and make not thy heritage a reproach" (2:17). Will you utterly destroy your people, the house in which you dwell? Look upon our solemn assembly and leave a blessing in your wake, for indeed your Day is at hand.

The Valley of Decision

"The sun shall be turned to darkness, and the moon to blood" (2:31) on the day God sits in judgment. He will draw all the nations before Himself; all the warriors with their swords shall stand in His presence. And on that day Egypt and Edom, Tyre and Sidon and the Philistines, will be made a desolate wilderness: all those who have done violence to Judah will be no more as the LORD avenges His people. He will be a refuge to His Chosen and Jerusalem shall again be holy.

"The mountains shall drip sweet wine" (3:18), for YHWH will have pity on His people. He will drive their oppressors from them and make their land fruitful once more. The fields will be green and the threshing floor full of grain when the LORD God restores the fortunes of Israel, counteracting all the punishment He has inflicted on them and taking away their shame for ever.

The LORD will be in the midst of His chosen ones and will pour out His Spirit upon them that day. From young to old, all shall prophesy, as vision returns to His fold. Like rain streaming down and watering the earth, so shall His Spirit be after He has judged the nations and brought justice to Jerusalem, requiting all her enemies who have sold her into slavery and made her practice harlotry.

Yes, the LORD dwells in Zion, and all souls shall know the truth of His presence among men.

AMOS

After roaring against Damascus and Gaza, Edom and the Ammonites and Moab, for ripping up women with child, carrying Israel into exile, and burning the bones of kings; after prophesying that these – along with Judah, for her rejecting the Law of God – will be beset by fire which will devour their strongholds and cause them either to perish or be sent into exile… Amos' attention is turned to the principal object of the LORD's condemnation, Israel.

Old Testament

O how the LORD will punish His chosen people for all their iniquities! How wicked their deeds have become: selling the righteous and the needy into slavery, trampling the heads of the poor, and profaning God's holy NAME by giving themselves in lust and drunkenness to every false god they encounter. Though the LORD destroyed giants before them as He brought them up from Egypt to the Promised Land, the mouths of the prophets they now close, as from their God they resolutely turn their heads.

And so the mighty shall fall to the dust and their swift horses be stopped in their tracks as their adversaries indeed descend upon them and violently plunder their land. They shall be cast out of the LORD's sight with but a bare remnant rescued from the mouth of the lion. Their vain altars and great houses shall come to an end.

Darkness

YHWH tries to warn His people, sending punishments on them that they might turn from sin: withholding bread and rain; raining on one city and not another, one field and not another; laying waste garden and vineyard; sending pestilence and slaying their young men with the sword; burning some places like Sodom and Gomorrah... yet they do not return to Him "who forms the mountains and creates the wind" (4:13), who "darkens the day into night" (5:8). And so, what remains but for them to fall and rise no more, to be taken every one into exile from His sight?

"Prepare to meet your God, O Israel!" (4:12). For all your transgressions against the LORD and against His righteous poor, for your failure to "let justice roll down like waters" (5:24), you shall know the utter darkness and gloom of His coming Day. There shall be wailing in the streets, in the farmlands, and in the vineyards. Those who stretch themselves on beds of ivory and drink bowls of wine shall be the first to know great woe, but none shall be spared – not a soul, not a bone, shall be left within a single home, as all houses are smashed to pieces. There shall be revelry no more.

The LORD will not accept your sacrifices, nor does He listen to the noise of your songs; for He knows your hearts are set on the gods in your hands, the vain images you create in opposition to His holy NAME. And so the sun shall set upon you.

Exile

Though the LORD withhold locust and fire, a plumb line shall be set in the midst of Israel: its king shall die by the sword and all its people go into exile. Though the priest of Bethel attempt to silence Amos' tongue, the word given this poor herdsman shall come to pass.

The songs of the temple will become wailings for Jacob's trampling on the needy and dealing deceitfully – they spurn the Sabbath and so will sink to the depths for their pride. On that day the sun shall go down at noon and all the people mourn as for an only son. There shall be a famine for hearing the Word of God and even the young shall faint for thirst. And though they hide in the pit of Sheol or on the heights of Carmel, the LORD will find them and cast them forth, for His eyes are on them "for evil and not for good" (9:4).

God in His mercy will not utterly destroy Jacob as other nations; the house of David will be rebuilt and plowman shall overtake reaper on the day Jesus sits on His throne… but though their fortunes shall be thus restored, none will escape now the hand of the LORD or the exile that is upon them. They shall know that YHWH is God, "He who touches the earth and it melts" (9:5).

OBADIAH

The prophecy against Edom, land of the brother of Jacob: he who is proud shall be utterly despised. He who made his dwelling on high, saying, "Who will bring me down to the ground?" (3), is pillaged by the LORD… and of him nothing remains. For he has done violence to his brother Jacob; he has rejoiced over the ruin of Judah, looting his goods and delivering up his survivors on the day of his distress. On the day foreigners came to carry Jacob away, Edom acted like one of them.

And so he shall be punished with all the nations on the day of the LORD; then all his deeds will return upon his own head. Those in whom he trusted shall cut off every man among them by slaughter.

Old Testament

For God will save His people: in Mount Zion alone shall be those that escape. Jacob shall return to his possessions, but Esau shall be burned to stubble by the flame that comes from the house of Joseph.

The exiles of Israel will return and take possession of the cities of Edom: "Saviors shall go up to Mount Zion to rule Mount Esau" (21). For it is the LORD to whom the kingdom belongs; it is He alone in whom all must trust.

Let all men turn away from sin, from their vain boast, and look kindly on their brother... lest they be brought down to the dust.

JONAH

The Father has pity on all who repent of their sin, for all are His children, made by His hand and given breath by the power of His Spirit. And should we wish to see evil done to any man?

Jonah must learn this lesson. Though he is of the chosen race and worships the only true God of Heaven and earth, he and his people do not alone have a home in the YHWH's compassionate heart. Even their enemies He will bless if they heed His warning against them and humble themselves before Him.

Jonah does all he can to escape the LORD and the word He has placed on his soul. He is called to proclaim destruction upon Nineveh, to cry out against the great city, a city which has been Israel's oppressor. But his greatest fear is that the people (and beasts) of Nineveh will repent at his word and God will have pity on them.... He thinks that if he doesn't speak, they will simply perish.

Jonah is willing even to die to see his enemy destroyed. And so he takes a ship in the opposite direction; and so when his guilt is discovered he tells the mariners to throw him into the raging sea. These pagans react with horror at how he has spurned the call of the LORD God. Indeed, they seem to have greater faith than the great prophet himself, hesitating to throw him into the sea to calm its waves, and then sacrificing to the LORD upon being saved.

But from the belly of the whale, from the depths of Sheol, Jonah finally cries out (and so is spewed out)... and then does as God commands. And the Ninevites repent and are spared.

The waters of selfishness and pride and anger close in on all of us, and they grow more tempestuous as we continue to harden our hearts. Who will thank the LORD for the mercy He offers all souls? Who will repent of his sins in sackcloth and ashes? Who will praise God for His blessings, even when they are taken away? Who can love even His enemies?

MICAH

The Word of the LORD against Samaria and Jerusalem for all their sins and transgressions: a heap of ruins they shall become, for God goes forth to tread upon them.

O what iniquity Israel has learned from the nations around them and from their idols! What wickedness is in their hands – how they oppress the peaceful of the land! Flaying their skin and breaking their bones and grinding them up like meat to feed their greedy bellies... and shall their prophets declare "Peace"?

"The sun shall go down upon the prophets, and the day shall be black over them" (3:6). In darkness they dwell and to darkness shall all the people come who listen to these seers that seek only to fill their stomachs and their pockets. The true prophet is told not to preach, not to speak of the imminent destruction coming upon such a wayward nation – it is only the preaching of wine and strong drink Jacob heeds.

Even to the gates of Jerusalem has such evil come, and so the Word of God cannot remain in the land. Disgrace will indeed overtake Israel and Judah, and the Spirit upon Micah be proved true. Let them be silent before Him. Let them cover their lips, those who abhor justice and build Zion with blood; and the LORD will gather a remnant from among them.

Old Testament

Jesus Prophesied

From Bethlehem shall come forth "One who is to be ruler in Israel, whose origin is from of old" (5:2), even the Son of God, the Lord Jesus Christ. Though Israel be given up to travail until His time, though she writhe and groan like a woman about to give birth until the day the Savior stands in our midst, it shall indeed come to pass in the latter days that Zion shall be as the highest of mountains and all nations will stream toward the Word of the LORD that goes forth from Jerusalem.

He shall judge the nations and make all peoples "beat their swords into plowshares" (4:3), for He will be peace for every soul who walks in the LORD's holy NAME. For ever the Son will reign over the remnant of God's Chosen. Though now they cry aloud, though now a siege is laid against them and they are taken to Babylon, the poor and lame will arise with their Servant King and trample down their enemies, destroying horse and chariot and all the evil images from disobedient lands.

The LORD cannot forget the wicked treasures stored up by rich men of violence and lying tongues, and so He must smite their evil with a desolating hunger; "all lie in wait for blood" (7:2) and, as Jesus has said, a man's enemies are of his own house (cf. Mt.10:36)... yet the saving acts of God will again be known – His redemption shall indeed come. The nations shall tremble in fear before Him who rules all as He brings forth light to those who walk humbly. On that Day the compassionate heart of YHWH shall be fully revealed as He treads down our iniquities and "cast[s] all our sins into the depths of the sea" (7:19). Praise the LORD for His steadfast love, brought to us in His only Son!

NAHUM

Nahum prophesies against Nineveh, the bloody city, for there is none upon whom her unceasing evil has not come. The LORD will break her yoke off the neck of His people and so free them from affliction. Though Assyria be numerous and strong, YHWH, whose "way is in whirlwind and storm" (1:3), who rebukes the sea and dries up rivers, before whom mountains quake and the earth is laid waste... will pour out his burning wrath like an overflowing flood, and she shall be reduced to dust.

Thus does the LORD do to all who plot against Him, who worship graven images and lead others to such desolation. Their violence and lies will come back on their own heads; the horses and chariots with which they trample the innocent underfoot will come rumbling out of Heaven against them – flashing like flame they come charging, leaving heaps of corpses behind.

This is Good News to God's people; it is the declaration of peace in the mouths of His apostles and prophets: eternal ruin crashes down on those who trust in their own strength as their little ones are dashed to pieces, but eternal life is found by the LORD's holy ones in the wake of His devouring fire.

The vengeance of the LORD against His adversaries is sure as the rising sun; though He is slow to anger, He will "by no means clear the guilty" (1:3).

HABAKKUK

Habakkuk stands on the tower to watch and wait for answer from the LORD, who sends the Chaldeans forth swift as eagles to devour the land with violence and carry off captives like sand. Why is this dread nation permitted to work terror and plunder many peoples; why do the wicked surround the righteous, perverting justice and shedding their blood? Why are those whose own might is their god, who worship the work of their own hands, trusting in idols with no breath in them... why are these given free reign for evil?

And to Habakkuk answer comes. Indeed, the LORD chastises His people. For a time He allows such punishment to come upon them – but He shall remember His mercy. Brightness shall flash forth from the hand of Him who makes the mountains writhe and the sun and moon stand still in the sky. He shall unsheathe His bow and "bestride the earth in fury" (3:12); for the salvation of His anointed, He will crush the head of the wicked, bringing upon them lasting woe.

Believe. Believe and know. Learn from the faith of Habakkuk who, though there be no sheep in the pasture or fruit on the vine, though terror surrounds him on every side, still rejoices in God and takes refuge in His strength. "For the earth will be filled with the knowledge of the glory of the LORD" (2:14), despite the impending darkness. The vision is sure. Find your hope in the eternal God.

ZEPHANIAH

The LORD again promises to restore the fortunes of Israel and Jerusalem; but, again, not before His chastising hand falls heavily upon them. For they do not seek Him but follow in the ways of the idolatrous nations around them.

Indeed, "all the earth shall be consumed" (3:8) in the jealous wrath of the Most High, for violence and fraud pollute all nations and peoples. And so, Moab and Ethiopia and Nineveh and all the cities that exalt themselves as gods shall become a waste for ever, lands without bird or beast or inhabitant of any worth – a salt pit like Sodom and Gomorrah. These wicked nations who have led Judah astray with their lies will be destroyed for their taunts against the children of God. And though in Jerusalem a remnant shall thus be found, she shall not be spared His wrath for her sins against Him.

The Day of the LORD will come with great fury and men will cry out in anguish and distress; the trumpet shall blast and the lofty battlements be torn down as the blood of the arrogant is poured out on the ground. But there is hope for the morning after: when YHWH has removed all the haughty from His sight, He will rejoice in His lowly ones and sing over them as at festival... and they shall rejoice with Him. Even those of distant nations shall have their speech purified that they might call on the NAME of God.

And so, do not fear, you humble ones who love the LORD and all that is good: your shame shall be taken away and your name be remembered and praised on that day.

HAGGAI

The people of Judah have recently returned from exile in Babylon, but they do not fare well. Rain is withheld and so the earth does not produce fruit. The LORD smites their land with blight and mildew and hail, and they have nothing to show for the work they have done: "he who earns wages earns wages to put them into a bag with holes" (6).

Why do the returning exiles experience such futility? Why is the LORD set against them? Because they dwell in paneled houses while the temple lies in ruins. They care more for their own concerns than the worship of God. And so the Word of YHWH comes to Haggai to encourage the governor and the priest and all the people to build the house of God that they might find the blessing of His presence among them.

What a state the temple is in! It is as nothing compared to its former glory. Yet the LORD assures governor and priest and people that His Spirit abides with them, and that He will again fill His house with splendor, a splendor greater even than the former one.

Three months later when the foundation is laid, the LORD still berates His people for the uncleanness of their offerings; but He also promises that from this day forth matters shall be different. From this day He will bless them with seed and wine and fruits, and more than this – He shall shake the heavens and bring the treasures of the nations into their house! The strength of kingdoms will be overthrown and the king of Judah shall be the LORD's chosen One. Set your hearts on that Day.

Old Testament

ZECHARIAH

Zechariah prophesies at the same time as Haggai, as the exiles rebuild the temple. He calls them to learn from their fathers' errors and return to God. A number of visions Zechariah is given as the Word of the LORD and His angel come to him to reveal the compassion He shall have on Israel – Jerusalem will again prosper.

The four horns that have scattered Judah will be driven down by four smiths. A man goes forth to measure Jerusalem, which shall be inhabited by such a great multitude that walls shall not contain it – the LORD Himself will be their wall, for He will dwell in their midst. He rouses Himself from His holy dwelling to plunder the nations and so save His Chosen. (Be silent before Him.)

Joshua the high priest and Zerubbabel the governor shall be blessed to stand beside the all-seeing power of God. Filthy garments are removed from Joshua as Satan is rebuked and the iniquity of Jerusalem taken away. Clothed in grace, by the Spirit of God Joshua and Zerubbabel shall accomplish the LORD's will… though the true Branch of His holy vine is yet to come.

A flying scroll goes out to consume the house of the thief and the liar; a leaden cover is thrust down over the ephah holding wickedness… and the four chariots with their horses go to the four winds of heaven to patrol the earth, whose rest shall not last long.

Let Joshua be crowned and the temple rebuilt, and let all "diligently obey the voice of the LORD" (6:15).

Fasting to Feasting

Great wrath has come upon God's people for their disobedience to His Word. He called them to kindness and mercy but they oppressed the widow and the orphan instead, devising evil in their hearts. And so their land was made desolate. And so they were scattered to foreign nations. And so they were made to fast.

But now the LORD purposes to do good to Jerusalem, to bring them peace and give their land its increase. He shall turn their fast days into feasts, and "the city shall be full of boys and girls playing in its streets" (8:5). There shall be great rejoicing at the marvels YHWH accomplishes in their midst – it "shall be as though [He] had not rejected them" (10:6).

He will tear down the nations that enslaved them; stripped of their wealth they shall writhe in anguish and remain uninhabited, their abominations ripped from their teeth and their idols forgotten for ever. Chariot and horse and battle bow shall be cast from Jerusalem and its survivors be made strong as a mighty warrior. People of every tongue will take hold of the Jew and beg to be brought to the temple, that they too might know God.

And so, let us not be afraid: the LORD will appear over us and march forth with His flock. We will be blessed with showers from on high and abundant grain, for our King comes to us "triumphant and victorious... humble and riding on an ass" (9:9). Rejoice in Him!

The Shepherd

There are none but worthless shepherds throughout the land, false prophets and diviners who profess lies. And the people follow them; all the people follow them, even Judah, and so they wander like lost sheep.

At the word of the LORD Zechariah takes upon himself the implements of a worthless shepherd and becomes as shepherd of those doomed to be slain. Three shepherds he destroys but the people reject the Grace he brings to them, and so God's mercy is taken from them. The staff of Vision is also broken, destroying the brotherhood between Judah and Israel.

Yet the arm of the worthless shepherds shall be wholly withered, for the LORD Himself will become Shepherd of all. Though all fight against Him, though they pierce through the Son He sends, though those even in His own house count out thirty pieces of silver for the life of the Savior – taking Him to be as worthless as the shepherds they follow so assiduously... yes, though the Shepherd be struck and the sheep scattered, though two-thirds of the people be cut off and the other third be refined as in fire (as they mourn as an only Son Him whom they have crucified), yet the feet of the Holy One will stand on the Mount of Olives and the LORD God come and dwell with His redeemed.

Old Testament

Though all the nations, including Judah, fight against Jerusalem, and their flesh and eyes and tongues rot upon them, there shall be a remnant from all the ends of the earth that will worship the Most High in His holy City. There a cleansing fountain is poured forth from Jesus' side for the salvation of souls, and no more does night remain: "Every pot in Jerusalem and Judah shall be sacred to the LORD of hosts" (14:21); all souls will glory in His NAME!

MALACHI

Malachi speaks the word of God against Israel and Judah, especially against the priests of the temple in Jerusalem, the sons of Levi. The LORD has favored Israel beyond any other nation, even his brother Esau, yet he despises his Father who loves him. Levi indeed stood in awe of the NAME of YHWH and offered true instruction and holy sacrifice; but now the priests offer polluted food on His altar. The blind and the lame and the sick they sacrifice to God, thinking Him worthy of nothing more... and of His tithes they rob Him.

Among the nations the NAME of the LORD is great and greatly respected, but His own people break His Covenant with them and so turn their blessing into a curse. They yoke themselves to a foreign god, despising the purity of the wife of their youth, and so producing no godly offspring. Rather, they call the arrogant blessed and desire the prosperity of evildoers, saying it is vain to serve the LORD.

But God will come burning like an oven, refining in fire the souls of all. On that day He will reduce to stubble the sorcerers and adulterers, the oppressors and all the wicked. But those who fear God and speak of His NAME, He will spare – His Son shall rise upon them with healing rays and they will rejoice in His glory.

Now the LORD sends forth His messenger to prepare His way; Elijah goes before Him to warn of the great and terrible Day coming upon all mankind. Let the hearts of fathers turn to their children and the children's to their fathers... and let all hearts turn to the Father of all!

1 MACCABEES

After Alexander defeats Darius and becomes king of Persia and the Medes (in addition to the Greeks), he advances to the ends of the earth, plundering many nations and putting their kings to death. Puffed up by pride he falls sick, but before he dies divides his kingdom among his officers, who cause many evils on the earth.

Under Antiochus Epiphanes, lawless men from Israel make covenant with the Gentiles. A gymnasium is built in Jerusalem, and the men cover their marks of circumcision and abandon themselves to iniquity. Then after Antiochus conquers Egypt, he comes to Jerusalem and takes all of value from the sanctuary, stripping it bare of silver and gold and all its treasure. Young men and old mourn throughout Israel.

Two years later the king's tax collector falls suddenly upon the city, plundering it and burning it with fire, then making it their citadel. Jerusalem becomes a dwelling of strangers where innocent blood is shed. Finally, the king demands all nations become one people, each abandoning its own customs.

And so, in 167 B.C. a desolating sacrilege is erected on the altar in Jerusalem, the books of the Law are torn to pieces and burned, and anyone found adhering to the Law is put to death – "and they hung the [circumcised] infants from their mothers' necks" (1:61). Many stand firm and choose to die, but what great wrath is upon Israel for its apostasy, for its turning so blatantly from the ways of the LORD to court the evil power of this world.

Mattathias

Seeing the blasphemies committed in Jerusalem, Mattathias takes his five sons and goes to Modein. There he laments the ruin upon his people and the holy city. The glory of the Jews is laid waste and her babes killed in the streets – who does not seize her spoils? And so Mattathias and his sons put on sackcloth and mourn.

Soon the officers of the king come to Modein to impose the unholy sacrifices. They approach Mattathias first, since he is a great leader, and attempt to seduce him with the king's honors. But Mattathias loudly proclaims his faithfulness to the Covenant and utterly refuses to obey the king's command. When a Jew comes forward to offer sacrifice, Mattathias is filled with the zeal of Phinehas and kills him upon the altar. He also kills the king's officer, tears down the altar, and calls all faithful Jews to follow him into the wilderness.

Troops from Jerusalem pursue them to their hiding place, and on the Sabbath day slaughter a thousand souls who refuse to fight. But Mattathias and his friends decide thereafter to take up arms to save the nation even if it be the Sabbath. Joined by mighty warriors, they proceed to strike down sinners, destroy their altars, and circumcise all the boys... thus rescuing the Law from the hands of the Gentiles.

When the day draws near for Mattathias to die, he invokes the names of Abraham and Joseph, Joshua and David, Elijah, Daniel, and all who put their trust in God and so find His blessing. He calls his children to be courageous and gives command of the army to Judas Maccabeus.

Judas Maccabeus

Judas takes command of the army of Israel and fights valiantly for his people and his God. A giant of war roaring like a lion, he destroys the ungodly from the land and delivers Judah from all its enemies, gaining great renown for his bravery.

First he defeats a large force from Samaria, taking the sword of their commander. Next with but a small company he crushes a strong army of ungodly men from Syria, declaring, "It is not on the size of the army that victory in battle depends, but strength comes from Heaven" (3:19). And so, like David, in the NAME of the LORD he mows down armies of increasingly greater size. And terror falls upon the Gentiles.

When Antiochus hears of the great victories of Judas, he gathers a large army of his own and has them sent against Judah. But this force of forty-seven thousand is no match for the three thousand with Judas

Maccabeus, for they fast and pray in the trampled temple, crying unto Heaven for help. As YHWH overwhelmed Pharaoh and his forces at the Red Sea, so He crushes the army of this evil king. Yes, smoke rises from their burning camp. A greater force of sixty-five thousand is also routed at the hands of Judas and his men, who are ever ready "to live or to die nobly" (4:35).

Encouraged by their success, Judas and his brothers turn their sights to Jerusalem; they go up and cleanse the sanctuary and rededicate it. They tear down the altar that had been defiled and remove the stones to a separate place. A new altar and a rebuilt sanctuary with all new accouterments they dedicate in great joy, three years from the very day the Gentiles profaned the holy place. This feast shall be remembered for eight days every year hence... and Mount Zion is fortified with high walls and strong towers.

Saving Their Brethren

The Gentiles round about become very angry when they hear that the Jews have rebuilt the altar and rededicated the sanctuary, and so they begin to destroy the Israelites living among them. But Judas makes war on those who lie in wait for Israel, delivering them a heavy blow – burning the towers in which they hide and crushing all before him.

Judas and his brothers then receive letters from Gilead and Galilee, begging that they come and rescue their fellow Israelites from annihilation at the hands of the Gentiles gathering against them. So Simon, Judas' brother, is sent to Galilee with three thousand men – who crush the Gentiles there (killing three thousand of them) – while eight thousand men are sent with Judas and his brother Jonathan to fight in Gilead. There they take city after city.

Judas comes to one city where Jews are already being attacked by a large company and crying unto Heaven. He encourages his men to fight for their brethren: so they sound their trumpets and cry aloud in prayer, and when the army before them realize it is Judas, they turn and flee... and eight thousand of them fall. The same commander gathers a larger force, but Judas does not hesitate at the stream between them. Every man is exhorted to attack, and as they cross the water en masse, again their enemies are destroyed... and they flee before them.

Both Simon and Judas gather the Israelites they have saved and lead them all together on pilgrimage to Jerusalem. Judas is forced to raze and plunder a town that does not let them pass through, but soon all come to the temple to praise and worship the LORD of all in great joy. The forces that remained in Jerusalem failed to listen to Judas and went out into battle to make a name for themselves, and so a number of them have fallen – but of those who went forth with Judas and Simon, not one was killed. And the brothers continue to conquer the nations round about.

Antiochus and His Son

After failing to take a rich temple in Elymais of Persia, Antiochus flees to Babylon. There he hears that his armies have been routed in Judea, and of how strong the Jews have become. On being told that they have broken down the abomination he erected in Jerusalem and that Judas and his men have surrounded the sanctuary with high walls again, in deep grief he takes to his bed sick, dying in this foreign land. Before he perishes he repents of the evils he has done in Jerusalem, having fallen upon it without cause – he knows it is for this he now dies. He leaves his young son and so his kingdom in the hands of Philip, but it is his commander Lysias who sets the boy up as king.

Back in Israel, Judas resolves to destroy those left in the citadel who trouble them. A few escape and with ungodly Israelites go to the new king to complain of the hostility of Judas and the threat the Jews are to his reign. Enraged, the king sets out for Judah with an army of one hundred and twenty thousand. Judas marches out to meet them, but their ranks are most impressive; arrayed around a number of elephants, their shields of gold and bronze set the hills ablaze. The Jews manage to kill a number of them, but when one valiant soul is crushed under the weight of an elephant he has killed, they flee before the army's royal might.

Jerusalem is besieged and it does not look good as the people have little food (this being the seventh year, when the land lies fallow). But when Lysias hears of his rival's attempt to seize the government in Antioch, he makes peace with the Jews, allowing them to follow their laws, so he can return and retake his own city... though not before breaking his word and tearing down the walls of Zion.

Treachery

Lysias and Antiochus are seized and killed, and Demetrius takes his seat on the throne. Led by one who covets the high priesthood, ungodly men from Israel come to the latest king with their accusations against Judas and his brethren. So the king sends a large force with them to take vengeance on Israel.

Some are duped by the peaceable terms Alcimus treacherously offers, but when these foolish ones and others who have deserted Israel are mercilessly slain, Judas stands up against the damage being done to his people – even greater than those wrought by the Gentiles are the evils of Alcimus. Seeing Judas' strength, the traitor returns to Demetrius seeking reinforcement.

Nicanor now comes with a larger army and likewise offers peaceable terms in Jerusalem. Judas becomes aware of his treachery and with the priests offers to God his prayer for help against this blasphemous man who promises the destruction of the temple. The LORD answers their hopes for deliverance. Nicanor is killed first in battle, and his army flees. They are pursued throughout Judea and not one of them is spared the sword. It is on the feast of Purim this great victory occurs, and so the day is renewed as one of great celebration. And Judah has a brief period of rest from its enemies.

Jonathan

Judas hears of the Romans' great strength and wisdom, and their loyalty to their friends, and so he makes alliance with those who subdue kings near and far. The Romans crush some countries and impose tribute on others, but Judas is most impressed by their lack of a king – as well as pride and envy – governed as they are by a Senate of 120 men constantly deliberating the welfare of the people and choosing a different man each year to rule over them. A bronze letter they send back to Jerusalem stating that each party will fight for the other and not support their enemies.

Yet Bacchides and Alcimus soon return to encamp against Jerusalem and, though he fights bravely despite being deserted by most of his army, crushing and pursuing his enemy in raging battle... Judas is eventually pursued himself, and he falls. And there is great mourning throughout Israel.

The lawless begin to take hold in the land, and so great distress is upon all. Jonathan is chosen to rule in his brother's place and Bacchides pursues him in the wilderness. Closed in on all sides, Jonathan and his men find their strength and cry out to Heaven for deliverance... and they defeat their enemy. Bacchides fortifies his strongholds throughout Judea, but when Alcimus is struck dumb and paralyzed after giving command to tear down the inner wall of the temple, he returns to his king. Two years later he comes back, but is soundly crushed, and takes his vengeance on the lawless men of Israel who caused him to return. He leaves making peace with Jonathan, and even restores captives to him. The sword then ceases and Jonathan has time to root out the ungodly from Israel.

Courting Jewish Favor

After five years Alexander son of Antiochus comes down against Demetrius, and both begin to court Jonathan's favor, that they might have his support in battle. First, Demetrius gives him authority to build an army, and releases the hostages in the citadel at Jerusalem. Jonathan starts to rebuild and fortify the city, and so the foreigners left in strongholds round about flee in fear.

Then Alexander hears of Jonathan and all his brave deeds and asks: "Shall we find another such man?" (10:16). He entreats him to be his ally, giving him a purple robe and a golden crown and declaring him high priest.

When Demetrius hears of Alexander's move, he makes Jonathan and the Jews great promises: he will release them from all taxes, set free all their captives, give them additional lands, pay for the rebuilding of the sanctuary and provide regular funds for its service.

But the Jews do not believe Demetrius, remembering all his evil against them, and so give their favor to Alexander.

Alexander crushes and kills Demetrius and then establishes alliance with Egypt, marrying Cleopatra, the daughter of Ptolemy, and Jonathan is invited to the celebration. Alexander decrees that no lawless man is to bring charges against Jonathan, and enrolls him among his chief friends.

A few years later when the son of Demetrius returns to his land, Alexander makes a retreat. But Jonathan stands strong against Demetrius' proud boasts and overwhelms his army in battle, plundering their strongholds and burning their temple. He then gains even greater honor from Alexander.

Changing of Kings

Ptolemy goes through Alexander's kingdom and takes its cities by trickery. In his covetousness he devises great evil against his son-in-law, even taking Cleopatra and giving her to Demetrius to make alliance with him. He puts on the crown of Asia as well as Egypt.

Alexander hears of it and comes against him, but is put to flight and beheaded by the Arabs with whom he takes refuge. Three days later Ptolemy also dies, so Demetrius then becomes king. Jonathan wins Demetrius' favor, and the new king honors him and declares to the Jews the return of their land and release from all taxes.

But Demetrius' troops and people rebel against him and cause him to take sanctuary in his palace. He calls to the Jews for help, and three thousand of them kill one hundred thousand men in Antioch in a single day; they thus save the king and return to Jerusalem with much spoil. Yet Demetrius begins to greatly oppress Jonathan.

When Trypho, who had served in Demetrius' army, returns with Alexander's son Antiochus, he routs Demetrius and takes control of Antioch. Antiochus curries Jonathan's favor, and makes him a great friend of the new king. Jonathan sets forth traveling beyond the river, finding welcome in some cities and destroying those who shut him out. When foreigners come to fight against him at Gennesaret, he stands with but three other men and a prayer to the LORD... and routs them all. He is soon joined in pursuit of his enemies by the men who had abandoned him.

Returning again to Jerusalem, Jonathan seeks to renew Jewish friendship with the Romans and the Spartans; he has not called on them because he has had the help of God, and some time has passed without communication. His letters find welcome and promise of alliance.

The Death of Jonathan

Demetrius returns to wage war against Jonathan, but Jonathan marches out of Jerusalem to meet him; and Demetrius' force flees in the night when they realize the Jews are ready for their surprise attack. Upon returning to Jerusalem, Jonathan sets about building up strongholds in Judea, isolating the citadel and raising the walls of the holy city.

Trypho marches toward Judah with plans to kill Jonathan, but Jonathan meets him with forty thousand troops. So Trypho receives him with honor and gifts, deceitfully telling him he is sent to give him Ptolemais to rule. Jonathan takes only one thousand men with him – leaving another two thousand in Galilee – all of whom are killed by the men of Ptolemais when they close the gates upon them. Jonathan, too, is believed dead, and is mourned; but the two thousand in Galilee remain strong and turn back Trypho and his troops.

Simon stands up to take the place of his brother and so rekindles the spirit of the people; but when Trypho comes to invade Judah again, against his better judgment Simon appeases the people and gives Trypho a hundred talents of silver and two of Jonathan's sons as hostages, to insure the release of Jonathan. Trypho breaks his word but is prevented from invading by a severe snowfall. He turns back to his own country, but not before killing Jonathan. All Israel bewails the death of Jonathan many days, and Simon erects a monumental tomb for his family – a pyramid for each member.

Trypho kills Antiochus and becomes king in his place, but Simon makes peace with Demetrius, who grants him full release from taxation. Thus the yoke of the Gentiles is removed from Israel, and the first year of Simon's independent rule is recognized by all.

1 Maccabees

Peace under Simon

"The land ha[s] rest all the days of Simon" (14:4). He captures major cities and the citadel, showing mercy to their inhabitants but cleansing their houses of all idols and setting faithful Jews in their place. At the expelling of their enemies from the citadel in Jerusalem, the Jews rejoice with songs of praise, and Simon decrees it to be a feast to be celebrated each year.

Simon "extend[s] the borders of his nation, and gain[s] full control of the country" (14:6). The land is tilled in peace as old men sit and talk in the streets and every Jew reclines under his vine and fig tree, for all the lawless and wicked men are done away with and the sanctuary is made quite glorious.

To the ends of the earth Simon's renown spreads. Rome and Sparta renew their friendship and alliance with the Jewish nation; and on a bronze tablet of their own the people inscribe the great deeds of Simon and his brothers – it is placed on a pillar on Mount Zion. These brothers have brought great glory to Israel by the battles they have won and their faithfulness to God.

All things prosper at Simon's hands and so the Jews make him governor and high priest for ever. He takes charge of the sanctuary, and all contracts in the country are written in his name. All agree to give Simon such powers, and to punish any who nullify them. Amen.

John

Antiochus, son of Demetrius, determines to return to his country and retake it from Trypho. Before he invades he writes to Simon, confirming all the promises his father had made – they will be able to keep their lands and remain free of taxation.

As Antiochus holds Trypho under siege, he receives a letter from Rome sent to all countries, declaring her renewal of friendship with Simon and the Jews. None are to seek their harm or aid those who do. When Simon sends troops to help Antiochus, he rejects them and proceeds to break his agreements with the Jews (perhaps envious of the large gold shield they had sent as a gift to Rome). He demands return of lands they've taken and tributes they haven't paid. When

Old Testament

Simon offers only a small sum and insists he will hold to the lands of his inheritance, Antiochus sends an army to invade Judea (while he pursues Trypho, who has escaped).

Simon calls on his sons to take his place in war. John puts to flight the invading forces and returns safely to Judea, but a treacherous governor within the country kills Simon and two of his other sons while at banquet in his presence. However, John seizes and kills the men sent to destroy him... and the book ends telling us that the brave deeds of John are inscribed in another chronicle.

2 MACCABEES

Before explicating the purpose of this book, the authors present two letters written by the Jews in Jerusalem to those dwelling in Egypt. It is the year 124 B.C. and they are entreating their brethren to celebrate the purification of the temple by keeping the feast of booths as they themselves prepare to do so in the holy city.

They briefly state how Jerusalem was saved from the impious Antiochus, and then proceed to recount some of the history surrounding the exile to Babylon, particularly the way some of the fire of the altar was preserved in a hidden cistern, and that upon returning, Nehemiah discovered it as a thick liquid. He had it sprinkled on the wood and the sacrifice, and a great fire blazed up when the sun shone upon it. Nehemiah prayed to the LORD to accept the sacrifice and to preserve Israel and make it holy, gathering it from all nations. Seleucus, the king of Persia, was so impressed by the finding of the liquid and its miraculous burning, he had the place it was found enclosed and made sacred.

Also recounted is Jeremiah's sealing up the tent and the ark and the altar of incense in a cave on the mountain where Moses had vision of the Promised Land. The way there has been forgotten, and Jeremiah has declared it will be unknown until all Israel is gathered as one in God's glorious presence. The books containing these records, and the entire library of Hebrew scriptures Nehemiah collected, are in possession of the Jews and their brethren are welcome to read them.

As for the purpose of this book: it is to condense the mass of material on Judas Maccabeus and his brothers into a single, readable volume (not unlike what is intended here for the Old Testament).

Onias

Jerusalem is in unbroken peace, the laws of God being well observed by the pious high priest Onias. The kings honor the temple with presents and the king of Asia himself has his revenues deferred to service of the sacrifices.

Then a troublesome man from among their own ranks plots against the holy city because of his disagreement with the blessed Onias. Through a governor he gets a message to the king that there are untold fortunes in the temple, of which he could take control. So the king sends his emissary to obtain them.

Though Onias informs Heliodorus there are but limited funds in the temple (along with a sum a righteous man has entrusted into the temple's care), and that these are set aside for the widows and orphans... because of the king's command, Heliodorus insists on taking the money. And so, Onias and the whole people make entreaty to God to save the temple from such violation. Most pitiable is their prostration.

YHWH hears their prayers, and when Heliodorus enters the sanctuary with his retinue, a magnificent horse and two strong men appear to him; the horse strikes him with its front hoofs, and the men scourge him to the point of death. Only the atonement made by Onias saves his life.

Upon recovering, Heliodorus heeds the two men, who appear again and tell him to be grateful to Onias. He witnesses to all, even the king, the power of God dwelling in Jerusalem. But when the troublesome Simon refuses to cease his slander against him and the city, Onias goes to the king to preserve peace in the house of God.

Onias Murdered

But the peace in Israel does not last long as the brother of the good Onias takes the high priesthood from him by bribing the new king, Antiochus. He quickly destroys the lawful practices of the Jews and introduces Greek customs, founding a gymnasium in Jerusalem to turn the young men's hearts toward Greek forms of prestige, and causing even the priests to despise the sanctuary and neglect the sacrifices.

Jason's treachery is soon answered by the treachery of the brother of the troublesome Simon, who himself secures the high priesthood by promises of moneys to the king. In his great cunning and by offering gold vessels he's stolen from the temple, Menelaus bribes the king's deputy to kill the just Onias, who has exposed this wicked man's thievery.

Many peoples are displeased at the murder of Onias; Antiochus himself is grieved, and so he has Andronicus killed in the very place he murdered Onias.

The Jews rise up against Menelaus and his brother for their evil connivance, but though they are able to put the temple-robbing Lysimachus to flight when he comes with troops against them, the men who bring charges against Menelaus are themselves put to death when the king's mind is swayed by promise of another substantial bribe. And so Menelaus remains in office and his wickedness continues to grow.

Slaughter

For forty days the Jews see golden-clad horsemen charging through the sky brandishing shields and drawn swords in fiery battle. But this is not now the good omen they pray it will be: the hand of God is upon them to punish them for their sins.

First the traitorous Jason returns from exile with a thousand men to slaughter his fellow citizens. But this wicked rebel meets a just end as he fails to take control of the city and is pursued from place to place in hatred by all – he dies in exile with no one to mourn him.

Then Antiochus comes raging to Jerusalem, indiscriminately slaughtering all Jews in his path, killing eighty thousand in three days and selling as many into slavery. Elated with pride he enters the temple and takes the holy vessels and votive offerings; the LORD allows such sacrilege because of the iniquity of His people. Antiochus leaves barbarous men to govern in Judea, including Menelaus, and makes another slaughter for good measure.

Great evil comes upon the Jews as they are forced to forsake the laws of God and participate in pagan sacrifices. The temple itself is dedicated to Zeus and defiled with abominable offerings and grave debauchery. Those who do not worship the false gods of the Greeks are ordered slain. Two women who circumcise their sons have them hung from their necks, and are hurled headlong from the wall. Those who hide in caves to observe the seventh day are burned together for their piety…

How long, O LORD, will you discipline your people? Whence shall come our salvation? It is in your kindness you punish us!

Eleazar and the Seven Sons

O what tortures come upon the people at the hands of Antiochus! The divine author recounts two incidents for the edification of his readers.

First the elderly Eleazar, a noble man, spits out the swine's flesh forced into his mouth, for he has "the courage to refuse things that it is not right to taste" (6:20); indeed, he will not go against the law set down by the Almighty. And though false friends attempt to seduce him into pretending to eat the banned meat, offering to provide secretly an acceptable substitute, this noble soul refuses to give bad witness to the young and to all the nation… and so he willingly and even gladly endures terrible sufferings and death, though he could save himself. (What a witness to the suffering of Christ he is!)

Then we hear of seven brothers who, one after the other, bear horrible tortures at the command of the raging king. He has their tongues cut out, their scalps torn off, their hands and feet chopped off, and what remains fried in a pan. But with their last breath they declare their allegiance to God, who will raise them up to life for their faithfulness to His laws.

The mother gives remarkable testimony to the LORD by her courage in witnessing the torture and death of all her sons. (O how like Our Lady she is!) She urges the youngest not to fear the butcher before him but to be strong as his brothers in believing in the One who made the heavens and the earth and shaped him in her womb. And he proves most courageous in his faith in God and condemnation of the king. And so he is tortured worse... and so is the greater blessed.

Judas Maccabeus Arises

During this great persecution of the Jews, Judas Maccabeus flees to the wilderness with his kinsmen to avoid defilement. He and his companions enter villages by stealth and gather about themselves six thousand men. They beg the LORD to have pity on the people, the temple and the city, and to remember the lawless destruction of innocent life and the blasphemies committed against Him.

Judas and his army begin to attack towns by night, taking strategic positions, and the Gentiles cannot withstand them. Soon Nicanor, one of the king's chief friends, is sent with an army of twenty thousand to wipe out the race of Judea. This wicked man plans to sell the Jews as slaves, ninety for a talent. But Judas encourages his men to fight nobly, exhorting them to remembrance of the outrages committed against them and the holy place, and of their trust in God. He recalls great victories of Jews in the past, and his troops thus become ready to die for their country and its laws.

And indeed Nicanor's army is soundly defeated: nine thousand are killed and the rest flee. The Jews take the money of those who would have bought them as slaves, and they pursue their enemy until the Sabbath comes... whence they turn home to praise the living God and share their spoils with the widows and orphans of those tortured.

They proceed to conquer other forces that come against them as well, continuing to take much plunder for themselves and the needy. Nicanor himself is made to flee like a runaway slave, and he begins to proclaim the Jews invulnerable because of the One who defends them.

2 Maccabees

The Sanctuary Purified

Antiochus Epiphanes is turned back in shame from his invasion of Persia, and hearing of the defeat of his forces by the Jews is transported with rage; he calls on his charioteer to drive immediately to Jerusalem, that he might make it into a cemetery.

But YHWH strikes him in his tracks. As soon as he has given his command, he is seized with pain in his bowels and suffers "sharp internal tortures" (9:5). This only increases his rage and his arrogant determination to destroy the Jews... but he is soon thrown from his chariot and must be carried away on a stretcher.

His body swarms with worms, his flesh rots, and the stench is so great none can remain in his presence. When even he cannot stand his own stench, Antiochus begins to come to his senses and repents of the evil he intends. He declares God's supremacy and promises freedom to the Jews, saying he will furnish the offerings in the temple (signaling also in letter the kind rule of his son)... and that he will even become a Jew himself! But justice for his wicked deeds yet takes his life in a most pitiful state far from his homeland.

Back in Jerusalem, Judas and his men recover the temple and purify the sanctuary, renewing the sacrifices two years to the very day it was profaned. They prostrate themselves and beg the LORD never to let them be handed over to a barbarous nation again... and then celebrate eight days with hymns of thanksgiving for the purification of the holy place, calling all Jews to yearly observance of this great feast.

God's Victories

Though they have the good will of one governor, those in power under the new King Antiochus overwhelm him and seek repeatedly to overwhelm the Jews. But repeatedly Judas and all the Jews prostrate themselves before the LORD, fasting and weeping and begging His intercession against their enemies – and so a string of victories in battle comes to them, led even by horsemen from Heaven. They slay twenty thousand here, twenty-five thousand there, burn others alive...

and are undeterred even by traitorous acts from within their own ranks.

After they defeat a force of the leader of the Greek government, he makes peace with them, realizing the Jews' invincibility under the might of God. But some of the governors round about do not recognize this treaty, and so Judas and his army have soon to set forth again, gaining another series of victories with the help of the LORD. They destroy Joppa and Jamnia, Charax and Carnaim, and Arabs along the way, often inspired with zeal against the blasphemies hurled at them by men in presumed strongholds. No walls can stand in their way.

They spare a town that has given good treatment to Jews, but after celebrating Pentecost return to conquering their enemies. Some of them die in one battle, and tokens of idols are discovered under the clothes on their corpses. But the Jews perform the holy and pious deed of making a sacrificial offering as atonement for the sins of these poor souls.

The king himself then comes against them with a tremendous force, but YHWH again hears their prayers. Judas and his men fight nobly and gain victory, so the king is forced to make peace and give generous pledges to the Jews.

Final Victory

Three years later Demetrius captures the Greek throne. Under Antiochus the traitorous Menelaus is thrown from a tower into a heap of ashes, but then Alcimus, a defiled high priest, goes out from among the Jews to convince the new king by deceit that Judas causes the nation great misfortune. Others jealous of Maccabeus join in the slander, and Demetrius appoints Nicanor governor of Judea and sends him off to destroy Judas and his men.

But the Jews again gather and pray, and word of Judas' valor convinces Nicanor to make a pledge of friendship with him; warmly he welcomes him into his presence. To counter this peace, Alcimus falsely accuses Nicanor of disloyalty to the king... and so he must turn on his friend and seek to kill him.

2 Maccabees

Judas successfully hides from Nicanor's newfound wrath, so instead he stretches out his hand against the sanctuary and looks to take Razis, a noble elder who risked body and life during the persecution. This man dies dramatically, first falling on his sword to avoid capture, then casting himself into the crowd and throwing his entrails at his enemies. But Nicanor exalts himself above even the Sovereign of Heaven, mocking the Sabbath day.

Then Judas inspires his men with a dream he has had of Jeremiah handing him a golden sword. They attack bravely and kill thirty-five thousand in battle, including the wicked Nicanor, whose head they cut off (with his arm) and hang upon the citadel in Jerusalem. This day is declared a feast to accompany the one that celebrates Mordecai's victory when it seemed the Jews would be annihilated. Long live the Jews and YHWH their LORD! May His kingdom come now in His only Son.

Here ends our going through the Old Testament. Where it is well-written, it is God's hand at work; where "poorly done and mediocre" (15:38), it is undoubtedly my own.

ADDENDUM:

The Finding of Jesus in the Temple
(and other Marian Mysteries)

> The things which Mary pondered in her heart,
>   how can we know?
> Her relationship with her divine Son,
>   how can we understand?
> How can we overhear the interchange between them?
>
> Let us look at the Word of God
> and prayerfully seek Our Lady's guidance.

Addendum

1. The Finding of Jesus in the Temple

"How is it that you sought me? Did you not know that I must be in my Father's house?" (Lk.2:49). Let us begin by looking at this statement of Jesus to His Mother when she found Him in the temple while He was yet a boy. It seems straightforward enough, and so, how is it Mary and Joseph "did not understand the saying" (2:50)? The question must not be as straightforward as it seems.

To understand this scene, first see that when Mary and Joseph discover Jesus in the temple, He is "sitting among the teachers, listening to them and asking them questions." And notice that the verse following says that "all who heard Him were amazed at His understanding and His answers" (2:46,47). It should intrigue us that He who is asking questions is somehow answering as well. Is the Word of God confused; is there some mistake?

We can better understand how questions may show understanding and be answers in themselves if we recall Jesus' discussions with these same teachers of the faith during His (adult) public ministry – how often He taught them by asking questions! "Is it lawful on the Sabbath to do good or to do harm, to save life or to destroy it?" (Lk.6:9). "Was the baptism of John from heaven or from men?" (Lk. 20:4). "If David thus calls Him Lord, how is He his son?" (Mt.22:45). Countless times the Lord taught His hearers with questions; and He does so now with the teachers. And He does so now with His Mother.

Mary and Joseph have been looking for Jesus; they have been searching the temple area, but He is not about. The anxiety of separation is upon the one who gave Him birth. Then she overhears His voice in the court reserved for the priests and teachers of the Law – a place especially excluded to women and children – and she is driven toward Him.

She likely runs into a guard whose duty it is to prevent those prohibited from entering. She pleads with him to let her see her Son, but he responds, "O woman, what have you to do with me?" (cf. Jn.2:4). Perhaps at this moment she hears Jesus pose this question to the teachers: "What then is this that is written: 'The very stone which the builders rejected has become the head of the corner'?" (Lk.20:17).

The Finding

    In great fear she cries out, "Y'shua!" In shock the teachers look up, and nod to the guard to let her enter. And so she runs to her Son, falls on her knees, begs an explanation... then hears His profound response: "Did you not know that I must be in my Father's House?"

    What does He mean by this? What is He trying to tell His dear Mother (and the Mother of us all)? If He is a worthy Son – and none is more worthy than He – He would do His best to settle her heart, to remove her very apparent anxiety. And this He does, with great love.

    What is He telling His Mother but that He is with her, always, that He has never left her? She is the Temple in which He dwells! What is He doing here but foretelling the destruction of the temple in which He has been teaching the elders and indicating the new Temple being constructed, the New Jerusalem, His Church, of which Mary is Mother and Model, and in which we all find our home... even as we find Jesus dwelling in us?

    And so, the Lord speaks to us all what He whispers so gently to His Mother – It is in you I remain; you are my Father's House. And so we should never fear but always realize the blessing upon our souls, the Spirit that is within us. "Do you not know that you are God's temple and that God's Spirit dwells in you?" (1Cor.3:16).

    But it is not simply this separation from her Son that has caused such fear in the Blessed Mother; it is not just that she has seemed to lose Him upon this earth. What her heart is pondering, and what she becomes terribly aware in finding Him here among the teachers, is His call to crucifixion. The Cross begins to overshadow her and she now senses the sword Simeon prophesied would pierce her heart even as it pierces that of her beloved Son.

    It is the ministry of Jesus that will bring His death, His speaking the truth that will arouse murderous jealousy among the leaders of the people. And though now that anger may be muted by the age of the Child, Our Lady can see it on the horizon... and so she takes Him from the temple, seeking to preserve the life of her Son.

    The boy Jesus might have begun His ministry here, at this time, but He is obedient to His Mother and Joseph, and leaves with them. It cannot but be that He remain in His Father's House, and so He stays with Mary. He continues at her side as she shall be at His side when the time for His ministry comes, when she comes to understand He will never leave her and calls her grown Son to reveal Himself, to do His Father's will... at the wedding feast of Cana.

Addendum

2. The Annunciation
(and the other Joyful Mysteries)

Before we move forward to consideration of the start of Jesus' public ministry at Cana, let us take a step back to the mysteries preceding the finding in the temple.

We have already spoken of the sword prophesied by Simeon to pierce the heart of Mary even as it pierces the body of her Son. Another related matter to note about the presentation of Jesus in the temple is the two turtledoves offered as sacrifice according to the dictates of the Law. We should see that these two innocent doves represent Jesus and Mary and the sacrifice the Savior makes for our sins, in which His Mother so intimately shares (and in which we are all called to share as well). One sees them being slaughtered even as Simeon declares his prophecy to Mary.

The birth of Jesus in Bethlehem is a mystery most profound. All I will say of it is that this dark cave, home to the lowest of animals, becomes the brightest and most pleasant place on earth, transformed as it is by our Savior's presence.

Mary's visitation to Elizabeth offers us much to consider about the role of Our Lady in the salvation of the world, particularly her effect on her Son's precursor, who will go before Christ to prepare His way. She indeed goes before the Baptist, as it were, bringing Jesus to him and serving to awaken him in his mother's womb.

The stirring of John in the womb of Elizabeth at the sound of Mary's voice is a mystery not often considered in all its depth. It is more than that he is happy to be in the presence of God. It is enough to fill Elizabeth with the Holy Spirit and move her to proclaim Mary Mother of the Lord... and Our Lady to answer just as inspired.

What is not realized in pondering this mystery is that Elizabeth has secluded herself for the first five months of her pregnancy, and that it is likely she is still in seclusion when Mary visits. It also seems forgotten that Elizabeth is of advanced years – thus her seclusion, that by such rest she might better protect the child in her womb.

But the most poignant matter overlooked is that John has likely remained dormant all this time, and so when he leaps in his mother's womb it is the first time that he has moved, that he has shown life (like the awakening of the old Law to the presence of the new Way!).

The Finding

Thus the awesome wonder upon Elizabeth's soul, and thus the expression of such blessed joy. One sees Mary coming to her reclining kinswoman, the curtains drawn... and bringing the light of day into the room.

Now as we come to consideration of the Annunciation, we will look more closely at the relationship between Mary and Elizabeth, for it will shed further light on this essential mystery of the Gospel.

The angel's proclamation that Mary will be the Mother of the Son of the Most High is indeed the key mystery in the history of the salvation of man. I believe there are two particularly important things to point up regarding this sacred event: Mary's vow of perpetual virginity and the source of that vow.

First, that Mary is vowed to perpetual virginity could not be made more apparent than it is in the angel's visit. (Why it is not seen in its unmistakable, simple clarity, I do not understand.) Gabriel declares the favor of God upon Mary and that she will give birth to the Savior. Mary responds, "How can this be, since I have no husband?" (Lk.1:34). Now, at this time Mary is betrothed to Joseph; they are as good as married. In fact, Matthew calls Joseph "her husband" (1:19). Common sense would tell us that if it were announced to any woman about to be married or as good as married that she is going to give birth to a son, her understanding would undoubtedly be that her husband or husband-soon-to-be would be the father of that child. Yes? Then why does Mary question the angel as she does? Why does she not acknowledge Joseph as her husband? The only possible reason for her question is that she does not expect to have relations with Joseph – and so with no man – that she has taken a vow of perpetual virginity. The question makes no sense otherwise. She cannot be saying (as many falsely presuppose): "I don't have a man to father this child," for she clearly has a husband at hand.

I would like next to explore the origin of Mary's vow, considering further her relationship with Elizabeth. One should remember first that what causes Mary to accept the angel's announcement and give her full consent to God's will is Gabriel's statement that Elizabeth is now in her sixth month. Till this moment Mary has been fearful of the angel's presence and uncertain of his word, and of his origin (though his explanation of how this will be has probably begun to sway her).

Addendum

As an aside, and to further solidify the case for Mary's perpetual virginity, it should be recognized that Mary's doubt is not like that which causes Zechariah to be struck dumb. His is a doubt of the LORD's power to do as He says. Mary does not doubt God's power, and so she is not chastised for her question. She inquires of the angel because what he says seems to go *against* the will of God, against the vow she has so solemnly made. She does not wish to break her vow and can only hesitate at the bidding of any being who seems to invite her to do so.

Then why does she change, why does she immediately give her wholehearted acceptance of the LORD's call, losing all doubt about the angel and his message, at the pronouncement of Elizabeth's being with child? It is not simply because the power of God has been proven to her. (Again, she does not doubt this.) It is because this word *confirms* her vow of virginity – it comes as an answer to her deepest prayer.

I propose, indeed I see in my mind's eye (and it inevitably brings tears) that Mary made her vow in the temple in her youth as a prayer to the LORD to take away her beloved kinswoman's reproach and bless her with a child. In an absolutely Christlike gesture – one which already reveals her union with her Son's selflessness, with His sacrificial love for others – Mary offers her own hopes for motherhood that Elizabeth's hopes might be fulfilled.

I believe that Elizabeth came like Hannah to the temple to beseech YHWH for the blessing of a child. (We note that upon the meeting of these two women and their sons in the womb, it is Hannah's song (cf. 1Sm.2:1-10) Mary echoes at the prompting of the Holy Spirit.) Whether Mary was present in the temple because she lived there from her youth as Tradition holds or because she had come there with all good Jews (including Elizabeth) for the Passover feast or another feast, it matters not. Mary overhears Elizabeth's heartfelt prayer (and her tears), and in response makes her vow and her prayer to God.*

And so when she hears the angel's marvelous words, she is completely overwhelmed with joy that God has answered her prayer, that Elizabeth is so remarkably blessed… and in that joy, and great love, all doubt and fear flee and she says: "Behold, I am the handmaid of the LORD; let it be to me according to your word" (Lk.1:38)! And so she will be both Virgin and Mother. So she is enveloped by the marvelous love and awesome wonder that is God.

3. The Wedding Feast at Cana

After Jesus is taken from among the teachers in the temple by Mary and Joseph, we do not encounter Him again until His Baptism in the Jordan by John, until He is thus prepared for His public ministry. And His public ministry begins at Cana, where He reveals, particularly to His disciples, that the Spirit of God is upon Him, that He is the One promised by the prophets. He does this by changing the water for washing into delectable wine.

It is, of course, at His Mother's request that the Son of God accomplishes this miracle. And this is no mere coincidence: it hearkens back to the finding in the temple. It seemed Jesus might begin His ministry then, but He was obedient to Mary and Joseph, who had no word of His revealing Himself at such a young age. He makes allowance for His Mother's fears and remains particularly subject to our humble condition in the home at Nazareth.

But at Cana Mary sees it is time to let her Child go into the world, to take the first step on a path that will lead invariably to the Cross. She knows what awaits Him but is ready now to accept the Father's will. And so she encourages Jesus to go forward on the narrow path… for we are very much in need of salvation.

I believe the Lord's words to His Mother – "O woman, what have you to do with me?" (Jn.2:4) – are the same as those that were spoken to Mary by the guard who restrained her from entering the restricted area of the temple, where her Son sat among the teachers. Jesus employs them, along with the following statement ("My hour has not yet come" (ibid)), to emphasize to His Mother what she is now calling Him to do. He is not refusing to do as she requests but making sure she is ready for the consequences, consequences she was not prepared to face in the temple in His youth.

There is great poignancy in Jesus' question here, for beyond asking if she is ready to have Him begin His ministry, if she realizes what the consequences will be – that this first step indeed leads to the Cross – He is making apparent to her, and to us all, how much her concerns (and ours) *are* His concerns. Far from denying His assistance to those in need, He is revealing by His question how deeply He cares for all souls, how much He makes our troubles His own… to the point, of course, of dying on the Cross for our sins.

Addendum

Yes, His Mother's concern affects Him deeply, and therefore He cannot turn from her plea. But here we see as well how Mary takes our concerns upon herself, and then brings them to her Son. We see not only Jesus taking up His Cross, but also His Mother allowing her heart to be pierced – so much does she have to do with Him.

And so, from now to the end of His ministry upon the wooden beams, Mary will remain at her Son's side, joined with Him in His sacrifice. She shall not shy away from walking with Him along the via dolorosa; she shall not fear standing beneath His bleeding body or cradling His lifeless corpse. She will remain strong, knowing in her heart the glory to which He leads all who follow in His way.

And to glory she shall be the first to come, following Him closely into the kingdom. She is made Queen of Heaven and earth by the holy offering of her life in union with Jesus' own; filled with the Spirit of God, she is raised to the gates of Paradise, and there enters to shouts of joy from the angels as she takes her place at the King's side.

And we shall join her; we shall come to the eternal gates if in this life we give ourselves in union with her Son as she has done. If we accept the call of the LORD, if we set our hearts on doing His will... if we take upon ourselves the Cross He offers for our salvation and that of the world, we will soon follow Him through the gates of the kingdom.

Have no fear. You are the temple of YHWH and He is with you. The grace upon His Mother, He would share with you; and so, give your "yes" to His call, and be prepared to lay down your life for all.

■■■

*Notes on Mary's vow of perpetual virginity:

Perhaps upon seeing Elizabeth so distraught, Mary prays, almost without thinking – so imperated by charity is she – something like, "LORD, take my own fertility that my sister (mother/kinswoman) might be blessed," then places her arms around Elizabeth and speaks gently into her ear: "The LORD hears your prayer."

We should remember, too, that Mary is immaculately conceived, and so, though she could not say "I am the Immaculate Conception" at this time, in her heart she must have some sense of her call, some inclination to the blessing she will know as the Virgin Mother of the Son of God.

Finally, she may not have been able to reveal her vow to Joseph at their betrothal, having to go on faith, trusting as Abraham that the LORD would somehow make her path clear.

Other Books by James Kurt

Our Daily Bread:
Exposition of the Readings of Catholic Mass –
A page of writing for every Mass of the liturgical calendar for the Roman Rite; reflections drawn from the readings. 727 pp. 2004. w/ imprimatur.
Our Daily Bread: Lent – 86 pp. 2019. w/ imprimatur.

Prayers to the Saints (Updated) –
A page of prayer to each saint on the General Roman Calendar for the U.S.A. 237 pp. 2019 (original 2007). w/ imprimatur.

"TURN and Become like Children":
Refuting the Presumed Contradictions of the Jerusalem Bible
Old Testament Commentary –
A case study recounting the problems afflicting modern biblical scholarship as exemplified in the JB. 188 pp. 2019.

"Into Your Hands...":
Distillation of the Letters of Fr. Jean-Pierre de Caussade –
Reflections of the profound counsel of Fr. de Caussade to embrace the Cross and find the Lord's will (and joy) even in our greatest sufferings. 82 pp. 2019.

Remembrance of Things Present –
A mystical work seeking the presence of the LORD in the moment, where He dwells at all times. 100 pp. 2018. w/ imprimatur.

Two Books: Paradox and the Christian Faith /
          Hippie Convert –
The apparent contradictions of the Faith are explained for those who seek wisdom; and a member of the flower generation addresses true love and peace, in poetic form. 238 pp. 2016/2019. w/imprimatur.

Lines of Grace: Meditations on Verses of Holy Scripture,
The Stations of the Cross, and The Most Holy Rosary –
A Catholic devotional especially for the encouragement of the practice of plenary indulgence. 195 pp. 2016.

Blessed Guilt (A Universal Conversion Story) –
On the life-giving repentance found in Jesus' blood; vaguely autobiographical but without particulars, thus making it a universal story of conversion. 119 pp. 2013. w/ imprimatur.

Chapters of the Gospels –
Exposition of the four gospels, chapter by chapter; in the style of *Our Daily Bread*.
114 pp. 2009. w/ imprimatur.

The Most Holy Trinity and The Four Corners of the Universe –
A collection of writings on the Trinity and its reflection in Creation;
founded upon the Shema. 300 pp. 2008. w/ imprimatur.

YHWH: Order of the Divine NAME –
On the significance of the contemplative silence that is the NAME of God,
and its application to a spiritual life. 260 pp. 2008/2019. w/ imprimatur.

Turn of the Jubilee Year: A Conversion Song –
Autobiographical depiction of vocation search through pilgrimage to Medjugorje
and stays at a hermitage or two. 230 pp. 2004.

***Songs for Children of Light*: Ten Albums of Lyrics** –
White on black conceptual work with simple drawings for each song.
150 pp. 2003.

silence in the city –
short contemplative poems; moments of divine silence in the midst of city life.
148 pp. (74 pieces). 2003.

author's website:
www.writingsofjameskurt.org

podcasting site:
www.hermitinthecity.libsyn.com

www.ingramcontent.com/pod-product-compliance
Lightning Source LLC
Chambersburg PA
CBHW030309080526
44584CB00012B/506